The Irish regional press, 1892–2018

The Irish Regional Press, 1892–2018

Revival, Revolution and Republic

IAN KENNEALLY & JAMES T. O'DONNELL

editors

FOUR COURTS PRESS

Set in 10.5 pt on 12.5 pt Ehrhardt MT for
FOUR COURTS PRESS LTD
7 Malpas Street, Dublin 8, Ireland
www.fourcourtspress.ie
and in North America for
FOUR COURTS PRESS
c/o ISBS, 920 NE 58th Avenue, Suite 300, Portland, OR 97213

A catalogue record for this title is available
from the British Library.

ISBN 978-1-84682-655-9

Printed in England
by CPI Group (UK) Ltd, Croydon CRO 4YY

Contents

Acknowledgments

We would like to acknowledge the support of Local Ireland, the Newspaper and Periodical History Forum of Ireland and The Old Athlone Society in bringing this book to publication. We would also like to thank the many reviewers, whose comments and suggestions made valuable contributions to the chapters and, of course, the authors without whom this book would not have been possible.

The origins of this book are in a conference held at Dublin City University in December 2014, and many of the chapters are based on papers presented there. We would like to thank the School of Communications, DCU, the Department of History at NUI Galway and the Newspaper and Periodical History Forum of Ireland for their support in taking that first step towards this publication.

Foreword

JOHN HORGAN

The essays in this book have a simple, overall unity: they comprise illustrations and analyses of the rich variety of the print media at a local or provincial – as compared with national – level in Ireland over more than a century in which profound social, economic, political and technological developments have been taking place. But that simple unity masks a political, social and economic complexity that provides almost inexhaustible opportunities for scholarship, for analysis, and for exploration of the varied relationships between local print media and communities in an era that witnessed profound social, political and economic change. The US politician Tip O'Neill once remarked sagely that 'all politics is local'. To the extent that this is still true, local and regional print media in Ireland continue to play a vital role. The local and regional print media fulfil this role, despite near universal access (at least throughout the developed world) to the instruments and technologies of electronic communication, despite the threats posed by current economic crises, and despite the growth of free media across the Internet. This role involves – as well as its traditional aspect as a marketplace for goods, ideas and information – framing political issues and establishing (or, less frequently, challenging) social and political priorities. Local and regional media have also played a vital role in providing their communities with fora for self-reflection, growth and development.

Scholarship about the Irish print media in general, about the regional media in particular, and about journalism in Ireland as a profession, was for many years episodic, and, until the latter part of the twentieth century, confined to a scattering of articles in academic journals that reflected the interests of individual scholars rather than the emergence of a sustained historiographical trend. From then on, however, substantial academic publications by individual authors or by groups of authors began to reflect a growing interest by historians and scholars in all Irish media, and led to the emergence of media studies itself as a recognizable academic discipline in Irish universities.

These developments ran parallel to a strand of the writing about the print media since the 1950s that tended to showcase highly colourful personal memoirs. Entertaining though these frequently are, particularly for journalistic contemporaries of the authors, they were generally inadequately garnished with specific publication data or other bibliographic data that might have been of use for scholarly investigation. Although there had for many years been episodic publication of articles in academic journals about many aspects of Irish print media, and to a lesser extent about journalism itself as a profession, it was not until the latter part of the twentieth century that academic publications by individual

9

authors or by groups of authors began to reflect a growing interest by historians and media scholars.

It is also important to remember – although no research model or technique could adequately respond to the challenges involved in tracing the complex linkages – that there have always been important relationships between the regional and the national media. The regional media were, for example, at least until the middle of the last century, the breeding and training ground for the many aspiring journalists who used them as a stepping stone to national careers of considerable significance, not only in print journalism but also in broadcast and, later, Web-based media. In the early days of RTÉ after 1962, for instance, the RTÉ newsroom, which served both television and radio, was almost entirely staffed by journalists who may have been recruited by RTÉ from the national print media, and whose primary journalistic experience had very commonly included many years, and a considerable amount of informal training, in the regional press. This early training and experience was strongly focused on the underlying characteristics of regional media: factual accuracy and political neutrality. These characteristics had, by the early twentieth century, in these newspapers generally (although there were exceptions) largely supplanted the high-profile editorial individuality and partisanship characteristic of the era of conflict and high political drama during which many of them had originally been established and flourished. There are deep echoes of this period in the first section of this book.

The developing editorial neutrality – or the decline of overt partisanship – had strong political benefits, and was also, of course, commercially advantageous. This was particularly the case in the immediate wake of the war of independence, when some smaller regional newspapers that had originally been established to cater for the small, albeit prosperous, middle–class unionist readership, began to wither on the vine.

The six essays in the first section of this book wisely eschew the impossible task involved in presenting any kind of a panoramic vision of the complex regional media landscape, both north and south, of what became the international border after partition. Instead, and valuably, they focus primarily on a number of regional titles that provide an intriguing selection of the journalism that reflected important aspects of the social and political complexities of this period. Inevitably, these essays have a strong political tinge, reflecting the tensions – subterranean or obvious – that were endemic in Ireland during this period.

The second section of the book contains essays that focus on the regional press more generally and thematically, providing a valuable overview of the varied and interrelated social, political and economic realities within which the regional press evolved. They bridge the gap between the heady days that followed Irish independence and the more complex, commercially and editorially challenging realities of the late twentieth and early twenty-first centuries.

These economic realities had – and still have – a profound effect on the fate of the Irish language in the regional press, which mirrored its national difficulties in the wake of its dramatic decline in the second half of the twentieth century. It is difficult, in this context, to underestimate the roles of the Catholic church and the educational system in facilitating and in all probability enhancing the language shift that took place during this period, and that was profoundly reflected in the rise of the *Nation* and the always problematic status of Irish language in the regional press, even in the revolutionary period of 1916–22.

British rule over the greater part of the island, and the strength of constitutional Irish nationalism until after 1916, was mirrored in the continuing survival throughout the pre-independence period of a large number of unionist regional titles. The catalogue of those titles – some of them, like the *Achill Island Missionary Herald and Western Witness* (1837–69), unashamedly Protestant, even quirkily so, in origin and tone – reflected either commercial or social realities; but not all had a specifically unionist origin. The local or regional newspaper casualties resulting from Catholic emancipation and resurgent nationalism were many, although a few nationalist regional papers also went to the wall, simply eliminated by the iron laws of competition. The flavour of this sub-current in Irish journalism – the organs of the religious minority as well as the commercial failures – can be gauged, even at this remove in time, by their titles. They included the *Athlone Conservative Advocate* (1837), the *Ballina Journal* (1882–95), the *King's County Chronicle* (1845–1922, and until 1963 under the less unionist appellation *Offaly Chronicle*), the *Carlow Sentinel* (1832–1920), the *Mayo Constitution* (1812–72), and the *Cork Constitution* (1823–1924), whose political inclinations hardly need to be guessed at. Similarly revanchist tendencies supported, until they disappeared under the rising tide of political nationalism and the weakening of unionist businesses after 1922, the *Kilkenny Moderator* (*c.*1775–1924), the *Leitrim Advertiser* (1870–1916), the *Skibbereen and West Carbery Eagle* (1857–1929) and the *Sligo Times* (1909–14).

As Christopher Morash has pointed out in his wide-ranging study of Irish media, almost 150 Irish newspapers (including those in Dublin and Belfast, which are not included as regional newspapers for the purposes of this essay) were founded between 1885 and 1910, and most of these 'were not simply regional papers, but nationalist/regional newspapers'.[1] This editorial and political vitality, in many cases embedded in, and an outgrowth of, the pre-existing local printing industry, also benefited from a technological revolution which, in a very short period of time, established a hegemony of the linotype machine that was to survive well into the second half of the twentieth century. This reduced labour costs, magnified the speed and accuracy of newspaper production, and remained the staple technology of many regional newspapers up to and in some cases even after the introduction of offset printing technology.

Even as these newly minted nationalist regional newspapers played a potent

1 Christopher Morash, *A history of the media in Ireland* (Cambridge, 2010), pp 116–19.

role in coalescing and giving a voice to emergent nationalism in many areas, some of the more 'moderate nationalist newspapers provided a steady stream of exotic stories: Gordon at Khartoum, opium wars in China, Scott in the Antarctic and so on'.[2] By and large, this interest in the world beyond the borders of Ireland was confined to the Dublin press, although, as James O'Donnell's essay in this book points out, a wider historical perspective up to the mid-twentieth century encouraged some of these regional newspapers to spread their editorial wings, even if they rarely covered as much territory as the *Skibbereen Eagle*, a west Cork newspaper that solemnly warned its readers on 5 September 1898 that it would 'keep [its] eye on' the tsar of Russia and his nefarious activities.[3]

By far the most useful overview of this period, and the twentieth century generally, is the *Irish bibliography of press history* published by the Newspaper and Periodical History Forum of Ireland.[4] Here, can be found many individual titles dealing with aspects of these media, including Marie-Louise Legg's seminal work *Newspapers and nationalism: the Irish provincial press, 1850–1892*, Mark O'Brien and Felix M. Larkin's edited collection *Periodicals and journalism in twentieth-century Ireland*, Kevin Rafter's edited collection *Irish journalism before independence*, and the present writer's history of Irish media.[5]

Although the number and vitality of many of these regional titles precludes an exhaustive survey, certain key periods were marked by change and challenge. The 1916–23 period, for example, was characterized by heavy censorship (both by the British administration and by the Free State administration that succeeded it). Although constitutional nationalism was still politically pre-eminent, the political divisions were – as Christopher Doughan's and Elaine Callinan's essays demonstrate – still relevant to some degree. The heavy hand of the authorities of course affected revolutionary titles, and the early mosquito Republican publications in Dublin more directly than those in the provinces, although nationalist stirrings in the more established regional newspapers published in the more populous (or better-educated) conurbations such as Kilkenny, Limerick, Cork and Belfast were also subjected to some colonial invigilation. Nor did the creation of the Free State result in the total liberation of the provincial press, as Ó Drisceoil points out: although mosquito Republican papers were, during the civil war, the prime targets of the Free State censors, the new Free State government was, particularly after de Valera's accession to power in the early 1930s, the author of occasional, indirect and not always successful, efforts at censorship tactics involving the withholding of government advertising. The complicated realities of the late nineteenth and early twentieth centuries had

2 Ibid., p. 121.   3 *Eagle and County Cork Advertiser*, 5 Sept. 1898.   4 *The Irish bibliography of press history*, newspapersperiodicals.org/bibliography, accessed 27 Nov. 2017.   5 Marie-Louise Legg, *Newspapers and nationalism: the Irish provincial press, 1850–1892* (Dublin, 1998); Mark O'Brien and Felix M. Larkin (eds), *Periodicals and journalism in twentieth-century Ireland: writing against the grain* (Dublin, 2014); Kevin Rafter (ed.), *Irish journalism before independence: more a disease than a profession* (Manchester, 2011); John Horgan and Roddy Flynn, *Irish media: a critical history* (Dublin, 2017).

settled down by the end of the 1940s, as the weaker provincial titles went to the wall, at which point there was probably little anticipation of further dramatic change in the media landscape.

A number of factors, however, combined to disturb this placid, and occasionally complacent, landscape from the latter part of the twentieth century onwards. One, which might not have been easily foreseen, and which was at first only incremental but later dramatic, was the change in ownership patterns of the regional press, particularly in the later decades of the century.

The changes, when they came, were both profound and rapid. Technologically, web offset printing replaced the linotype machines that had been the mainstay of both national and provincial newspaper production since the 1880s. This led to the almost total elimination of one highly skilled but now almost obsolete group of newspaper workers – the printers – and to rapidly rising production values.

In many cases, too, the closely knit family structures that had often established, and still owned, a lot of the more significant regional titles began to break apart. As the career paths of the younger generations of regional newspaper owners began to diverge, the newspapers that had been established, in many cases, by their grandparents or great-grandparents, were increasingly seen as assets for sale rather than as family businesses. Another relevant factor was the cumulative disappearance of many of the smaller regional titles that had originally been established to represent and reflect the commercial instincts of the Anglo-Irish sections of the community. Many members of this community simply migrated to Northern Ireland; and the advertising revenues from the dwindling numbers of Protestant-owned enterprises outside Dublin were not enough, in themselves, to sustain those elements of the regional press that had hitherto profited from commercial support from Protestant-owned advertisers.

As the twentieth century morphed into the twenty-first, the large numbers of independent publications owned by individual families began, as succession and family issues arose, to be redistributed into groups of regional newspapers. The most significant of these was (especially and initially in the more prosperous and populated eastern part of the country) comprised of publications acquired by the national Independent Newspapers group.

Weaker, less adequately capitalized newspapers began to fall by the wayside during this period. The process of consolidation, in which the Independent group had originally been the largest player, subsequently evolved into a dogfight over ownership in which some of the provincial titles changed hands for eye-watering amounts of money. The new factor in this process was the growing interest of UK regional newspaper groups, from England and Scotland, in acquiring Irish regional titles. The boom in newspapers generally faltered in 2001–2, but this did not deter investors, some of whom (particularly the UK-based ones) committed extraordinarily large sums to the purchase of Irish regional titles – sums which, in retrospect, could not have been justified by any intelligent calculations. At the same time as the regional press began to diversify into local radio, the major Irish newspaper publisher, Independent News and Media (which already had substantial radio interests) contemplated extending its regional newspaper footprint even further by adding a number of regional titles to its existing stable. But this initiative foundered in 2017 when INM walked away from its proposed purchase of five regional print titles following an examination by the Department of Communications, Climate Action and Environment of the issues raised, and subsequent recommendations made by that department's minister. This in all probability put the question of acquiring further regional print assets very much on the back burner.

In summary, while the story of the regional print media had been one of almost uninterrupted prosperity for many years – modified and characterized by the survival of the fittest – global media, over-hasty centralization and technological developments have created a much more challenging future, in which the particular strengths of a vibrant regional press (including their involvement with new media) will have to be accurately identified and built upon to secure their future.

It would not be an exaggeration to say that the present state of the regional press is one of considerable flux and uncertainty as these publications try to chart a path through the convergence of the print and electronic media (including the Internet) in a manner that will guarantee their future. The problems of identifying their continuing strengths, and adapting these to a multimedia environment whose effect on revenue streams is at best unpredictable and at worst threatening, are considerable. Underlying all of this is an issue with which public policy and regulators have grappled only rarely, and not particularly successfully: the extent to which the marketplace can, or should, continue to be the sole yardstick and determinant of the fortunes of a free and socially significant regional media which – despite its acknowledged structural and other weaknesses – can chart a future that will be as relevant as its past.

I

The regional press in Ireland's provinces

Journalism and the local newspaper industry in Sligo, 1899–1922

MARK WEHRLY

Favourable political and economic conditions – especially for nationalist newspapers – and the development of journalism for mass audiences formed the backdrop for the exponential growth in the local newspaper industry in Sligo at the beginning of the twentieth century. Throughout Ireland, from the formation of the Irish National League in 1882, the national question had become a central focus of local politics. Whereas local life in Ireland in the mid-nineteenth century was dominated by issues such as 'pregnancy and the price of tea',[1] from the mid-1880s local newspapers frequently published reports from the meetings of dozens of local branches of the Irish National League, the Gaelic Athletic Association, the Catholic Literary Society and other such organizations. This brought the national question significantly to the forefront of local affairs and, in a relatively short space of time, the effects were noticeable in most localities.[2] In Sligo, this process was described by the chief secretary, George Wyndham, in 1900, when he called the *Sligo Champion* 'a leading source of mischief in Sligo and surrounding counties. Where it circulates, the people live in dread of having their names published as guilty of committing offences against the Land League'.[3]

Newspapers could not have had such a capacity to facilitate the National League and other such organizations if the conditions in which they were operating had not been so favorable. Rising literacy levels specifically benefitted Catholics in Sligo – as elsewhere in Ireland[4] – something that gave local nationalist newspapers an audience to match their purpose. Illiteracy among Catholics in Sligo fell from 56,176 (58 per cent) in the 1861 census to 11,913 (17 per cent) in that of 1901. The more literate Protestant population of the county also saw a proportional fall in illiteracy, from 1,300 (14 per cent) in 1861 to 227 (4 per cent) in 1901, with similar declines among Presbyterians, Methodists and 'Others'. The greater increase in literacy among Catholics meant that the Catholic proportion of the overall literate population of Sligo increased from 84 per cent to 90 per cent during this period. Between 1891 and 1911, the number of jour-nalists and printers in Sligo significantly increased – as did the Catholic proportion of these professions:[5]

---

1 K.T. Hoppen, *Ireland since 1800: conflict and conformity* (London, 1989), p. 117.   2 Marie-Louise Legg, *News-papers and nationalism: the Irish provincial press, 1855–1893* (Dublin, 1998), p. 11.   3 Quoted in Íde Ní Liatháin, *The life and career of P.A. McHugh: a north Connacht politician* (Dublin, 1999), p. 41.   4 Legg, *News-papers and nationalism*, p. 12.   5 *Census of Ireland, 1891* [C. 6885–iv], HC 1892, xciii, 572. *Census of Ireland, 1901*, 72 [Cd. 1059–iv], HC 1902, cxxix, 801. *Census of Ireland, 1911* [Cd. 6052–iv]. HC 1912.

Table 1.1: Sligo journalists by religion

	Total	Catholic	Protestant	Presbyterian	Methodist	Other
1891	4	2	1	0	0	1
1901	9	6	2	1	0	0
1911	15	10	2	3	0	0

Table 1.2: Sligo printers by religion

	Total	Catholic	Protestant	Presbyterian	Methodist	Other
1891	29	22	2	3	2	0
1901	44	41	2	0	1	0
1911	46	44	1	1	0	0

In addition to the growth of an audience, and of the professions of journalism and printing, industrialization offered significant technological innovation in both printing and paper production – the first appreciable advances in those fields for 300 years. Mass production thus became affordable, and newspapers became cheaper again at the point of consumption when the repeal of taxes on newspaper stamps was finalized in 1855, after which came the proliferation of penny newspapers and – by 1900 – halfpenny newspapers.[6] Journalism became increasingly professionalized during this period – although it was somewhat slower to do so in Ireland than in the UK[7] – and with this development came a new style that was more suited to mass consumption (and which was derided by Matthew Arnold as 'pandering to the prejudices of the proletariat'[8]). The 'new journalism' of W.T. Stead and T.P. O'Connor may have been slower to take hold in Ireland than in Britain, but there were still many examples of its practice in Sligo and elsewhere in the late nineteenth and early twentieth century.[9]

A further development that directly contributed to the rise in newspaper production in Sligo at the turn of the twentieth century was the passage of the Local Government (Ireland) Act of 1898.[10] This reinforced the extent to which socio-economics were inextricably linked with the political climate in heightening such activity in local newspaper production. Prior to the passage of the act, the home rule movement was well served by the *Sligo Champion*, which in turn was heavily subsidized by the Irish Parliamentary Party.[11] In addition to political contributions, another source of revenue was viewed as crucial by the

6 Piers Brendon, 'When the press went pop' in *Powers of the press: a special supplement to the David Low exhibition with BBC history magazine*, 3:2 (May 2002), p. 20.   7 Michael Foley, 'Colonialism and journalism in Ireland', *Journalism Studies*, 5:3 (2004), p. 374.   8 Matthew Arnold, 'Up to Easter' in *The Nineteenth Century*, 123 (1887), pp 629–43.   9 Mark Wehrly, '"Blessed with the faculty of mirthfulness": Arthur Malley, the "new journalism" and the local press in Sligo at the turn of the twentieth century', *Irish Communications Review*, 12 (2010), pp 103–14.   10 Local Government (Ireland) Act, 1898 (61 & 62 Vict., c. 37) (21 Feb. 1898).   11 Legg, *Newspapers and nationalism*, p. 178.

Champion and its competitors: public printing and advertising contracts that were granted on an annual or multi-annual basis by local public bodies.

Between 1885 and 1898, the Co. Sligo grand jury paid a variety of printers £1,417 for the printing of the county register and announcements. Among those who received these contracts were the printing businesses operated by the *Sligo Champion* and its unionist rival, the *Sligo Independent*.[12] The *Roscommon Constitutionalist*, owned by the Protestant printer Stuart Griffiths, was also successful in winning the contract for three years, from 1888 to 1890. The printing contract was granted annually, with the *Sligo Champion* only winning the tender on two occasions during this period while Protestant printers won it the remainder of the time – with the exception of Thadeus Kilgannon's winning of the 1894 contract. However, the *Champion* did win the contract for the printing requirements of the office of the clerk of the crown and peace, which was a lucrative sum of £166 per annum, from 1893 until 1899.[13]

The 1898 act placed political power firmly into the hands of nationalists.[14] This, in turn, led to the *Sligo Champion* receiving a significantly larger share of such contracts than had previously been the case – but it also brought the prospect of funding other sustainable newspapers of a nationalist hue in Sligo town. In the first quarter of the twentieth century, the *Champion* faced significant competition from the Healyite *Sligo Star* from 1899 to 1902 and the radical *Sligo Nationalist* (later the *Connachtman*), from 1908 until 1925. A vast amount of editorial comment was devoted to the destination of these contracts – itself evidence of the increasingly self-conscious nature of journalism at the turn of the twentieth century.[15]

THE BATTLE FOR PUBLIC CONTRACTS

It was in these changing circumstances that Patrick Aloysius McHugh arrived as editor and proprietor of the *Sligo Champion* in 1885. A secondary school teacher with no journalistic experience, McHugh was the *Champion*'s seventh editor since its establishment in 1836. The impact of his tenure would be noted in the newspaper's centenary edition:

> When the late P.A. McHugh acquired the property ... it had almost ceased to exist. His advent, however, gave it new life. Its columns at once reflected the strong personality of its new proprietor, and throwing the full weight of his forceful character and outstanding journalistic ability on the side of the downtrodden peasantry, the *Sligo Champion* became one of the foremost of Ireland's provincial newspapers.[16]

---

12 The proprietor of the latter was Alexander Gillmor (until 1893) and then Jane Gillmor, under whom Bob Smyllie was employed as editor of the paper from 1899 until 1908.   13 Sligo grand jury county-at-large presentments, Sligo County Library, no. 922, vol. 3.   14 Desmond Roche, *Local government in Ireland* (Dublin, 1982), p. 78.   15 Wehrly, 'Arthur Malley', p. 107.   16 *SC* centenary number (1936).

This view of McHugh's tenure was not shared by his contemporaries. A common theme in their columns was the overt favoritism to his newspaper which they perceived in the granting of public printing and advertising contracts. In addition to his work as a journalist, McHugh also had a significant political career, with roles including mayor of Sligo (on five occasions), chairman of the county council established in 1899 after the passage of the Local Government Act, and member of parliament, first for North Leitrim from 1892 and then for North Sligo from 1906 until his death in 1909.[17]

Particular animosity existed between McHugh, who had become a principal organizer of the United Irish League in Sligo in 1900, and another nationalist journalist, Michael Dowd, a Healyite and prominent organizer in the People's Rights Association. While this animosity derived from the factionalism of nationalist politics in the late nineteenth century,[18] it also bore a commercial hue. Notable in the editorial jousts between the *Sligo Champion* and Dowd's newspaper, the *Sligo Star*, were disputes over the destination of public printing and advertising contracts – now in the gift of the predominantly nationalist public bodies. Dowd devoted two full leader columns to the county council's consideration of tenders for general county printing for 1900. Tenders had been received from the *Sligo Champion*, the unionist *Sligo Independent* and from local printer Thadeus Kilgannon, on whose premises the *Sligo Star* was printed. Reporters were denied entry into the council chambers and the price of the respective tenders were not made public. The outcome of the deliberation was a proposal by Councillor Peter Cawley, a prominent UIL activist, to consider a selection of single items of printing out of 144 cases in all – in which case the *Sligo Independent* and the *Sligo Star* both argued it would be possible to claim that any of the tenders was the cheapest. When the *Champion* was awarded the contract, Cawley was the subject of withering criticism in the *Star*, with the paper featuring him in a cartoon depicting an overfed boar bearing the name 'Sligo Champion' being stall-fed by Cawley from a trough full of public money. Describing the whole affair as a 'farce', Dowd proclaimed of McHugh's victory in the matter that 'The public do not know the names of the firms from whom tenders were received nor the manner in which the decision to declare McHugh the contractor was arrived at', adding that if this was what was coming with home rule, then 'may God deliver us from it'.[19]

The artist responsible for the cartoon that punctuated Dowd's argument, Alfred McHugh (no relation to P.A.), had been recruited by the *Star* in 1900 after an altercation with Jasper Tully, the editor and proprietor of the *Roscommon Herald* and close ally of P.A. McHugh. Among other things, Tully was the owner of the first motor car in Boyle, and was depicted by the *Star* with a similar disdain to that normally reserved for P.A. McHugh – the paper referring to him

---

17 J.C. McTernan, *A Sligo miscellany* (Dublin, 2000), p. 534.   18 F.S.L. Lyons, 'The aftermath of Parnell, 1891–1903' in W.E. Vaughan (ed.), *A new history of Ireland*, iii: *Ireland under the union, ii, 1870–1921* (Oxford, 1996), pp 82–3.   19 *SlSt*, 5 July and 12 July 1900.

as 'the Shah of Boyle'. Tully had a political career – like P.A. McHugh – sitting in parliament from 1892 until 1906.[20] He also wielded, as a result, significant influence in garnering public printing and advertising contracts in Roscommon.[21] Alfred McHugh worked for a brief period at the *Roscommon Herald*, but it was reported by the *Star* that he had become growingly resentful of Tully's demands regarding the content of his cartoons. On one occasion, when Alfred McHugh flatly refused this direction, an argument ensued in the office of the *Herald* in which a window was reportedly broken and the cartoonist was said to have 'attempted with qualified success to inflict similar injuries on the cranium of the proprietor'.[22] Legal proceedings followed, in which Alfred McHugh was imprisoned for a month; upon his release he was swiftly recruited by Dowd to join the *Sligo Star*. Dowd's interest in the whole affair had a commercial context, as the *Star* relied heavily on a circulation in north Roscommon, and carried a large column of news and notes from Boyle. The animosity between the two newspapers was further evidenced in November 1900, when Jasper Tully's brother, George, was fined 7s. 6d. for 'assaulting several newsboys who were selling the *Star* on the streets of Boyle'.[23] In 1902, the importance to local newspapers of revenue from public printing and advertising was highlighted when the *Star* went out of business; an editorial explained to readers that the principal reason was not a lack of readership or sales, but a failure to make an impact in bidding for public printing and advertising contracts.[24]

The *Sligo Independent*'s editor, Robert Smyllie, for his part, was broadly indignant at the new regime that had come about with the passing of the Local Government Act in 1898. He strongly criticized the county council for reportedly considering reopening a tendering process for the erection of an ornamental railing for the 1798 centenary monument in Sligo because the person who had been initially granted the contract was not a Catholic.[25] Smyllie satirically commented on the conflict between the *Champion* and the *Star*, attempting to reconcile conflicting reports in the two papers of a local concert in October 1900 in which Dowd had been a participant – the *Champion* claiming he had 'warbled a patriotic ditty' to a reception of 'groans ... welcomed by bricks', whereas the *Star* claimed he 'received an ovation for his melodious vocalism'.[26] But while such incidents may have been amusing to Smyllie and his readers, and while the *Independent* won a reasonable share of advertising revenue from Sligo's local public boards,[27] Smyllie would be – like Dowd – frustrated by the perceived favoritism shown to the *Champion* in county printing contracts. The *Champion* won the contract for the printing of forms, lists and registers in June 1901 despite tendering at a significantly higher price than the *Independent* – and also the *Star* – which offered the cheapest rate. In this matter, Smyllie and Dowd were concordant in their criticism of the process. 'In ordinary

---

20 Michael Wheatley, *Nationalism and the Irish Party: provincial Ireland, 1910–1916* (New York, 2005), p. 99. 21 *SlSt*, 9 Aug. 1900. 22 Ibid., 23 Aug. 1900. 23 Ibid., 27 Sept. 1900. 24 Ibid., 30 Oct. and 8 Nov. 1902 25 *SI*, 4 Nov. 1899. 26 Ibid., 13 Oct. 1900. 27 Ibid., 16 Apr. and 7 May 1901.

fair play – and particularly in the interest of the ratepayers – the contract should have been given to the company who offered it at the lowest price,' Smyllie wrote in support of the *Star*'s tender.[28]

Frustrated as he was, Smyllie would show remarkable pragmatism when, in 1909, he ended his relationship with the Gillmors and established his own newspaper, the *Sligo Times*. The editorial approach of his new paper was pragmatic, projecting a middle-ground persona in an attempt to appeal to the largely nationalist public boards for what was traditionally seen as the unionist share of public advertising. With some reason, Smyllie presumed Sligo's public bodies had an obligation to ensure their announcements were also read by Sligo's sizeable Protestant minority. This was an approach that had some success, and one which also placed him in direct opposition with the *Sligo Independent* more than with any nationalist newspaper.[29] However, broader controversies would arise in the even more competitive arena of public printing, where Smyllie's aggressively low tenders prompted a debate on fair wages that cut across political lines. The county council's deliberation on tenders for general county printing and the printing of the electoral register for the years 1911 to 1914 saw this debate in its sharpest focus. Smyllie's tender was significantly lower than that of any other newspaper, with only the *Leitrim Observer* coming close (see table 1.3).

Table 1.3: Bids for Sligo county council printing contracts, 1911–14

Paper	County register	General county printing
Sligo Times	£265 10s.	£248 10s.
Sligo Nationalist	£317 5s.	£350
Sligo Champion	£595 10s.	£300 10s.
Sligo Independent	£750	£320
Leitrim Observer	£279	n/a

The *Observer* was eliminated from consideration by the council on the grounds that local industry should be supported. Questions were raised about how Smyllie was able to offer such a cheap rate, to which he answered that he was the only qualified master printer in Sligo town and was the only printer equipped with the latest Linotype technology, which had cost £800. Smyllie contended that this machine could account for the output of seven typesetters working manually, but an alternative view was put forward by the council that it actually only accounted for four. In 1899, the council had passed a fair-wages resolution, and compelled those tendering for all public contracts to comply with this. The local branch of the Typographical Association also became involved, warning

28 Ibid., 4 June 1901.   29 Thadeus Kilgannon, *Kilgannon's almanac and directory of Sligo, 1907* (Sligo, 1907), pp 16–17; Sligo Musical Society concert programmes, 1883–1963 (Sligo County Library, ANN 23); *SI*, 2, 9 and 16 Jan. 1909.

that competition among nationalist and unionist newspapers would lead to an all-out price war in the printing sector.[30] The result of these ruminations was that the *Sligo Champion* was granted the contract, with Councilor Peter Cawley once again arguing strongly in its favor. His main point was that the *Champion* had a larger staff, whose employment relied on such contracts being granted. It would have been a shame, he contended, were the council to take a decision which would directly impact on local employment.[31]

Smyllie had been a natural champion for the interests of the ratepayers, as many of the business owners in Sligo town were Protestant. The council's bruising rebuff of Smyllie in the matter of the county printing contracts in 1911, on the grounds of workers' rights, was spun as a slap in the face to the ratepayers of the town.[32] However, the *Sligo Times* would not survive long enough to derive satisfaction from the vindication which was to follow. In 1913 it was reported that Tullus paper merchants of Edinburgh had brought a suit against Smyllie for debts of £78. The *Champion* asked, 'could the taking of contracts at unprofitable prices be accountable for this?'[33] However the *Times* was, by then, in total disarray, for reasons other than its cheap printing and advertising rates. The business never recovered from a fire that destroyed its premises in 1912, and in its aftermath, the business side of the newspaper fell into neglect. Recent accounts suggest Smyllie never had much aptitude for the business side of the newspaper at any rate,[34] but from 1913 his disorganization became particularly evident when he was late in with his tender for printing for Sligo agricultural committee and was disqualified, with the contract going to the *Sligo Nationalist*.[35] Whatever about Smyllie's enterprising approach to journalism, the day-to-day realities of business appeared beyond him. No more evidence of that was needed than the incident which led to the demise of the newspaper. Smyllie had employed an accountant who, unbeknownst to him, had been pocketing most of the money that had come in from the public and private advertising contracts for which he had fought so hard in the columns of his newspaper. The man, who was a relation of the Maguire family that owned the Brown Thomas business in Dublin, subsequently fled the country with approximately £15,000 before Smyllie knew what was happening, leaving his business in tatters. Smyllie declined to prosecute despite his friendship with the local Royal Irish Constabulary.[36] The issue of the *Sligo Times* was abruptly halted in February 1914, and the following month an item appeared in the *Sligo Champion* taken from the most recent edition of *Stubbs' Weekly Gazette* which confirmed that Smyllie had gone bankrupt.[37] Smyllie's son, R.M. (or 'Bertie'), would eclipse his father's journalistic career, becoming editor of the *Irish Times* in 1934 and holding that position for twenty years.[38]

30 Sligo county council: minute books, 1909–1914 (Sligo County Library, no. 931, vol. 3). See also *ST*, 3 June and 8 Sept. 1911. 31 *ST*, 8 Sept. 1911. 32 Ibid., 15 Sept. 1911. 33 *SC*, 10 May 1913. 34 Tony Gray, *Mr Smyllie, sir* (Dublin, 1991), pp 12–13. 35 *SN*, 20 Sept. 1913. 36 *II*, 20 Jan. 1914; *MC*, 11 Apr. 1914. 37 *SC*, 13 Mar. 1914. 38 John Horgan, *Irish media: a critical history since 1922* (London and New York, 2001), pp 44–5.

CHANGING ATTITUDES

The economic impact of the First World War changed attitudes towards competition for printing and advertising. The *Sligo Champion* and *Sligo Independent* agreed universal rates for personal advertising, and a tendering pact to ensure both received shares of public printing and advertising, with the overall goal of keeping employment in Sligo town. This pact was closely supported by the Sligo Trades Council, and was extended to include the radical nationalist newspaper, the *Connachtman* (initially established in 1908 as the more moderate *Sligo Nationalist*).[39] In the deliberations on the contract for county printing in 1921, this pact resulted in the tenders from the *Western People* and the *Roscommon Herald* being summarily excluded from consideration. At the council meeting, which was open to reporters, Robert George Bradshaw, the editor of the *Connachtman*, was accused by a representative of the *Western People* of perpetuating a 'ring' in Sligo town.[40] It was a view of such practices that was shared elsewhere, with a 'newspaper manager' quoted in the *Irish Independent* in 1917 as proclaiming:

> The members of the Typographical Association are playing a dangerous game just now in forcing the managers of provincial newspapers to pay wages which reduce the various properties to almost a state of bankruptcy. Do the printers forget that the war must come to an end very shortly, and hundreds of men will be looking for jobs? The men who are 'hustling' employers will not be readily forgotten, and their rapacious methods will win no sympathy from firms which have kept on the old and decrepit.[41]

In response to the *Western People*'s criticism, Bradshaw was reported to have said:

> It is to the mutual interests of those whom we employ ... that proper prices are paid by public bodies for work done. There is nothing very serious in that, and that 'ring' as you call it, will continue and will be maintained unbroken so long as the vital interests of our respective businesses are concerned, and so long as we are convinced we are inflicting no injustice on the ratepayers and the public.[42]

Bradshaw's final caveat was telling, as the playing of politics with local public printing and advertising contracts greatly contributed to the collapse of the borough's finances in 1917.

As the dire financial situation of Sligo borough council revealed itself fully in late 1917, a broad-based coalition of business owners had formed the Ratepayers' Association, campaigning vigorously for electoral reform as a panacea for the problems of one political grouping dominating local government. The association received its wish with the imposition of

39 *SC, CM, SI*, 17 Sept. 1921. 40 Michael Farry, *Sligo, 1914–1921: a chronicle of conflict* (Dublin, 1995), p. 130. 41 *II*, 6 July 1917. 42 Quoted in Farry, *Sligo, 1914–1921*, p. 130.

proportional representation in the Sligo Corporation Act of 1918 and the ensuing borough elections of January 1919.[43]

There were two great ironies in this. The first was that the *Sligo Champion* was now front and centre in campaigning for this reform, with its new editor, James Flynn, writing:

> The object of a borough council is not for nation-building or high-fa-luting political aims, but for ... regulating in a business-like way the public services of a particular borough ... . The Sligo corporation has always been elected on the political issue. The political bias has been the secret of its failure. In unionist hands the corporation went into debt. In nationalist hands it continued and advanced in that debt. In Sinn Fein [*sic*] hands the climax has been reached and it has become a perfect muddle.[44]

Necessity and revisionism were clearly the mother of invention for the *Champion*, as their continued support for home rule in the aftermath of the 1916 Easter Rising – and even after the general election of 1918 – meant they were no longer in the political ascendancy. Sinn Féin, now establishing political control in Sligo, were to be made scapegoats. Before losing his seat in an acrimonious campaign in North Sligo in that general election, Irish Party MP Thomas Scanlan made great haste in sponsoring the Sligo corporation bill in parliament, with his party colleague in South Sligo, Thomas O'Dowd (likewise defeated in that election), also instrumentally supporting the bill.[45]

The second great irony of this affair is that the Ratepayers' Association would have won more seats in the 1919 borough election under the old system than they did under proportional representation. With eight seats available in each ward, nine of their candidates (four in the west, two in the east and three in the north) polled in the top eight in their respective wards, yet only eight were elected. Despite gaining seven more first-preference votes than Sinn Féin's Thomas Flanagan in the west ward, ratepayer candidate James Hamilton was eliminated on the twelfth and final count, while Flanagan was returned six counts earlier. The same fate befell James Campbell on the eleventh count in the north ward, despite gaining eight more first preferences than a Sinn Féin candidate who was elected with relative comfort. In all, Sinn Féin ran five fewer candidates than the Ratepayers' Association, and were facilitated in their better vote management by the apparent enthusiasm of voters for the new system (many exercising up to eight preferences, having been well informed by instructions and illustrations in all of the local papers).[46]

The *Sligo Champion* survived beyond the civil war – indeed it is still in operation at the time of writing. But after the diminishing of home rule as a political force, the newspaper was rapidly depoliticized and frequently sermonized about the

43 Jennifer Hart, *Proportional representation: critics of the British electoral system, 1820–1945* (New York, 1992), pp, 199–206. See also Local Government (Ireland) Act, 1918 (8 & 9 Geo V) (30 July 1918) (cited in main text as the Sligo Corporation Act, 1918). 44 *SC*, 8 Sept. 1917. 45 Ibid.; *SI*, 26 Jan. 1918. 46 *SC*, 25 Jan. 1919.

dangers of national politics dominating local affairs – a marked contrast with the paper's approach under P.A. McHugh two decades earlier.[47] The *Sligo Independent*, too, abandoned its overt unionism under William Peebles, who rarely commented on national politics following his taking over both the editorship and proprietorship of the paper in 1920.[48] The *Connachtman*, meanwhile, did not survive beyond 1925. Unlike the *Champion* and the *Independent*, it never shook off its politics and, having been on the losing side in the civil war, its survival beyond 1922 was an achievement in itself. That year, it gave testimony of the extent of the struggle involved in producing an anti-treaty newspaper in an editorial on 23 September that noted that the present publication was undertaken with 'considerable difficulty' as 'many of those who have been employed in its production are on active service with the forces of the Republic, and the fight has put others off'.[49] But covering events during the civil war from a journalistic, rather than a political, point of view did not prove expedient either – the initial attitude of the Free State government towards the press following the war was one of distrust precisely because of this move away from partisan coverage.

Despite pleas from many local newspapers for a new source of national advertising revenue to replace many of the contracts that had sustained them in the past, there was a discernible lack of interest from the new Free State government in helping them.[50] But as the demarcation between national politics and local affairs continued, and as the number of different newspapers in Sligo diminished (only the *Champion* and the *Independent* remained after 1927), there was, too, a recession in the volume of newspaper content protesting at the destination of public printing and advertising. This was a consequence not only of the de-politicization of these newspapers but also of the trauma of the borough's 1917 bankruptcy, which necessitated the projection of corporate responsibility in how such matters were handled.[51]

A CONTEXT FOR HISTORICAL SCHOLARSHIP

It may seem too obvious to state that newspapers are one of the most important primary sources for the study of nineteenth and twentieth century history, but until recently the manner in which such material was used by historians has been criticized for lacking consideration of the context in which they were produced. Marie-Louise Legg and Stephen Koss have both contended that while newspapers were widely regarded as a historical source, too many histories involving a predominance of newspaper material treated the source material in such an arbitrary way that they were 'assembled rather than written'.[52]

47 Ibid., 28 July 1923.   48 *SI*, 4 Aug. 1923.   49 *CM*, 23 Sept. 1922. See also McTernan, *A Sligo miscellany*, pp 531–2.   50 Dept. of Finance: advertisements: applications from newspapers for government advertisements (National Archives of Ireland, attached to FIN1/2340).   51 *SC*, 4 Aug. 1923; *SI*, 4 Aug. and 18 Aug. 1923.52 Legg, *Newspapers and nationalism*, p. 11; Stephen Koss, *The rise and fall of the political press in Britain*, i: *The nineteenth century* (London, 1981), p. 7.

As has been highlighted in this chapter, a combination of complex factors greatly influenced the words on the pages of newspapers, underscoring the importance of this context in using such sources for historical study. In Sligo, politics and socio-economic considerations were inextricably linked in the production of newspapers at the turn of the twentieth century. The manner in which national politics permeated local life during the era of Parnell made this inevitable, and collaborated with industrial developments to spur on a boom of newspaper production in the early twentieth century. In all, thirteen different newspaper titles were produced between 1885 and 1927 in Sligo town. Two survived the period – the *Sligo Champion* and the *Sligo Independent*. The others were the *Sligo Chronicle* (1850–93), *Connacht Leader* (1885–7), *Sligo Gazette and Western Advertiser* (1888–91), *Sligo Advertiser* (1892–3), *Sligo Chronicle* (1896–9), *Sligo Star* (1899–1902), *Sligo Nationalist* (1908–20), *Sligo Times* (1909–14), *Connachtman* (1920–5), *Solais an Iarthair* (1926) and the *Sligo-Leitrim Liberator* (1927).[53] The prolonged coverage in the columns of the most prominent of these newspapers of the destinations of public printing and advertising can be attributed to the preponderance of national politics in local public bodies – and consequently in local journalism – but it also betrayed the self-consciousness of the emerging journalistic and printing professions in an era of great change. However, in the aftermath of the First World War, and with the financial collapse of the borough of Sligo, the disentanglement of local newspapers, as with local politics, from national affairs was well and truly underway by 1922.

---

53 McTernan, *A Sligo miscellany*, pp 531–7.

Evolving nationalism:
Michael McDermott-Hayes and the
Westmeath Independent, 1900–20

JOHN BURKE

The Irish provincial press assisted greatly in fostering the conditions that led to the redefinition of Ireland's political fortunes after 1900. In towns, villages and rural areas across the country, while many businessmen and big-house owners leafed through the national dailies, it is likely that the majority of people turned to the local newspaper for information. In a well-researched and general-interest provincial newspaper, people received a précis of much of what the national dailies, weeklies and some international publications had reported. The editors of these titles were figures of authority, whose editorials provided not only information, but guidance. The capacity for influencing political discourse did vary from publication to publication, yet, in many cases, it was substantial. Indeed, many political figures, MPs, ideologues and commentators owned, operated and edited their own provincial news title for this reason. In Athlone, the most important press title was the *Westmeath Independent*, the archetypal independently owned Irish provincial newspaper. Largely free from the direct influence of any MP, political party or ideology, it realigned its editorial opinion as Ireland's political situation evolved. While the title tended to support the most popular nationalist movements, that support was never slavish; its editorials were critical, even condemnatory, when necessary. Its editor for the majority of the period, Michael McDermott-Hayes, became a prominent pressman, one whose work not only informed and influenced local opinion, but also fed the national drive for Irish autonomy, something for which he endangered both his personal reputation and the newspaper itself.

By 1900, the *Westmeath Independent* was a stalwart of the Irish press scene. Established in Athlone in 1846 under the name *Westmeath Independent and Agricultural and Commercial Journal*, it was founded at a time when the Famine continued to claim thousands of lives and force the emigration of thousands more.[1] The newspaper maintained production throughout the crisis, outlasting the *Athlone Sentinel* (established in 1834), which closed in 1861, and the *Athlone Times* (established in 1886), which ceased production in 1902. It was produced in the Athlone Printing Works, a company owned and managed by the Chapmans, a Dublin family that purchased the concern in the 1880s. By

---

1 John Burke, *Athlone in the Victorian era* (Athlone, 2007), p. 285.

the end of the century, the *Westmeath Independent* dominated the newspaper market in the southern districts of Westmeath and Roscommon, while also circulating in Longford, Meath, Queen's County (Laois), Galway, Leitrim, Mayo, Sligo and King's County (Offaly), where a re-tailored version, the *King's County Independent*, was the most popular title in the west of that county. The supremacy of the *Westmeath Independent* ensured that the views of Athlone's citizens were influenced primarily by one newspaper. In contrast, Mullingar – in the east of the county – hosted up to four titles at various points during the period under study, with the consequence that particular political ideologies were catered for in dedicated publications. It was therefore necessary for the *Westmeath Independent* to present an editorial line that appealed to as wide a constituency as possible, ensured a good commercial return and limited the scope for a competitor to enter the market.

From its inception, the *Westmeath Independent* established an ability to vary its political allegiances. In the 1850s, the paper often promoted Conservative policies, in the 1870s it backed Liberal Party views and then in the 1880s and 1890s it made a definitive move to Irish nationalism, when Charles Stewart Parnell was increasing his profile through his work with the Land League, Irish National League and Irish Parliamentary Party (IPP).[2] The editorial line remained Parnellite after Parnell's death in 1892.[3] During the subsequent political turmoil the *Westmeath Independent* bemoaned the absence of unity in Irish nationalism, and it was not until 1900 that the newspaper again had a popular nationalist movement to which it could lend its support, when the United Irish League (UIL), the latest organization to concern itself with Irish land-ownership issues, gained additional prominence. When John Redmond, elected as IPP leader that same year, adopted the UIL as the party's grass-roots organization, the *Westmeath Independent* had a political personality to follow. Also in 1900, a young journalist named Michael McDermott-Hayes was added to the newspaper's staff; he would be the man who would lead the *Westmeath Independent* through the period when home rule and rebellion defined Irish politics.

Limerick-born McDermott-Hayes began his career with the *Limerick Leader* before moving first to the *Kilkenny Journal* and then to the *Midland Tribune*, eventually working with the *Daily Express* in Dublin.[4] He moved to Athlone in 1900 upon gaining a position with the *Westmeath Independent*, and was promoted to editor soon after. During his tenure, he increased the newspaper's size, coverage and distribution, at times claiming to edit the largest provincial newspaper in Ireland, which released up to 20,000 copies each week.[5] He promoted many nationalist causes but did not seek political office, as did many contemporary newspaper men, such as J.P. Hayden of the *Westmeath Examiner*.

2 Marie-Louise Legg, *Newspapers and nationalism: the Irish provincial press, 1850–1892* (Dublin, 1998), pp 44, 48, 220. 3 Burke, *Athlone in the Victorian era*, pp 183–202.   4 *WI*, 17 Feb. 1912.   5 Ibid., 15 Dec. 1900, 12 July 1902 and 31 Mar. 1906; *Leader*, 7 Apr. 1906

Seán Mac Eoin, stationed as the Irish Free State army officer-in-command in Athlone in 1922, noted in a 1966 article, 'The lone patriot', that McDermott-Hayes was 'very energetic [and] deeply interested in Irish affairs', but that his efforts and influence had been largely ignored.[6]

During the early years of his editorship, the *Westmeath Independent* attracted the attention of other Irish pressmen. UIL founder William O'Brien's *Irish People* repeatedly referred to the *Westmeath Independent*'s reports, such as in 1907 when the Irish council bill, a Liberal Party sop to the IPP designed to dampen the desire for home rule, was being excoriated in the Athlone paper's columns.[7] Consistent support also came from editor D.P. Moran of the Dublin weekly the *Leader*, who lauded the *Westmeath Independent* for its commitment to Irish industry and 'excellent' reports.[8] Criticism too came, especially from minority press titles such as the *United Irishman*, edited by Arthur Griffith. The *United Irishman* criticized the *Westmeath Independent*'s use of 'green paper of foreign manufacture', accusing the publication of trying to be 'all things to all men', and contrasting its support for the Gaelic League with its reports on British army sports.[9] In general, however, research has shown that the *Westmeath Independent* was a respected news source, which, by 1913, when the need came to drive the formation of a nationalist militia, had a strong enough voice to ensure that the idea reached areas distant from Athlone.

An important step in gaining this authoritative voice was establishing the *Westmeath Independent* as an influential advocate for the strongest political ideology at the time in Ireland: constitutional nationalism. McDermott-Hayes was at the forefront of efforts to reinvigorate local nationalism in the wake of IPP reorganization, issuing strong editorial directives to Athlone's citizens. From 1900 to 1912, the *Westmeath Independent* promoted Irish Party candidates in elections, Irish Party endeavours at Westminster, as well as nationalist meetings in the town and the formation of Athlone's UIL branches. It was the primary motivator in encouraging locals to contribute to the parliamentary fund, the revenue source for IPP activities.[10] Given the considerable energies invested, it was unsurprising that when the IPP held the balance of power between Conservatives and Liberals in the House of Commons in 1910, and appeared capable of leveraging home rule for Ireland, McDermott-Hayes redoubled his efforts.

The *Westmeath Independent* editor was not the only Irishman to increase his political activism in the face of home rule. Unionists concentrated in the north-east of Ireland viewed home rule as a threat to their political and economic existence. They were convinced that a Dublin parliament dominated by nationalist Roman Catholics would act in ways inimical to unionist interests. In early 1912, as the home rule bill took shape, unionists established a militia to complement their

6 Seán Mac Eoin, 'The lone patriot', *Comorú na Cásca Digest*, 8 (1966), pp 189–90.   7 *IP*, 14 Sept., 28 Sept. and 2 Nov. 1907.   8 *Leader*, 7 Apr. 1904, 18 Nov. and 10 Feb. 1905, 12 May 1906, 19 Jan. and 23 Mar. 1907, and 11 July 1908.   9 *UI*, 17 Sept. 1904.   10 John Burke, *Athlone, 1900–1923: politics, revolution and civil war* (Dublin, 2015), pp 12–42.

existing political agitation. The introduction of the threat of force led McDermott-Hayes to enter his most politically charged editorial period yet.

From late spring 1912 to the summer of 1913, McDermott-Hayes' polemics were informed by two main ideas. First, that the introduction of the 'adequate and generous'[11] home rule bill was inevitable, and second, that unionist threats were a bluff. His relevant editorials during this time were suffused with upbeat yet realistic assessments of home rule's progress, as well as references to unionist activities, which he often dismissed out of hand. The *Westmeath Independent* referred repeatedly to the 'fallacious' arguments promulgated by unionists, describing their push for a 'violent refusal' of home rule as 'blackguardism'.[12] The creation in September 1912 of the Solemn League and Covenant, a written declaration of unionists' intention to resist home rule, drew yet more criticism from McDermott-Hayes who singled out Edward Carson, the Ulster Unionist Party leader, for censure. Carson – or 'King Carson', or 'General Carson' – was the manufacturer of 'an exploded squib',[13] the orchestrator of a theatrical ploy.

From early 1913 it became apparent that McDermott-Hayes, like many people across Ireland, began to take the threat of unionist violence more seriously. The main factor in this change of attitude was the Ulster Unionist Party's adoption in January 1913 of the unionist militia that would become known as the Ulster Volunteer Force (UVF). That month, the House of Lords rejected the home rule bill for the first time. The rejection was expected – the Lords could reject a bill three times before it was passed over their heads – but the adoption of the UVF appeared to be an ominous portent. This impression grew as time passed, and while the *Westmeath Independent* described the anti-home rule overtones of the unionists' marching season in July 1913 as displaying 'corner boy character-istics', Carson's promise to source arms for the UVF caused the editor to reassess unionist actions and complement his activism on the printed page with a more tangible counterbalance to unionists' activities.[14] In September 1913, along with a number of Athlone men, McDermott-Hayes formed the Midland Volunteers Force (MVF), twentieth-century Ireland's first organized nationalist militia, a group whose influence has been dramatically underplayed in Irish historiography.[15]

The reportage on the formation, development and influence of the MVF provides good evidence of the *Westmeath Independent*'s ability to influence the nationalist agenda. In articles published in the 11 and 18 October editions of the paper, McDermott-Hayes presented exaggerated reports on the parades of the MVF, replete with eye-catchingly large estimates of the numbers of men involved, and warnings to unionist agitators.[16] Whatever the details, the reputation of *Westmeath Independent* was such that many other publications accepted the articles' veracity. On 14 October, the *Evening Herald* ran an article on the MVF, followed the next day by the *Freeman's Journal* and *Irish Times*,

---

11 *WI*, 13 Apr. 1912. 12 Ibid., 3 and 10 Aug. 1912. 13 Ibid., 28 Sept. 1912. 14 Ibid., 5 and 19 July 1913. 15 Burke, *Athlone, 1900–1923*, pp 84–9. 16 *WI*, 11 and 18 Oct. 1913.

the latter the only publication to refer to the parades as 'alleged'.[17] The *Irish Independent* ran an article the following week, as did the *Derry Journal*, which dedicated a full column.[18] The November edition of the advanced nationalist *Irish Freedom* engaged, albeit in critical fashion, while the news also made the *Manchester Guardian*, the IPP's most prominent British supporter. The articles were noticed by political figures including Laurence Ginnell, the firebrand independent Irish nationalist MP, and the Gaelic League's Eoin MacNeill, assisting him in his decision to form the Irish Volunteers (IV) in late November 1913, a body which the MVF would join one month later.[19]

With the formation of the IV, the influence of the MVF was attenuated in the short term. However, as the passing of the home rule bill came closer during early 1914 and increasing tensions between the IV and UVF threatened to derail it, the Athlone force was to be an important player in justifying John Redmond's logical decision to seize control of the nationalist militia. Redmond's 'adoption' in May disgruntled advanced nationalists within the IV, yet the majority of their fellow members, letting their views be known via the press in June and July, supported Redmond's right to direct and control the IV, adverting to Athlone's founding role in creating the militia as a constitutional nationalist force in the first instance.[20] This debate took on a more cut-throat appearance in September 1914 after Redmond delivered a speech at Woodenbridge, Co. Wicklow, in which he stated that IV members should fight for the British army in the recently declared Continental war. Redmond's speech led to a split in the volunteers and on this occasion, McDermott-Hayes was at the forefront of the debate.

As was case with most political debates, each side argued their points using newspapers. The *Irish Volunteer*, previously the voice for all volunteers, was, after the fracture, now dedicated to promoting the advanced nationalist group, the IV, with the newly founded *National Volunteer* promoting Redmond's Irish National Volunteers. McDermott-Hayes spearheaded the promotion of the Redmonite line, with his first swipe at Eoin MacNeill and his colleagues being a letter to the *Freeman's Journal*. In its 26 September edition, McDermott-Hayes, described as 'Chairman of the First Organising Committee', lambasted the 'ridiculous pretensions of the Dublin "Unknowns"'. The *Westmeath Independent* editor demanded it be acknowledged that the MVF was set up, 'to lend whatever assistance was possible to Mr Redmond and the Irish Party'.[21] His letter was reproduced in the 17 October edition of the *National Volunteer*, under the headline 'Genesis of the Originals'.[22] The debate on the origins of the movement was only part of a wider argument, however, as advanced nationalists understood that to effectively undermine the MVF they needed to denigrate its most vocal defender.

17 *EH*, 14 Oct. 1913; *FJ*, 15 Oct. 1913; *IT*, 15 and 18 Oct. 1913 18 *II*, 25 Oct. 1913; *DJ*, 27 Oct. 1913.
19 *MG*, 24 Nov. 1913; *CT*, 27 Dec. 1913; Burke, *Athlone, 1900–1923*, pp 85–94. 20 For examples, see: *CT*, 6 June 1914; *SSt*, 6 June and 13 June 1914; *FJ*, 8, 10 and 16 June 1914, 14 and 21 July 1914; *SF*, 13 June 1914; *Leader*, 20 June 1914; *WI*, 20 June 1914; *II*, 20 June 1914 21 *FJ*, 26 Sept. 1914. 22 *NV*, 17 Oct. 1914.

Attacks on McDermott-Hayes came from a variety of sources. A former supporter of an Athlone origin for the IV, D.P. Moran, was the most prominent critic, as he was profoundly opposed to Irishmen enlisting in the British army. He attempted to undermine Redmond's right to direct the IV in the *Leader*'s 3 October edition: 'Some ... force was started in Athlone ... [W]e understand it was more or less of a hoax ... [A]n Athlone ... paper, of which a Mr Hayes is editor ... wrote the matter up as ... fact; we understand that it was ... farcical'.[23] This attack on the *Westmeath Independent* editor's professional reputation was followed by another from Ballaghadereen man M.J. Judge, a contributor to the *Irish Volunteer*: '[T]he Athlone Volunteers ... had no existence save in the wild fancies of a journalist who had ... indulged too freely in the "glowing cup".'[24] This charge was believed by others, such as a prominent advanced nationalist, Corkman Liam de Róiste, who stated in his personal diary that: 'The whole affair existed in the mind of a journalist of the town [Athlone] on a "booze".'[25]

While the criticism from advanced nationalists was strong, it represented the views of a minority. In late 1914, most Irish press publications supported an Athlone origin for the IV, Irish recruitment and Redmond's enlistment call. It is consistent then, that as recruitment calls were made, the *Westmeath Independent* was a supporter of Irish enlistment. McDermott-Hayes, like many of his contemporaries, believed that Irish enlistment would show gratitude for home rule legislation and prove that Irishmen would assume their responsibilities as members of the British imperial network. Over the eighteen months from the commencement of the war to Easter 1916, he provided strong support for 'the effort', criticizing the enlistment-shy – the 'craven-hearted curs' – in Connacht.[26] He crowed about Westmeath's recruitment record, which, by the end of 1915, he stated, was proportionately better than that of any other county.[27] As recruiting levels fell in late 1915 and early 1916, McDermott-Hayes supplemented his efforts by publishing 'galleries of heroes', images of local men fighting at the front.[28] He continued to provide backing for the IPP, congratulating them for ensuring that Irish conscription was not introduced, while also taking the time to evaluate the efforts of the most prominent anti-enlistment party, Sinn Féin, whose anti-war actions he viewed as patriotic, if misplaced.[29]

However, the rebellion staged during Easter 1916 was to see McDermott-Hayes re-evaluate his views. In the 29 April edition of the *Westmeath Independent*, he lambasted the rebels who initiated the rebellion, condemning them for jeopardizing home rule; 'the work of so many years'.[30] One week later, after eight leaders had been executed, his views softened considerably, along with those of many of his readers, and, along with others across Ireland, he called on the government to moderate its response:

23 *Leader*, 3 Oct. 1914.   24 *IV*, 10 Oct. 1914.   25 U271/A/16, Cork City and County Archives, Liam de Róiste Diary, 11 Nov. 1914, pp 22–3.   26 *WI*, 24 Oct. 1914; 17 Apr. 1915.   27 Ibid., 31 July, 25 Sept. and 2 Oct. 1915.   28 See all editions of the *WI* from 8 Jan. to 18 Mar. 1916 inclusive.   29 Ibid., 25 Mar 1916.   30 Ibid., 29 Apr. 1916.

> [The] crime ... against Ireland has been a terrible one ... the poor dreamers ...
> deluded by German intrigue ... It is the duty of Ireland to plead for mercy for
> the misguided young fellows ... They are the class from whom has been drawn
> the Irish soldier ... [P]unishment if it must be for the leaders – but not ... death.[31]

In addition to his censure of the British, McDermott-Hayes was also annoyed with
the IPP for their inaction on behalf of those executed, and those who had been
arrested in the nationwide raids by crown forces that followed the rebellion. He
welcomed John Dillon's 'rivers of blood' speech in the House of Commons, which
appeared to presage a more vigorous IPP response, but soon had to accept it as
the largely empty rhetoric that it was, and set about engaging more actively in
agitating for a more appropriate response from the British authorities.[32] He and
Athlone Printing Works owner Thomas Chapman had to assume the responsibility of protesting vigorously on behalf of Athlone's internees, something that
McDermott-Hayes did so energetically that he was called to account by the local
military commander.[33]

McDermott-Hayes' need to act on behalf of the internees was fed by his growing
sense that the IPP was neglecting its duties, something his readers must have
recognized when digesting his editorials, editorials that in turn reflected their own
changing attitudes. He, like many others, believed that John Redmond did little to
moderate the British reaction to the Rising, a reaction which disregarded the sacrifices
of Irishmen at the front. He drew people's attention to the unchecked unionist
influence in the British cabinet, something that he believed was going to undermine
home rule and lead to Ireland being partitioned. In early June, McDermott-Hayes
condemned moves by British Prime Minister Lloyd George to move ahead with
home rule and partition; he did so in exceptionally strong language over three issues,
describing the proposals as 'bastard home rule', and stating his preference for martial
law as an alternative.[34] Given the by then obvious IPP acceptance of partition in some
form, the Athlone editor began to look ever more seriously at Sinn Féin arguments
during July and in the run-up to the execution of Roger Casement on 3 August. The
determination of the authorities to execute Casement confirmed for McDermott-
Hayes that Irish nationalists' views were of little interest to the British, something
he hoped the IPP would accept as a now indisputable fact. He wrote of one of Sinn
Féin's more positive effects on Irish politics and Redmond's party:

> No matter what else we owe Sinn Féin – we owe to it the awakening of the
> country and ... Irish Party to the ... danger we exposed ourselves [to] when we
> surrendered the ... weapon of independent opposition to all British parties.[35]

By September, his anger at IPP inactivity had boiled over, and he demanded
that the home rule bill, now certain to be compromised, should 'be given to the
flames'.[36] He began to now promote, rather than just comment upon, aspects of

31 Ibid., 6 May 1916. 32 Ibid., 13 May 1916. 33 Ibid., 10 June 1916. 34 Ibid., 10, 17 and 24 June 1916.
35 Ibid., 5 Aug. 1916. 36 Ibid., 9 and 16 Sept. 1916.

Sinn Féin's policy, as would become apparent when by-elections were staged for the constituencies of North Roscommon and South Longford the following spring.

Still not fully disengaged from constitutional nationalism, the newspaper's reaction to the win of Count Plunkett, the Sinn Féin-backed candidate in North Roscommon in February, was contextualized in terms of IPP reinvigoration at Westminster. McDermott-Hayes termed the Sinn Féin call for parliamentary abstention as 'foolish', given that he, like so many others, found it difficult to envisage Ireland gaining political autonomy simply by asserting her independence and disengaging from Britain.[37] However, simple, provocative acts, such as the prohibition of the 1917 St Patrick's Day parade in Athlone by the local RIC, exerted an influence that saw the *Westmeath Independent* lend additional support to Sinn Féin for the South Longford by-election in May.[38] Citing the likelihood of 'Headlong Orange triumph', given the 'deadly inaction' of the IPP on the issue of partition, the Athlone newspaper was foursquare behind Joe McGuinness, the representative of the party that promised action on the issue.[39] The newspaper's championing of the Sinn Féin candidate did come in for criticism, most notably from D.P. Moran in the *Leader*, who stated that the Athlone publication was happy to run recruitment advertisements, and was unlikely to support the republic that many Sinn Féin members were seeking.[40] McDermott-Hayes could not distance himself from the *Westmeath Independent*'s support for the war effort and neither, as became apparent, did he wish to. He viewed a victory for the Triple Entente as essential, and something that Ireland should have a role in; supporting Sinn Féin and victory in the war were not mutually incompatible, in his view. However, his support for the war effort was not unconditional or limitless, and during the summer of 1917, as the threat of Irish conscription loomed again, he moved definitively towards Sinn Féin, as did so many of his readers.

One of the obstacles that faced McDermott-Hayes' move to Sinn Féin was his poor understanding of its aims and potential, something that was apparent in the 23 June edition of the *Westmeath Independent*: 'Sinn Féin, whatever it may ultimately end in, has caught the fancy of the country.'[41] To combat this common problem, Sinn Féin campaigned across Ireland, holding meetings to advertise its main aims: resistance to conscription; representation for Ireland at the post-war peace conference; and complete independence from Britain. Deployed alongside these events were branch organization meetings to create a pervasive grass-roots Sinn Féin organization. The move of the *Westmeath Independent* to Sinn Féin became clear as both Thomas Chapman and McDermott-Hayes assumed committee positions in the Athlone branch that was formed in August.[42] Indeed, the latter's support for Sinn Féin at this time even led him to publish a retrospective article on the MVF, in which, with more than a little irony and less success, he attempted to trace the force's foundation back to a Sinn Féin meeting in Athlone during August 1913.[43]

37 Ibid., 24 Mar. 1917. 38 Ibid., 5 May 1917. 39 Ibid., 19 May 1917. 40 *Leader*, 12 May 1917. 41 *WI*, 23 June 1917. 42 Ibid., 18 Aug. 1917. 43 Ibid., 25 Aug. 1917.

As 1917 drew to a close, it became apparent that the IPP was not capable of faithfully representing Irish nationalists' concerns. The doomed Irish Convention, a political sop designed by British Prime Minister Lloyd George to pacify discontented American political opinion, had occupied much of the party's time, yet had yielded no useful result. The *Westmeath Independent* highlighted the impotence of the IPP as it made its definitive break from the party after the death while on hunger strike of Irish Volunteer Thomas Ashe. The *Westmeath Independent* published an account of Ashe's death, and McDermott-Hayes editorialized that 'the policy of Sinn Féin ... [was now the] only effective weapon to save the Irish nation'.[44] Like other commentators, he made a distinction between MIPs and MEPs – members of the Irish parliament and members of the English parliament – the former being those who 'scorn to touch the English bribe' of the £400 annual wage of MPs.[45] By early 1918 his opinion of Irish constitutional nationalism was as low as it had ever been; the IPP was nothing more than the epitome of the:

> sham constitutional movement prosecuted since the death of Parnell ... governed and dictated by English Liberals [which] was ... bleeding Ireland to death. [The IPP] was ... politically and morally atrophied when Sinn Féin stepped in.[46]

John Redmond's death soon after the *Westmeath Independent* published this did not soften McDermott-Hayes' views. While producing a balanced piece for Redmond's obituary, he excoriated the IPP for electing as his replacement John Dillon, a man McDermott-Hayes censured for criticizing 'the real national movement', Sinn Féin.[47] This criticism of the IPP increased when the party moved to share the same platform as Sinn Féin during the most heated anti-conscription campaign of the war.

During 1918, no other issue carried the political currency of Irish conscription. A diminished British army required recruits, and, since early 1916, Ireland had proved unwilling to supplement the ranks with the numbers required. The move by the British government to impose conscription on Ireland met with exceptional resistance and gave Sinn Féin a well-defined and emotive issue to focus on in the immediate term. The IPP's opposition to conscription, though consistent with Redmond's earlier stance, appeared to many observers, not least McDermott-Hayes, to be the adoption of Sinn Féin policy, something for which 'the miserable nondescript of a played out, beaten and discredited faction', should be ashamed.[48] Indeed, such was the paper's antipathy towards the IPP during this episode, that the *Irish Independent* noted that it was becoming known 'as one of the most outspoken critics of the Irish Party in the provincial press'.[49] As the *Westmeath Independent*'s vitriol peaked in late March 1918, alongside many of its readers' own opposition to conscription, the press censor adjudged that it

---

44 Ibid., 6 Oct. 1917. 45 Ibid., 22 Sept. and 13 Oct. 1917. 46 Ibid., 5 Jan. 1918. 47 Ibid., 30 Mar. 1918.
48 Ibid. 49 *II*, 6 Apr. 1918.

had breached the Defence of the Realm Act (DORA) and ordered its closure in April. The closure lasted just three weeks, but the censor believed that it 'had an effect of the most salutary nature on the whole Irish press', despite McDermott-Hayes gaining considerable publicity and support for his related protestations.[50] His efforts increased his profile further, and assisted him in securing the position of chairman of the Central Ireland Branch of the Irish Journalists' Association just two months later.[51]

Upon recommencing publication, the *Westmeath Independent* made no effort to change the editorial policy that had so antagonised the press censor. Two weeks after reopening, the title described General John French, the new Irish lord lieutenant, as a 'military dictator', instated to enforce the 'blood tax' of conscription.[52] By November 1918, McDermott-Hayes was publishing articles declaring the betrayal of Ireland by Lloyd George, reinvigorating his previous condemnations of moves towards partition and allying these with predictions that 'Midland and western counties [are] to be parcelled out among English and Scotch soldiers.'[53] Numerous editorials adverted to French's efforts to crush Sinn Féin, and also asserted that the imminent general election would prove that the Irish people had decided that Sinn Féin was the party which would best serve their interests. The *Westmeath Independent* championed the two local Sinn Féin candidates, Laurence Ginnell in Westmeath and Harry Boland in South Roscommon, and in doing so abandoned the two incumbents, IPP stalwart J.P. Hayden, and Sir Walter Nugent, by this point an isolated quasi-nationalist former IPP member. The victories of the local Sinn Féin candidates and seventy-one others on 18 December 1918 assured McDermott-Hayes that Ireland could now move forward; 'the obliteration of the Irish Party was essential'.[54] Three weeks later, after the inaugural meeting of Dáil Éireann, Ireland's national parliament, the *Westmeath Independent* proclaimed that, 'the ill-fated connection with Britain' was 'terminated',[55] a political reality that would require additional sacrifices.

The convening of Dáil Éireann suggested that Irish political autonomy would be achieved via a political process. However, on the same day, a fatal attack on RIC men carried out by members of the IV at Soloheadbeg, Co. Tipperary suggested otherwise. McDermott-Hayes described the attack as an 'appalling outrage and shocking crime', however, yet again, the British response would further radicalize the editor. He continuously promoted the image of a pernicious British administration through his publication of articles ranging from the short prison diary of local IV leader Seán O'Hurley, to extensive testimonies in court reports and editorials concerning the widely reported decision of a British army picket to charge a meeting held by Laurence Ginnell TD in Athlone during May 1919.[56]

50 British in Ireland Series, 'Press censorship', Apr. 1918, CO 904/166, pp 425–30.   51 *II*, 17 June 1919.
52 *WI*, 11 and 25 May 1918.   53 Ibid., 23 Nov. 1918.   54 Ibid., 4 Jan. 1919.   55 Ibid., 25 Jan. 1919.
56 Ibid., 8 Feb., 29 Mar. and 10 May 1919; *NG*, 10 May 1919; *IT*, 10 May 1919; *IM*, 10 May 1919; British in Ireland Series, 'RIC county inspector's report, Westmeath', May 1919, CO/904/109; British in Ireland Series, 'Republican suspects', Laurence Ginnell, 11 May 1919, CO 904/202/162, p. 156.

The *Westmeath Independent*'s castigation of the British government was hardly diluted by new press-censorship rules introduced in the late summer, with its editorial line continuing to be 'hostile to the government and openly sympathetic to Sinn Féin'.[57]

This sympathy for Sinn Féin was to be enhanced during 1920. As the structures of an administration loyal to Dáil Éireann were established, McDermott-Hayes' criticism of British political efforts increased. He described the drafting committee for the government of Ireland bill, as 'hateful ... to Irishmen', the scheme as a 'ridiculous farce' and its conse-quences as 'the Nation ... split in two, the bleeding of Irish wealth and resources is to continue'.[58] The *Westmeath Independent* promoted both Sinn Féin and Labour during the 1920 local-authority elections in January and June, reminding all such bodies of the need to affiliate with Dáil Éireann.[59] Strong support for the republican or Sinn Féin court system came too, as did promotion of the 'Republican Police', who supplanted the ostracized RIC, a force the *Westmeath Independent* accused of arresting Irish people for refusing to comply with unjust British laws.[60] The death of republican hunger striker Terence MacSwiney in September, and raids in the Athlone region by crown forces, the Black and Tans and RIC Auxiliary soon after, reinforced his views on the malignancy of British rule. His expressive editorializing greatly aggrieved members of these locally stationed forces, who decided in mid-October 1920 to permanently shut down the *Westmeath Independent*. After one attack on the paper's offices, McDermott-Hayes responded gravely:

> We ... condemn the administration ... which every day is reducing ... Ireland to rotten degeneracy ... [it] is an indication of the terrorism under which we live ... [we] denounced the ... misrule ... There is no bravado in this. We know the danger in which our property stands.[61]

Indeed, that danger was very real. Assurances gained from the authorities by the ailing Thomas Chapman's brother with regard to the protection of the Athlone Printing Works proved hollow, as an escalation in republican activity in the region saw crown forces seek out a soft target for retribution. On 3 November 1920, it was burned to the ground and the *Westmeath Independent* was forced out of production. It would not publish again under McDermott-Hayes' editorship.

By the time the *Westmeath Independent* restarted publication in February 1922, the political context in Ireland had changed quite radically. Rehiring McDermott-Hayes was never countenanced. A moderate voice was deemed more suitable in light of the schism in Irish republicanism that was then developing. Ivan Chapman, the late Thomas' brother, hired Cathal Ó Tuathail, an Irish-speaking nationalist; people were to read his editorials as the Irish Free State began to take shape.

57 CI Report, Westmeath, Sept. 1919, CO/904/110. 58 *WI*, 18 Oct. and 27 Dec. 1919. 59 Burke, *Athlone, 1900–1923*, pp 84–9. 60 *WI*, 10, 24 and 31 July, and 7 Aug. 1920. 61 Ibid., 23 Oct. 1920.

After the destruction of the *Westmeath Independent* offices in 1920 Michael McDermott-Hayes had attempted to set up a new newspaper in Tullamore. However, the challenge was insurmountable at a time when money was scarce and newspapers appeared to be risky ventures, especially one with a fiery editor at the helm. In 1921 he left Athlone after being hired by the *Irish News* in Belfast, initially as a journalist, then as a sub-editor on the international desk. His decision to work with IPP leader Joe Devlin's newspaper appears to have been one of necessity rather than of preference, yet it did allow McDermott-Hayes to again take up his pen and write his opposition to unionist activities. He remained on the staff of the newspaper until he died, largely impoverished, in 1924. He was 54 years old. His passing was marked in the *Freeman's Journal* and *Irish Independent*, both of which ran obituaries that reminded readers of his founding role in the Irish Volunteers.[62]

McDermott-Hayes was one of a number of Irish provincial press editors whose legacy has been largely ignored in modern historiographical works on early twentieth-century Ireland. It is certain however, that his contribution to Irish nationalism, both constitutional and advanced, was an essential aspect of its success, popularity and, indeed, failure in the areas in which the *Westmeath Independent* circulated. The establishment of the MVF provided proof that McDermott-Hayes was not content to simply observe and comment on the changes in Irish nationalism, but wanted to directly influence them. He was also able to recognize when allegiances needed to change, and when it was more important to say what was required, rather than what was permissible – something for which he and the *Westmeath Independent* paid dearly.

62 *FJ*, 4 Apr. 1924; *II*, 4 Apr. 1924.

'All the news of interest': the *Kerryman*, 1904–88

MARK O'BRIEN

Like many regional newspapers, the *Kerryman* emerged from the success of a printing business, in this case the Kerry Printing Company, established in 1902 with a modest £500 in capital, which allowed for little more than the purchase of a second-hand printing press and the hire of a Linotype machine.[1] The company was established by Maurice Griffin, his close friend Thomas Nolan, and the latter's cousin, Daniel Nolan – and in due course the *Kerryman* made its debut in August 1904. Of the three founding fathers only one had any experience in journalism. For some years Maurice Griffin had been a correspondent in his home town of Dingle for the *Kerry Weekly Reporter*. Having trained as an accountant and relocated to Tralee to take up employment at a building firm, Griffin met Thomas Nolan and the two became lifelong friends.[2] It was Griffin who most influenced the paper's editorial ethos. He joined the Sinn Féin movement in its original incarnation and supported the ideas of self-sufficiency and native industrialization espoused by Arthur Griffith. Indeed, one report in the *Kerryman* from 1906 noted that Tralee's Sinn Féin society held a meeting chaired by Griffin at the paper's premises.[3] Griffin was elected to Tralee urban district council in 1908 and served as the *Kerryman*'s managing director for many years. Complementing Griffin, Thomas Nolan's skills lay in editorial direction: he was, his obituary noted, 'widely read, a fluent writer and highly intelligent'.[4] Both Griffin and Nolan sat on the Kerry county board of the Gaelic Athletic Association (GAA), alongside other prominent persons, such as Austin Stack.[5] The third partner, Daniel Nolan, also trained as an accountant and devoted himself to the commercial side of the house following Griffin's death in 1928. Nolan also involved himself in the movements associated with the Gaelic revival: he served as secretary of the Tralee branch of the Gaelic League; and immersed himself in the life of the town, serving as secretary of the Tralee Sports Field Committee from 1903 to 1909.[6]

On its debut, the *Kerryman* entered a crowded field. Among the titles then circulating in the county were the *Kerry Evening Post* (1774–1917), *Kerry Sentinel* (1878–1918), *Kerry Weekly Reporter* (1883–1936), *Killarney Echo* (1899–1920), *Kerry News* (1894–1941), *Kerry Evening Star* (1902–14) and *Kerry People*

---

1 *IT*, 11 Dec. 1954, p. 2. 2 *KM*, 7 Apr. 1928, p. 5. 3 Ibid., 12 May 1906, p. 5. 4 Ibid., 8 Apr. 1939, pp 1, 6. 5 Ibid., 7 Oct. 1905, p. 3. 6 *IT*, 30 Apr. 1938, p. 8; *KM*, 23 Apr. 1938, p. 6.

(1902–28). Only one of these titles, the *Kerry Evening Post*, represented conservative (unionist) interests: the others represented the worldview of the Irish Parliamentary Party.[7] The *Kerryman* would outlast them all. Its first edition, with a print run of 1,200 copies and costing one penny, was published on Saturday 20 August 1904 and consisted of ten pages of news and adverts. Unlike the national daily press but similar to some of the more established regional papers, such as the *Anglo-Celt*, the *Connaught Telegraph*, the *Longford Leader* and the *Southern Star*, it placed news rather than adverts on its front page. Among its front-page stories were reports on emigration, the Tralee *feis*, the Cahirciveen petty sessions, and the meeting of Tralee and Fenit pier and harbour board, while inside pages carried reports of meetings from around the county, including reports on the Dingle board of guardians and Listowel urban council. Its adverts were drawn from well-known Tralee businesses including drapery store J. Revington & Sons, food merchants Latchford & Sons and coal merchants McCowen & Sons, and there also were a significant number of smaller adverts for Dingle businesses, reflecting perhaps, Maurice Griffin's Dingle origins. It also carried a story in the Irish language, 'Coiste gan capall' ('The headless coach') with an English translation alongside. Given the proprietors' interest in the GAA, the first edition was somewhat sparse in relation to sport: it carried a short report of a recent meeting of the Kerry county board. The first edition also carried a column of notes from the Kerryman's Association in New York. Headed 'American Letter' it declared that 'a journal run on manly and independent lines [that enunciated] nationalist principles and policies should certainly be a most important factor in the upbuilding of an Irish Ireland by inculcating among the people a spirit of self-reliance and self-respect'. Such a journal was needed, it continued, given that 'shoneenism and toadyism' were rampant in Kerry, which had been most recently demonstrated:

> during the recent visit of the king of England when the flunkeys of Tralee and Killarney went out of their way to present him with an address of welcome, thus disgracing Irishmen everywhere and bringing the blush of shame to the cheeks of Kerrymen all over the world.[8]

Its first leading article – 'About Ourselves' – was somewhat understated. It declared that it would 'be a straight, independent paper, conducted on sound Catholic and nationalist lines' and that it would give 'expression to what is sound and honest, in public opinion'. It also affirmed that it would 'devote such energies and ability as we possess to the development of those healthier phases of our national life' and declared that 'those young movements which are working in the reconstruction of an Ireland that will be really Irish shall have our best support, and the first claim on our space'.[9]

Edited jointly in its early years by Maurice Griffin and Thomas Nolan, the

---

7 For more on the *KS*, see P. Fitzgerald, 'The keys of the kingdom: the *Kerry Sentinel*, its commercial & political rivals', *Journal of the Kerry Historical and Archaeological Society*, 2:15 (2015), pp 103–20.　　8 *KM*, 20 Aug. 1904, p. 3.　　9 Ibid., 20 Aug. 1904, p. 4.

Kerryman devoted considerable space to the county's GAA activities – including Kerry's first All-Ireland football win in 1905.[10] It also devoted significant space to the activities of the local units of the Irish Volunteers, including the fact that the vast majority of members in Kerry sided with Eoin MacNeill rather than John Redmond when the movement split on the issue of whether Irishmen should enlist in the British army. It reported that, at a meeting of the Tralee Battalion, when Redmond's representative, Thomas O'Donnell MP, showed up uninvited 'only the stern sense of discipline of the corps saved him from being bodily thrown out of the hall'.[11] The *Kerryman* opposed Irishmen enlisting during the First World War and, when, in November 1914, fifty Belgian refugees – many of them men of fighting age – arrived in Kerry it declared that it was 'a matter of surprise that Irishmen should be asked to go out and fight for a country which these men have deserted'. The judicial division of the chief secretary's office noted that the paper 'had been especially and consistently disloyal'.[12]

The newspaper was, however, rather mute in the aftermath of the Easter Rising of 1916. It noted that the absence of any censor in Tralee impacted on the local press and declared that since it could find no authority to review its reports related to 'current political happenings' it had decided to omit these altogether. It did, however, carry the lord lieutenant's official statement on the shelling of Dublin's Liberty Hall and a short report on the chief secretary's account of the Rising to the House of Commons.[13] The subsequent issue, still devoid of a leading article on the rebellion, carried reports of the Rising from the *Illustrated Sunday Herald* and the *Weekly Dispatch* and also published the proclamation of independence.[14] Its first leading article to refer to the Rising was published on 13 May 1916, but even then it confined itself to criticizing the Irish Parliamentary Party for taking so long to criticize the actions of the British authorities in Ireland.[15] By this time, the British authorities had rounded up those suspected of sedition – including Maurice Griffin, who was arrested on 9 May 1916 and detained first at Dublin's Richmond Barracks and then at Wakefield Prison, Britain. He was released at the end of May 1916 and in an interview with the *Kerryman* recounted that at the time of his arrest the officer in command had told him that he would be shot dead if any rescue attempt was mounted on his behalf.[16]

In late August 1916 a party of British soldiers served a warrant on the paper that accused it of 'publishing on August 19 an article calculated to cause disaffection' and proceeded to remove vital parts of the printing press. Exactly which article caused the offence remains a matter of speculation. While the paper's fiftieth-anniversary supplement identified it as a reader's letter that welcomed Griffin's release and called for a campaign for others who had been 'unconstitutionally convicted', the *Irish Independent*, in its contemporaneous report on the raid, stated that it was prompted by a report on a resolution, passed by the

10 Ibid., 25 Oct. 1905, p. 5.   11 Ibid., 17 Oct. 1914, p. 4.   12 Ibid., 4 Jan. 1980, p. 13.   13 Ibid., 29 Apr. 1916, pp 1, 5.   14 Ibid., 6 May 1916, pp 2, 5.   15 Ibid., 13 May 1916, p. 2.   16 Ibid., 3 June 1916, p. 1.

Listowel board of guardians, which condemned the execution of Roger Casement two weeks previously.[17] The paper's editor, Thomas Nolan, immediately travelled to Dublin where he sought to lodge a complaint with the wartime press censor, Lord Decies. However, Decies informed him that the raid had nothing to do with his office and redirected him to the military authorities. While in Dublin, Nolan made arrangements to have the *Kerryman* printed by the Gaelic Press and smuggled to Tralee in the coal bunkers of the Dublin–Tralee train. Thus the *Kerryman* appeared as normal, though in much reduced form, throughout September 1916. In mid-October 1916 the confiscated printing parts were returned by the British military and the paper resumed normal publication.[18]

As the country swung behind Sinn Féin in the December 1918 general election, the paper again ceased publication – though for more prosaic reasons this time. In late January 1919 its Linotype machine ceased working: it was late March 1919 before the paper reappeared, announcing its purchase of a new Model 4 Linotype.[19] It was perhaps because of this eight-week interruption that it decided not to publish the Dáil Éireann loan prospectus later that year, thus avoiding the risk of suppression and further financial pressure. In September 1919 it reported the suppression of the *Kerry News*, *Kerry Weekly Reporter* and *Killarney Echo* for publishing the prospectus, and also noted that these were the only Kerry papers to publish it.[20]

Publication was again suspended for two weeks in November 1920 due to the extreme violence that erupted in response to the hanging of Kevin Barry and the death of the lord mayor of Cork, Terence MacSwiney. After IRA head-quarters issued orders for all units to engage in action, seventeen policemen and military personnel were shot, seven fatally, by Kerry IRA units in the space of twenty-four hours. The reprisals that followed shook the county. Temperance halls and creameries across Kerry were torched, while Tralee was put under siege by British forces which ordered the closure of all businesses in the town for seven days. With international press attention beginning to focus on the town, the siege was lifted on the orders of the chief secretary for Ireland, Hamar Greenwood. On its return to publication the *Kerryman* made no reference to the orgy of violence that had prevented its publication. The following year the paper suffered grievously at the hands of crown forces. On 18 April 1921 a notorious Auxiliary officer, Major John McKinnon, was shot dead by an IRA sniper at Tralee golf links. Later that day crown forces visited the *Kerryman* and demanded that its twice-weekly evening paper, the *Liberator*, be printed in thick black-ruled columns as a mark of respect to their dead colleague. The proprietors decided not to publish on that day.[21] Two days later the military returned and ordered everyone out of the building. Three

---

17 *II*, 20 Aug. 1916, p. 3.   18 On resumption it published an edition dated 2, 9, 16, 23, 30 Sept. and 7 Oct. 1916. See *KM*, 11 Dec. 1954, pp 2–3 for an account of the surreptitious printing.   19 *KM*, 25 Jan., 1, 8, 15, 22 Feb., and 1, 8, 15 Mar. 1919, p. 1.   20 Ibid., 27 Sept. 1919, p. 8.   21 Launched in July 1914, the *Liberator* was published on Tuesdays and Saturdays.

loud explosions were then heard as the soldiers blew up the printing press, causing £4,000 worth of damage.[22]

The *Kerryman* did not resume publication until August 1923, when it re-appeared as a pro-treaty paper. As recalled by Thomas Nolan's son Dan, 'the country was on its knees in every respect following the Anglo-Irish struggle and the bitterly contested civil war. My father and his colleagues felt that the only hope was to work the treaty.'[23] In its leading article, the paper struck a note of optimism as it called on readers to 'complete, not wreck the marvellous work of those countless great heroes of ours who died so willingly so that Ireland might live'.[24] Although politically the paper remained a supporter of the treaty, its editorial ethos would be moulded by Con Casey, a new recruit to the reporting staff and an anti-treaty activist. Casey had played an active role in the IRA activities that had resulted in the siege of Tralee, before being captured by government forces and sentenced to death in 1922 – a sentence commuted to ten years' penal servitude.[25] He remained active within the IRA until 1926 when he became 'disillusioned' and decided to concentrate instead on 'the cultural side of the revival'. Having secured a job on the *Kerryman*, Casey, as he put it himself, 'kept the flag of Irish culture and nationalism flying in Rock Street'.[26]

The paper's return was unequivocally welcomed. Its initial circulation of 1,500 in August 1923 rose to 3,933 in January 1924 and to 8,286 in December 1924.[27] Expansion soon followed: in 1926 it acquired the premises and titles (*Kerry Weekly Reporter*, *Killarney Echo* and *Kerry News*) of John Quinnell & Sons. It was during this period too that the *Kerryman* played a key role in popularizing local history. In September 1926, Commander Donal O'Connell of Beaufort, Killarney wrote a letter to the paper asking readers to send him detailed descriptions of monuments in each townland. Whenever monuments of note were reported to him, O'Connell investigated and published his findings in a letter to the paper. Thus followed a publication (*Kerry archaeology survey publication no.1: letters to the* Kerryman) and the formation of the Kerry Archaeological and Historical Society.[28] This period of expansion was followed soon after by the deaths of the paper's three founding fathers. In March 1928, Maurice Griffin died; in April 1938, Thomas Nolan died; and in April 1939, Daniel Nolan died.

As the Second World War loomed, the future of the paper rested on the shoulders of Thomas Nolan's son, Dan, who assumed the position of managing director. By 1939, the *Kerryman* consisted of fourteen pages, cost twopence and had a circulation of 18,109 per issue. Though datelined as a Saturday newspaper, it was published on Fridays (it would not correct its dateline until October 1973); the company also published an evening paper – *Kerry News* – on Mondays and

22 *II*, 21 Apr. 1921, p. 5.   23 *KM*, 11 Jan. 1980, p. 14.   24 Ibid., 13 Aug. 1923, p. 4.   25 U. MacEoin, 'Con Casey' in *Survivors: the story of Ireland's struggle* (Dublin, 1980), pp 370–7.   26 Ibid., p. 377. See Casey's obituary in *KM*, 30 Aug. 1996, p. 32.   27 *IT*, 8 Jan. 1925, p. 3.   28 Ibid., 13 July 1939, p. 4; *KM*, 20 May 1967, p. 10.

the *Liberator* on Saturdays.[29] The war was a trying period for the company. The shortage of newsprint resulted in the cessation of publication of both the *Liberator* (in 1939) and *Kerry News* (in 1941), and the reduction of the *Kerryman* from fourteen pages to six pages per issue between August 1939 and August 1942. In addition, the *Kerryman* had to operate within the confines of a wartime regime whereby all content was censored to ensure it did not favour any belligerent nation or undermine the state's neutrality. Edited during the war years by Patrick Foley (nephew of Maurice Griffin and better known by his GAA moniker 'P.F.') and then, from 1944, Ted Gallagher (a Belfast man who later edited the *Irish News*), the paper had a sometime stormy relationship with the censor.[30]

For the most part it was innocuous breaches of the regulations that drew rebukes from the chief press censor, Michael Knightly, a Tralee-born journalist who had worked on the *Kerry Weekly Reporter* and the *Irish Independent*.[31] Early in the war, the censor noted the paper's report of the annual Puck Fair festival which declared that 'with the rest of the world in a state of unrest and Europe in a state of chaos; with small countries being wiped out and weak ones being absorbed; with kings disappearing and kingdoms crumbling; with dictators threatening and presidents unyielding, King Puck alone stands defiant', but took no action.[32] It was a report on the torpedoing of the *Langlee Ford* off the Kerry coast and the arrival of survivors at Kerry Head that prompted the censor's first protest. Such material should, the censor declared, have been submitted for prior approval. In response, Nolan stated that the *Kerryman* 'always exercised the most meticulous care in order to comply with the censorship regulations'.[33] In a later letter, Nolan noted that because of the paper's compliance with the regulations 'in so far as local affairs are concerned, we have frequently incurred the criticism of our readers on account of omissions of reports of several local happenings, which are well known among the general public'.[34] Another item that drew the censor's ire was the publication of an aerial photograph of Tralee that accompanied a report on the town's development plan.[35] And, in the closing days of the conflict, it earned a final rebuke for its extensive report (under the headline 'Did His Parents Come From Kerry?') on local speculation that the townland of Knockeen, Castleisland, was the birthplace of the father of Lieutenant-General Omar N. Bradley, senior commander of the US Ground Forces in Europe.[36]

It was, however, matters republican that caused the most angst between the paper and the censor. In September 1939, the censor noted the publication of a photograph of the Kerry football team parading around Croke Park behind a

29 Circulation figure from headed notepaper in National Archives of Ireland (NAI), Jus/93/1/47 (32). 30 For Foley's obituary see *KM*, 12 Nov. 1966, p. 8. 31 There was also a family connection to be considered: Knightly's sister Minnie had married Thomas Nolan, so the press censor was an uncle of the paper's managing director, Dan Nolan. For more on Knightly, see *II*, 21 Dec. 1965, p. 15. 32 National Archives, Jus/93/1/47 (32), hereinafter Jus/93; *KM*, 10 Aug. 1940, p. 6. 33 Jus/93, letter dated 26 Feb. 1940. 34 Jus/93, letter dated 27 July 1940. 35 Jus/93, letter dated 1 Nov. 1944; *KM*, 28 Oct. 1944, p. 1. 36 Jus/93; *KM*, 7 Apr. 1945, p. 1.

banner that stated 'Kerry Protests Against Arrests of Gaels' – a reference to the recent arrests and internments of republicans.[37] In November 1942 the censor took exception to the reports of the numerous expressions of sympathy passed by local organizations in response to the execution at Mountjoy Gaol of Kerry IRA Volunteer Maurice O'Neill. How to censure the paper without aggravating local feelings prompted a discussion among censorship staff, with one official noting that 'perhaps the most expedient thing would be to do nothing about this'. Ultimately it was decided to issue a warning by telephone.[38]

Two years later, the execution of the Tralee-born IRA chief of staff, Charlie Kerins, on the paper's day of publication resulted in a spat between the paper and the censor's office. A fractious Dáil debate on the eve of the execution (and the day the paper was printed) had resulted in the expulsion from the house of two Kerry TDs – Dan Spring (National Labour) and Patrick Finucane (Farmers' Party). The paper's subsequent letter of protest noted that it had the full report of the contentious Dáil debate from its own Dublin correspondent, but that when it rang the censor's office at 7:40 p.m. for the official release it had been given a short dictated statement and informed that if any more of the debate was passed for publication then the censor's office would telephone it through. Having not heard from the censor's office, the paper ran with the official report, whereas the national titles carried fuller reports – with more verbatim exchanges. As the letter ruefully noted:

> As two of the three deputies suspended were Kerry deputies, and as the debate arose out of the matter of the execution of Charles Kerins, no other paper in the country was more vitally interested in the story than ourselves, and the fact that we came out of it with nothing more than a bald statement has left us open, in the minds of our readers, to a charge of inefficiency or bias.[39]

For his part, the chief press censor, Michael Knightly, noted that he would not 'accept or admit any responsibility for the faux pas which occurred'. As he recalled the sequence of events, he had given the paper the statement at 7:45 p.m. and had offered to telephone any further releases through, but had been told that the paper was going straight to press. He would, he concluded, have telephoned if he had not been 'put off'.[40]

Ted Gallagher edited the paper between 1944 and 1956, and then returned to his native Belfast. He was succeeded first by Eoin Neeson (later director of the government information bureau) and then Tom Dunne before stability returned with the appointment of Con Casey, who edited the title from 1957 to 1974.[41] It fell to Dan Nolan, as managing director, to ensure continuity and growth. Nolan was, in modern parlance, an entrepreneur; he not only built up the company's

37 Jus/93; *KM*, 16 and 30 Sept. 1939, p. 1. 38 Jus/93, memo dated 26 Nov. 1942; *KM*, 21 Nov. 1942, various pages. 39 Jus/93, letter dated 4 Dec. 1944. 40 Jus/93, memo dated 7 Dec. 1944. 41 For Neeson's obituary, see *IT*, 8 Jan. 2011, p. 12; for Dunne's obituary, see *KM*, 2 June 2000, p. 14.

printing business, but also contributed significantly to the development of Tralee. Nolan was a key driving force behind the development of the town's racing park, its sports complex, its annual Christmas shopping festival, and the Rose of Tralee festival. He also expanded the *Kerryman*'s reach into neighbouring counties by publishing Limerick and Cork editions. So successful was the latter that in 1966 Nolan took the decision to establish the *Corkman*. He also established the Anvil Press publishing company, and *This Is Ireland* magazine – an annual holiday guide launched in 1950 and distributed primarily in Britain.[42]

By the mid-1950s the *Kerryman* consisted of sixteen pages, cost three pence and had a circulation of 27,790 per issue.[43] In 1953 it published a book – *With the IRA in the fight for freedom: 1919 to the truce* – written by 'former senior officers of the IRA'.[44] The following year it serialized the book – against the backdrop of IRA raids on British military bases in Northern Ireland. It was the publication of these articles that then minister for finance Gerard Sweetman probably had in mind when, in a speech to Tralee's chamber of commerce, he noted that:

> those who are in a position to influence public opinion have a specially grave responsibility; that in regard to unlawful armed activities, there should be no ambiguity of thought or attitude, and that no one can have it both ways in this matter.

Showing his steely side, Nolan responded that he was 'conscious of his responsibility and it was with a full sense of it that what had appeared in the *Kerryman* had been published. Since these articles, numerous letters had been received from people of all shades of political opinion.'[45] A hard-headed businessman, Nolan knew that keeping pace with technological developments was crucial. Addressing the Association of Advertisers in 1965, he noted that the future of newspapers lay in colour printing, and that given the large-scale capital investment that was needed, not all regional papers could remain completely in private family ownership.[46]

Less than seven years later, in September 1972, it was announced that Independent Newspapers had acquired the *Kerryman* for the sum of £378,000.[47] By then the *Kerryman*, with a circulation of 41,790 copies per issue, was the most successful regional title in the country.[48] While the change in ownership did not disrupt publication, the subsequent change in ownership of Independent Newspapers did. When, in March 1973, Tony O'Reilly acquired Independent Newspapers from the Murphy family, journalists at the group's Dublin titles held a mandatory meeting that kept papers such as the *Irish Independent* off the streets for five days. In solidarity, journalists at the *Kerryman* held a mandatory meeting that resulted in the non-appearance of the title for the first time since the war of independence.[49] Nonetheless, the change in ownership permitted greater

42 For Nolan's obituary, see *KM*, 15 Dec. 1989, p. 7. See also *KM*, 4 Jan. 1980, pp 13–14. 43 Dáil Éireann Debates, vol. 159, cols. 659–60 (24 Mar. 1955). 44 *KM*, 25 Apr. 1953, p. 2. 45 *Irish Times*, 21 Jan. 1955, p. 4. 46 Ibid., 11 Nov. 1965, p. 9. 47 Ibid., 8 Sept. 1972, p. 14. 48 *KM*, 20 Jan. 1973, p. 1. 49 *IT*, 14 Mar. 1973, p. 1.

investment: in 1973 the paper moved to new premises at Clash Industrial Estate on the outskirts of Tralee, which allowed for the installation of a new colour printing press. Throughout the late 1970s and early 1980s the new plant attracted a significant amount of contract printing, including titles such as *Hot Press* and *In Dublin*.

Shortly after the move, in February 1974, Con Casey retired as editor and was succeeded by Seamus McConville. Born in Navan, McConville began his career at the *Meath Chronicle* before working with the Irish News Agency. In 1957, he joined the *Kerryman*, for which he covered the infamous 1958 Moss Moore murder in Reamore that inspired John B. Keane's play *The field*. Like Dan Nolan, McConville played a key role in the development of the Rose of Tralee festival – it was his idea to link the eponymous ballad to the festival. He was also involved in the establishment of Siamsa Tíre, the national folk theatre.[50] McConville served as editor until 1988, and he continued to pen a column 'My Town' right up to his death in 2012.

On his first day in the editor's chair, McConville received a telephone call supposedly from the IRA threatening serious action if the paper published an article written by columnist Con Houlihan that was critical of the Price sisters (Marion and Delores), who were then on hunger strike, having been imprisoned in connection with a car bombing in London in 1973. As McConville recalled:

> I checked with republican sources to see if the threat was genuine or not and was told that it was. Despite pleas by friends in the republican movement not to publish I decided to stand over the paper's right to publish views whether it agreed with them or not.[51]

The paper's premises were put under round-the-clock garda protection. On publication day it led with a front-page article – 'A Matter of Freedom' – in which it observed that the last time it had been so threatened was during the war of independence, when 'the newspaper did not offer either the actual support – or the silence – which the British thought their policies deserved'. What the IRA wanted, it concluded, was silence and its motive was 'the same motive which impelled the Tans [and was] just as unsavoury'.[52] Houlihan's column – centred on a letter written to the *Irish Independent* by a Tralee-born, London-based nurse, Pauline Carmody, who had treated those injured by the Price bombs – was published on page eight. However, the following week, the *Kerryman* acknowledged that the 'nurse' had no connection with the Tralee address she had used in the letter and that the three London hospitals that had treated the bomb victims had no such nurse on their staffs.[53]

Local politics were equally fraught. During the 1977 general election, Fianna Fáil TD Tom McEllistrim broke with his party's view that supporters were free to vote for any of the three party candidates in the Kerry North constituency when he placed an advert in the *Kerryman* asking the electorate to vote for him alone – with no mention of the other two Fianna Fáil candidates, Kit Ahern

50 Ibid., 28 Jan. 2012, p. 12. See *KM*, 18 Jan. 2012, pp 14–17, for McConville's obituary. **51** *IT*, 27 Sept. 1983, p. 12. **52** *KM*, 8 Feb. 1974, p. 1. **53** Ibid., 15 Feb. 1974, p. 1.

and Denis Foley. However, as publication day approached, McEllistrim had second thoughts and called to the homes of editorial staff to seek – unsuccessfully – the advert's cancellation. On printing day, McEllistrim and a posse of supporters descended on the paper to again seek the advert's removal. This time editorial executives agreed to remove the advert but to keep the press running until the new page – minus the advert – had been made up. McEllistrim's offer to purchase all copies printed with the advert was rejected.[54] Demonstrating the adage that there is no such thing as bad publicity, McEllistrim topped the poll (Kit Ahern was also elected). There were lighter moments too. At a meeting of Kerry county council, Senator John Blennerhassett, a Fine Gael councillor, produced a whiskey bottle and a glass from his briefcase and poured a sample of Castleisland's water supply, which he claimed smelled like a well-known brand of disinfectant. He then invited those present at the meeting to taste the water. When the *Kerryman*'s reporter tried it and declared that he could find nothing wrong with it cheers erupted in the chamber.[55]

By this time, a new publication, *Kerry's Eye*, had been established in Tralee by Pádraig Kennelly. Originally a free sheet, published on Thursdays (a day before the Tralee edition of the *Kerryman*) with a circulation of 8,000 copies per issue, its attempt to capture some of the town's readership and advertising led to some interesting encounters – especially during the contentious eighth-amendment referendum of 1983. In February that year the *Kerryman* ran a story on how pro-amendment campaigners had criticized Dick Spring, a Tralee politician who was then Labour Party leader and tánaiste, for having expressed unease at the wording of the proposed constitutional amendment. Having failed to elicit a comment from Spring, the paper ran the story in its Kerry North edition without one; for the later, Tralee, edition the paper incorporated into the story a statement from Spring.[56] There the matter rested until the subsequent edition of *Kerry's Eye* claimed – under the page-one headline 'Dick Spring Was Badly Framed' – that senior personnel from Independent Newspapers had compelled Seamus McConville to include the Spring statement even if that meant reprinting the Tralee edition in its entirety. McConville initiated libel proceedings in the circuit court and was awarded £3,000 in damages.[57]

In the mid-1980s, events in Kerry put the county centre-stage in terms of news coverage. The interception of the *Marita Ann* gunrunning ship and the arrest of Martin Ferris (later a Sinn Féin TD) in 1984; the Kerry Babies case in 1984 and the subsequent tribunal of inquiry, which heard evidence in Tralee; and reports of moving statues in the village of Asdee in 1985 prompted much local and national coverage. Seamus McConville's retirement as editor in 1988 cut a longstanding link to the paper's founders, and in many ways presaged a new era for the regional press – some titles of which would sell for astronomical sums

54 *IT*, 16 June 1977, p. 5.   55 Ibid., 21 Aug. 1980, p. 11.   56 *KM*, 11 Feb. 1983, p. 1.   57 See ibid., 22 Apr. 1983, p. 1; *IT*, 27 Jan. 1984, p. 5; *KM*, 3 Feb. 1984, p. 2.

during the Celtic Tiger years. McConville's successor, Brian Looney, oversaw the transformation of the *Kerryman* into the country's first fully computerized regional title.[58] In 2006 the migration of the paper's printing to Belfast allowed its rival, *Kerry's Eye*, to claim that it was the only newspaper compiled and printed in Tralee, but this was tempered by the fact that the *Kerryman*'s editorial staff had returned to the town centre, ready to face the challenge of publishing a newspaper in the digital era.

---

58 Later editors included Ger Colleran, Declan Malone and Kevin Hughes.

The role of the provincial press in the development of association football in pre-First World War Ulster: the cases of Donegal, Fermanagh and Cavan

CONOR CURRAN

The twenty-first century has seen a huge increase in the volume of work published on the history of Irish soccer.[1] However, how the game was actually reported upon has received less attention. In particular, the role of the military in association football's growth in provincial Ulster in the late Victorian era and early Edwardian era has received little analysis from academics, although some assume it was substantial.[2] This chapter examines the impact of the military on the game in Cavan, Donegal and Fermanagh in the period from the early 1890s until the outbreak of the First World War. It will be shown that the impact of military teams was greatest in towns where they were stationed, and that they generally failed to branch out and challenge more outlying teams. While there is strong evidence that military selections were responsible for helping with the game's early development in Enniskillen, Belturbet and Ballyshannon, most clubs in west and south-west Ulster were set up independently of military assistance. The military's involvement in cup football will be examined, and their interactions with the local community will also be assessed. In addition, the role of the provincial press in promoting and drawing attention to the game will be explored, with particular emphasis on views expressed in a sample of nationalist, unionist and more moderate newspapers.[3] It will be shown that although the military did not have wide-scale involvement in developing soccer, cultural nationalists were eager to portray it as a 'garrison game' in the local press as part of their efforts to rid Irish society of this sport.

---

1 See, for example, Neal Garnham, *Association football and society in pre-partition Ireland* (Belfast, 2004); Tom Hunt, *Sport and society in Victorian Ireland: the case of Westmeath* (Cork, 2007); Cormac Moore, *The Irish soccer split* (Cork, 2015); David Toms, *Soccer in Munster: a social history, 1877–1937* (Cork, 2015); and Conor Curran and David Toms (eds), 'Going beyond the "garrison game": new perspectives on association football in Irish history', *Soccer and Society* special issue, 18:5–6 (2017), pp 599–799. 2 See the views of historian J.J. Lee in the documentary *Green is the colour: the history of Irish soccer* (Beaumex, 2012). 3 For an examination of the role of the press in facilitating the conflict between organizers of Gaelic football and soccer in Donegal in the opening decades of the twentieth century, see Conor Curran, *The development of sport in Donegal, 1880–1935* (Cork, 2007), ch. 7. The present chapter utilizes parts of this work, particularly ch. 6 and ch. 7, and is also partially drawn from *Sport in Donegal: a history* (Dublin, 2010).

THE DEVELOPMENT OF SOCCER IN IRELAND
AS SEEN THROUGH THE PRESS

Soccer was initially played in the province of Ulster in 1878, with the Scottish teams Caledonians and Queen's Park participating in an exhibition match in Belfast on 24 October.[4] This was advertised in the *Belfast News Letter* as a 'Grand Football Match' between the 'celebrated Glasgow clubs' at the Ulster cricket ground under the 'Scottish Association Rules'.[5] This distinction was generally made in these early reports of what is now more commonly known as soccer to avoid confusion with the laws of rugby. As the paper did not have a regular soccer section at that stage, the advertisement was placed in a column informing readers about other events in the city, such as the Belfast Musical Festival.[6] By 1890, along with the Irish Football Association (IFA), founded in Belfast in 1880, regional governing bodies for soccer were present in counties Derry, Antrim and Down, and a mid-Ulster association was also functional at this point.[7] Matches were being played in Donegal by 1881 and in Fermanagh by 1887, and clubs were in existence in Tyrone and Monaghan by the early 1880s.[8] The Leinster FA was founded in 1892, and the Co. Donegal FA was organized in 1894, while the Munster FA was not formed until 1901, illustrating soccer's uneven growth in Ireland.[9]

The general growth of sports clubs and competitions in Britain in the late Victorian era comprised what is commonly known as the sporting 'revolution', and this had a knock-on effect in Ireland. Reports of Irish soccer activity generally began to appear in the 1880s in the provincial press, although specialized newspapers dedicated to sporting developments – such as *Sport*, first published in 1880, and *Ulster Football and Cycling News*, available in 1887 – were also in circulation at this time.[10] However, it must be noted that regional news in these specialized publications pertaining to association football and other codes was generally taken from the provincial press, and many clubs in the counties under examination in this chapter did not receive regular publicity. Neal Garnham has stated that there were over one hundred newspapers published throughout the country by 1860, and that 'during the 1890s, at least a dozen newspapers that concerned themselves primarily with athletic and sporting news, most of which were admittedly short-lived, appeared in Ireland'.[11] Newspapers such as the *Donegal Vindicator* and *Donegal Independent*, which were both based in Ballyshannon, generally did not have sections dedicated to soccer matches at this point, with intermittent snippets of matches in local news sections more common, although, as will be seen, the lack of organization of the game there until the mid-1890s impacted on this. Similarly, readers seeking information on soccer in the *Anglo-Celt*, Cavan's main newspaper in the late nineteenth century, could occasionally find it in

4 Garnham, *Association football and society*, p. 4.   5 *BNL*, 24 Oct. 1878.   6 Ibid.   7 PRONI, Papers of the Irish Football Association, D/4196/S/1. Cash book of the IFA, 31 Aug. 1889 and 8 Jan. 1890.   8 Ibid., 7 Oct. 1882 and 6 Dec. 1884; *DV*, 25 July 1881; and *IR*, 27 Oct. 1887.   9 Garnham, *Association football and society*, p. 6, and *DJ*, 30 Mar. 1894.   10 Garnham, *Association football and society*, p. 9.   11 Ibid.

the 'Notes and Comments' section or under news relating to a particular village, although not always on a regular basis.[12] However, by the early 1900s this newspaper had a column entitled 'Sport and Sporting', with information compiled by 'Flapper'.[13] In the early 1890s, the *Fermanagh Mail and Enniskillen Chronicle* kept Fermanagh citizens up to date with the initial growth of soccer in the area. By 1905, readers could find reports on soccer proceedings in a more structured form, with information such as fixtures, tables, match reports and annual general meetings highlighted through more specialized sections such as the *Fermanagh Herald*'s 'In the Football Field'.[14] Matches of note, such as the visit of city clubs to Enniskillen, were also advertised, with dates, venues, kick-off times and admission fees clearly printed.[15]

At the most basic level, these newspapers informed their readers about fixtures and scores in a region generally dislocated from the heart of soccer activity in east Ulster, where the majority of professional teams were located. Most of these more regional clubs could be described as junior combinations, and the most ambitious of these competed in the IFA's Junior Cup. An assessment of finalists from the period when this was initiated, 1888 to 1914, shows that the majority of winners came from the east of the province, illustrating the strength of the game in this area.[16] A similar situation existed in regard to the Irish Junior League, which was operational by 1890.[17]

THE MILITARY AND ASSOCIATION FOOTBALL IN THE LOCAL PRESS

Early reports of soccer activity in the west and south of Ulster were generally restricted to a couple of paragraphs with a brief description of the weather, spectators and action on the pitch. Pictures of teams or action were rare. Yet regional newspapers allow for an examination of how significant the military was in spreading the game of soccer in this area. In general, despite the common perception that soccer in Ireland was a 'garrison game', evidence for this within the area covered in this chapter is patchy. A handful of clubs in Cavan, Fermanagh and Donegal did develop out of interaction between local and military teams. Soccer in Ballyshannon needed the participation of the military, stationed in the local Rock Barracks, to spread interest, and in this regard the town was unusual. Although there had been earlier failed attempts by civilians to encourage the game in the Ballyshannon area, a detachment of the locally based 2nd Dorset Regiment were said to have provided the inspiration for the founding of a number of soccer clubs there during 1896.[18] The first match in this soccer

12 See, for example, *AC*, 22 Aug. 1896 and 15 May 1897.   13 Ibid., 31 May 1902.   14 *FH*, 11 Mar. and 8 Apr. 1905.   15 Ibid., 12 Mar. 1904.   16 Ireland's Saturday Night *football and athletic annual, 1909–10* (Belfast, 1910), p. 50.   17 Ibid., p. 51.   18 *DV*, 19 Feb. 1897. See also *DJ*, 13 and 25 Oct. 1883 and *DV*, 23 Feb. and 20 Apr. 1889.

revival took place on Wednesday 11 March 1896, between newly formed Erne FC and the 2nd Dorsets. The *Donegal Independent* vividly described the event:

> A stranger coming in from Belleek on that day would believe he was very near the famous Derby race course, as the bright shining jerseys of the civilians, under their capt. Mr Rogan, marched onto the field and looked splendid. We believe they were specially ordered from the new hosiery establishment started by the Sisters of Mercy ... the soldiers were dressed differently, having come to the field with short trousers and shins bare. The ground being in a bad slippery condition it was a wonder none of them got hurt. The soldiers were by far the lighter team.[19]

Despite their lack of team shirts, the Dorsets apparently came out on top by 4–3. Prior to their departure in September 1896, the military men took part in eleven out of fifteen soccer matches held locally that year and were undefeated.[20]

Matches were often refereed by prominent locals such as members of the military and business men such as John McAdam, the proprietor of the *Donegal Vindicator* in the late 1890s.[21] However, this did not stop poor discipline and mis-understandings about the rules, and the local press often highlighted this in the hope that it would cease. Rough play continued to be a feature into the twentieth century and a lack of discipline and fitness was at times noted.[22] Newcomers to the game who struggled to master the skills of association football risked humiliation in the local press. After a match between Swifts and Ballintra, it was claimed that Swifts' goalkeeper gave a 'wretched display', and that Captain Hamilton's kicking was 'erratic'.[23] On a more serious note, it was also stated that 'the habit of quarrelling with the referee's decision must be stopped as it lowers the dignity of a club'.[24]

While soccer had been played in Donegal since the early 1880s, and clubs in Tyrone and Derry had a strong influence in the north-east, Cavan came to the sport late. In March 1893, Cavan club Belturbet Red Stars played in what is said to be the first association football game recorded in the county, a friendly against the West Kent Regiment, who were stationed in the village, which resulted in a draw before a large crowd with 'the play' noted as 'good'.[25] The *Anglo-Celt* reported that members of the military team gave a musical parade through the village before the match and again performed when it had ended.[26]

Throughout the rest of this decade and into the early twentieth century, the military gave exhibitions of skill and technique in their play, as well as providing opposition, officials and facilities for matches.[27] By February 1897 interaction between the Belturbet Stars and the military was apparently helping to strengthen local relationships between civilians and soldiers, and it was reported in the

---

19 *DI*, 13 Mar. 1896. 20 Ibid., 8 Mar., 2 June and 28 Aug. 1896. 21 See, for example, *DI*, 13 Mar. 1896 and 14 Feb. 1914. 22 See, for example, *DV*, 3 Apr. 1896, *FH*, 4 Mar. and 20 May 1905. 23 Ibid. 24 Ibid. 25 *AC*, 1 Apr. 1893. 26 Ibid. 27 See, for example, *AC*, 1 Apr. 1893; 28 Mar., 11 Apr. and 2 May 1896; 16 Mar., 20 Apr. and 2 Nov. 1901; 3 May and 6 Sept. 1902.

unionist *Impartial Reporter* that the soldiers were 'becoming quite favourites with townspeople'.[28] By the winter of 1902, competing in the inaugural Jackson Cup were Inniskilling Fusiliers and the Royal Field Artillery, along with civilian teams Belturbet United, Monaghan, St Michael's Hall Celtic (Enniskillen), Monaghan Wanderers and Cavan.[29] By the early 1900s Belturbet United were one of the strongest teams in south Ulster, winning the South Ulster League in 1903.[30]

Soccer in Fermanagh had an earlier start than in Ballyshannon and Belturbet. In Enniskillen, like in Ballyshannon, some local sportsmen were initially more interested in playing rugby, with a military detachment said to have been responsible for initiating this code there in 1885.[31] It was local bank official J.G.I. Vance who was said to have initially been responsible for organizing soccer selections in Enniskillen, with an intra-rugby club association football match taking place the following month. In February 1888 he organized a team composed of the local rugby club's players to face the band of the King's Royal Rifles in a soccer match, with a return fixture taking place a few weeks later.[32] During Easter of 1888 an Enniskillen club named Erne Ramblers travelled to Derrygonnelly for a match in the association code, while in October that year an Enniskillen team made up of civilian and military players journeyed there for another match.[33] As soccer grew in strength in Enniskillen, with Erne Ramblers taking on a more regular club structure by late 1890, rugby struggled to maintain its popularity, with the transfer of military players said to be a problem.[34] While a military barracks was also present in Belleek, there is little evidence that the development of the village's soccer club, which was in existence under the name 'Skirmishers' by 1889, was heavily influenced by the military.[35]

RAISING THE STANDARD OF THE GAME?

Matches involving military men could have their advantages and disadvantages. Military teams certainly provided locals with the spectacle of a higher standard of soccer than what was available locally, although there is no evidence in the newspapers covered here that they actually gave instruction in the skills of the game to civilians. The Loyal North Lancashire Regiment took part in what was said to be 'the fastest and most exciting game ever played on the Tempo grounds', against the local club in December 1890 in the Tempo Challenge Cup, the first soccer competition to be held in Fermanagh.[36] After the military team's easy victory in the final three months later, it was recorded in the *Impartial Reporter* that they were 'a well-trained body of men' who had a 'quiet, unassuming, and yet determined manner'. In contrast, their local opponents Colebrooke were said to be lacking in combination.[37] However, the regiment failed to enter the competition the following year, having lost a number of players who

28 *IR*, 25 Feb. 1897. **29** *AC*, 22 Nov. 1902. **30** *FH*, 6 June 1903. **31** *IR*, 19 Feb. 1891. **32** Ibid., 9 Feb. 1888. **33** Ibid., 5 Apr. and 4 Oct. 1888. **34** Ibid., 23 Jan., 20 Nov. and 11 Dec. 1890. **35** *FM*, 14 Oct. 1889. **36** *IR*, 18 Dec. 1890. **37** Ibid., 5 Mar. 1891.

had transferred to Derry, a common hindrance for the development of military teams.[38]

Some clubs were clearly unhappy about facing military men in civilian teams, and at times, representatives expressed their discontent publicly in the local newspapers. Trillick Ramblers objected to the composition of the Enniskillen Ramblers team before their Trillick Cup first-round match in December 1893, 'the grounds being the preponderance of military players, who were suspected not to be bona-fide members'.[39] The Enniskillen Association club were said to have broken the Tempo Cup competition's rules in 1895 when they fielded a number of military players in the final against Tempo Jubilee, the result being that the latter claimed victory in the press when Enniskillen failed to turn up for a replay ordered by the cup committee.[40] This involvement of military men in supposedly civilian teams was also a problem in other counties. One writer to the *Anglo-Celt* claimed that the Clones Blues club's heavy defeat against Belturbet Stars in April 1901 was the result of half of the latter team being composed of members of the 140th Artillery.[41] As well as drawing attention to the composition of teams, letters to the press could serve to inform the public of happenings on the football field, but at times these were used to highlight perceived injustices or were written in the hope of rectifying controversial matters.

By the winter of 1898 Ballyshannon's first soccer competition, the Vindicator Cup, was in operation, with a trophy donated by John McAdam. No military team was involved, illustrating the sporadic nature of military teams' participation in local soccer in provincial Ireland. The teams were all from local urbanized areas. The two primary clubs in Ballyshannon – Erne 98s and Swifts – registered, and Ballintra, Donegal Celtic and Belleek Rose Isles of Fermanagh also affiliated.[42] Newspaper reports of matches and the advertising of competitions allowed teams in other counties to become aware of opportunities to participate, and cross-county matches were becoming increasingly common at this time. The competition was played on a knock-out basis in November and December 1898, with the final between the Swifts and the Erne 98s played on 26 December. It was held on the Swifts' ground, and, according to the *Donegal Independent*, approximately 2,000 spectators attended.[43] The *Donegal Vindicator* claimed there were spectators present from Killybegs, Sligo, Enniskillen and Omagh, and that 'many ladies graced the enclosure with their presence'.[44] The Swifts protested to the cup committee after their 2–1 defeat, and a replay was decided upon following a ballot, but the match referee, clearly aggrieved, wrote to the editor of the London based *Athletic Record*, who replied, and agreed that his decisions on the field, and the result, were final.[45] The Erne 98s were declared winners, and this was brought to the public's notice in the *Donegal Vindicator*.[46]

Although not every civilian team was happy to face military opposition, and clubs' fielding of soldiers was problematic, some were grateful for their input, such

38 *IR*, 6 Oct. 1892.   39 Ibid., 28 Dec. 1893.   40 Ibid., 23 May 1895.   41 *AC*, 27 Apr. 1901.   42 *DV*, 7 Oct. 1898.   43 *DI*, 30 Dec. 1898   44 *DV*, 30 Dec. 1898.   45 Ibid., 10 Feb. 1899.   46 Ibid., 17 Feb. 1899.

as the Enniskillen Athletics club in 1893, as it was felt that 'there is no rough play and they know how to kick [a] football'.[47] Cup victories attracted varying levels of interest in the local community, and celebrations at times depended on the level of social backing behind the team, and the political allegiances of the local press. The *Impartial Reporter* was keen to portray a positive image of the military in the locality in the early 1890s through a description of how the Loyal North Lancashire Regiment's victory in the 1891 Tempo Cup final was viewed by their opponents, local youths and by those within the barracks. After the match the team spent 'a convivial half hour with their opponents and Tempo friends'. They then returned by wagonette to Enniskillen, where they were escorted by local youths 'seemingly delighted that the cup had come to their town'. Having been welcomed with a rendition of 'conquering heroes', played by the battalion's band, the team received 'an excellent dinner' in the barracks, where the cup was filled with sparkling wine and handed around. The players were then congratulated by the officers, and a concert was held until the singing of the national anthem at 11:30 p.m.[48] The success of the Enniskillen-based 2nd Battalion of the Queen's Own Royal West Kent Regiment over the Sherwood Foresters in the Army FA Challenge Cup final of 1893 in Aldershot was also well publicized in this newspaper and well-received locally, at least by the unionist element of the town.[49] It was reported that 'great enthusiasm prevailed among the inhabitants of this most loyal town' on the team's arrival home, with church bells being rung, a band present to lead the military procession and the cup put on display in the officers' mess.[50]

The presence of the military in Enniskillen and Belturbet probably helped to raise the standard of the game in these areas and military-civilian sporting relations were similar to those described by Garnham when he stated that 'on the sports field, as in the concert hall, the rank-and-file of the British military mixed with their civilian hosts on perhaps surprisingly good terms'.[51]

OPPOSITION TO THE PLAYING OF SOCCER

By publishing their letters and reports, some local newspapers also facilitated the claims of cultural nationalists that Gaelic games should be the preferred sports of Irishmen. In the late 1880s, soccer clubs in Galway came under pressure in the Connacht provincial press to transfer to Gaelic football.[52] Although Fermanagh's soccer clubs were being targeted in the local press as early as 1890, it was in the early 1900s that this criticism of the playing of soccer escalated.[53] By then, this type of rhetoric was becoming increasingly common within the nationalist newspapers of Ireland. The condemnation of 'English sports' was not uncommon in Westmeath around this time,

---

47 *IR*, 9 Nov. 1893. 48 Ibid., 5 Mar. 1891. 49 Ibid., 13 Apr. 1893. 50 Ibid. 51 Neal Garnham, '"The only thing British that everybody likes": military-civilian relations in late Victorian Ulster' in *Éire-Ireland*, 41:3–4 (Autumn/Winter 2006), pp 59–76, at p. 68. 52 Michael Leydon, *Dunmore MacHales: a history of football in Dunmore parish* (Dunmore, 1983). 53 *FM*, 23 Apr. 1890.

although the playing of cricket appears to have received most of the criticism in the local press there.[54] The standard of play in the latter sport was also ridiculed there, while an attack by leading Gaelic revival figure Seamus MacManus on the organizers of the Evans' Cup in Ardara in 1905 in the Donegal press appears similar to events in Fermanagh in the early twentieth century.[55]

Gaelic football had struggled to develop in Fermanagh in the late nineteenth century, with the local press used as an instrument to voice the concerns of the Catholic church in relation to matches being held on Sundays. In May 1889, Ven. Archdeacon Smollen noted 'the evils of kicking football on Sundays and holidays'. This was part of a wider directive within the Catholic church, with Dr Donnelly, bishop of Clogher, having 'consulted with his clergy' at conferences in Monaghan and Fermanagh, condemning it as 'a great evil'. The press reported on these clerical criticisms of Sunday football, as well as other clerical concerns, such as the fear that GAA clubs were being infiltrated by the Irish Republican Brotherhood.[56]

Local GAA clubs in Fermanagh appear to have taken to playing matches on Mondays, Wednesdays and Saturdays for a brief period, but given the sport's strong reliance on agricultural workers as players, this must have been difficult.[57] In October 1891, Enniskillen landowners were warned off letting their land to clubs on Sundays by Ven. Archdeacon Smollen during a sermon given at Mass, and this was publicized in the *Fermanagh Mail*.[58] Despite the presence of a county committee in the early 1890s, the GAA there went into decline and was not revived until the early 1900s, with a county board formed in 1904.[59]

This revival created a conflict between those attempting to organize soccer and Gaelic football in Enniskillen, and this was played out in the local press. The Fermanagh and south Tyrone association football league had also been formed there in 1904, and the playing of Gaelic games on Sundays again drew condemnation from the clergy, thereby heightening the difficulties of developing Gaelic football in Enniskillen.[60] At a meeting in November 1904 of Fermanagh GAA clubs held in that town, there was discussion about going ahead with matches on Saturdays, with the number of players per team reduced from seventeen to thirteen and playing fields reduced in size. Clubs were encouraged to appoint delegates to visit the clergy in their districts in regard to playing on holidays.[61]

Although not every Ulster county was affected – in Donegal, Bishop O'Donnell supported the GAA after the county board there was formed in 1905 – the conditions imposed by the clergy in the diocese in which much of Fermanagh lay, and the promotion of the idea, through the press, that soccer organizers were being well funded to counteract the development of Gaelic games, undoubtedly saw a rise in opposition to association football among some sections of society,

54 Hunt, *Sport and society*, pp 193–6.   55 *DJ*, 1 Mar. 1905.   56 *FM*, 23 May 1889.   57 See, for example, *FM*, 2 and 9 Apr. and 21 May 1890.   58 Ibid., 16 Oct. 1891.   59 Mike Cronin, Mark Duncan and Paul Rouse, *The GAA: county by county* (Cork, 2011), p. 149.   60 Conor Curran, 'Networking structures and competitive association football in Ulster, 1880–1914', *Irish Economic and Social History*, 31 (2014), pp 74–92, and *FH*, 5 Nov. 1904.   61 *FH*, 5 Nov. 1904.

particularly among clubs with allegiances to nationalist organizations such as the GAA, Gaelic League and the Ancient Order of Hibernians.

Given the cultural revival around the turn of the century, this is perhaps unsurprising. At their AGM in April 1905, with Cahir Healy presiding, the Fermanagh county board passed a resolution that 'any club having any association football players among its players be suspended from Gaelic football and hurling competitions'.[62] Healy was secretary of the first branch of the Gaelic League in Enniskillen, founded in 1902, and was a key organizer of local *aeridheachta* and *feiseanna*.[63] While GAA members had been banned since 1902 from participating in soccer, rugby, hockey or cricket, this proposed to go a step further by actually suspending clubs as well as individual players.

Military involvement in association football was also targeted by cultural nationalists in the provincial press, some of whom were keen to link the sport with the British military as part of a wider campaign to encourage native pastimes and activities at the expense of those they deemed to be 'foreign'. Pen names were often used although at times writers simply signed their names in Irish. One cultural nationalist, writing to the *Fermanagh Herald* under the guise of 'Aod Ruad', was particularly alarmed by the playing of soccer in Enniskillen on St Patrick's Day 1905.[64] The participation of a Sergeant Crawford from the Inniskilling Fusiliers as referee was also condemned. It was, however, the first public appearance of a newly formed band of the Devenish branch of the Irish National Foresters at the match that drew the bulk of the criticism, particularly their playing of 'a selection of national airs at intervals during this game', as apparently this showed that 'the spirit of seoininism is still strong in Enniskillen'.[65] The writer concluded by stating that he hoped that 'in a very short time we would see those foreign pastimes cleared from the county of the Maguires, which should be filled with spirits and traditions of their ancestors'.[66]

Despite such efforts, Gaelic football struggled to attract sufficient interest in Fermanagh at this time. Gabriel Brock has stated that 'lack of competition from soccer is probably the main reason why Teemore was the only club that managed to stay in continuous existence' in the opening decade of the twentieth century, illustrating how association football's development curtailed that of the Gaelic code in most of the county at the time. He has noted footballers transferring between the two codes due to 'the scarcity of players', with suspensions under the ban common, weakening Gaelic football selections.[67] Criticism of soccer in the local press was insufficient to prevent the game being played, while the presence of the GAA's ban was hindered by soccer's strong tradition in the area, low levels of population and the threat of emigration, which meant that GAA teams could not always afford to ignore offending players.[68] David Toms has illustrated in

62 Ibid., 22 Apr. 1905. 63 Helen Meehan, 'Cahir Healy MP, 1877–1970', *Donegal Annual: Bliainiris Dhún na nGall*, 62 (2010), pp 92–103, at p. 94. 64 *FH*, 1 Apr. 1905. 65 Ibid. 66 Ibid. 67 Gabriel Brock, *The Gaelic Athletic Association in County Fermanagh* (Enniskillen, 1984), p. 22 and p. 32. 68 Curran, *The development of sport*, p. 222.

his major study of soccer in Munster that 'for all these concerted campaigns on foreign games conducted in the press, they did not act as preventatives'.[69]

By the early 1900s, soccer in Enniskillen had developed sufficiently to see off the threat of rival sports. It also had a solid enough administrative system, and committed organizers who could draw on support through relationships with the IFA to withstand any pressure for its removal from society. The importance of the game there can be seen in a report published in the *Fermanagh Herald* in the summer of 1905 after Enniskillen Celtic's victory in the North West FA Junior Cup final in Derry city against holders Hibernian Seconds:

> The scene outside St Michael's Hall [where the club held their meetings] when the result became known was one of the greatest enthusiasm. Terrific cheers were raised, accompanied by the waving of hats, caps and handker-chiefs, and it was a considerable time before the excitement subsided. A move was soon made to give the victors a cordial reception on their return home.[70]

On arrival at the station, the players were carried to waggonettes, which were drawn by supporters through the town, and then the team were carried again into their club hall. It was stated that there were 'at least 2,000 people in the throng' and 'en route all creeds and classes joined in the demonstration'. The brass band of the Devenish branch of the Irish National Foresters, like the winning team, were evidently not put off by the earlier press condemnation they had received, and preceded the players on their journey.[71] Frequent reports published in the local press of matches and related events, such as celebrations after cup victories, meant that the public were well aware of the progress of the game there, and ensured that the pleasure and joy it gave to its players, organizers and supporters was sufficiently documented.

COMMUNITY

Of all the garrison towns in the area discussed above, Enniskillen was the one where soccer enjoyed the greatest advancement in the opening decades of the twentieth century, and this was particularly facilitated by the loyalist-leaning *Impartial Reporter*. The *Fermanagh Herald*, through its publication of material designed to damage soccer's spread, ultimately failed to stop the game being played there, although it must be stated that this newspaper covered all sports played locally. In Ballyshannon, Erne FC grew sufficiently in strength to enter the IFA Junior Cup in 1905, and defeated Omagh before succumbing to Strabane in the third round. The *Donegal Independent* noted this achievement with the first publication of a picture of a Ballyshannon soccer team. However, none of Ballyshannon's teams affiliated with the Fermanagh and Western District FA, which came into existence in 1906 but did not have a regular playing field.[72]

69 Toms, *Soccer in Munster*, p. 112.   70 *FH*, 27 May and 10 June 1905.   71 Ibid., 27 May 1905.   72 *FH*, 6 Oct. 1906.

With the failure of the Donegal Football Association in the 1890s, the organization of soccer in Donegal was restricted to inconsistently arranged, localized cup competitions until the 1930s. It was the GAA club in the town, formed through the Gaelic League in 1909, which later attracted the most support and had developed the leading football club there by the 1920s.[73] In addition, the GAA in Donegal made better use of the press to promote their codes than soccer organizers did, with the *Donegal Democrat* becoming the mouthpiece of the new county board in the 1920s.[74]

After the burst of soccer activity in Cavan in the 1890s, a revival in GAA activity was experienced between 1900 and 1903, most notably across the centre of the county, with Killeshandra as its heartland.[75] While the foundation of the GAA county board there in 1903 strengthened the GAA's position within Cavan society, soccer at the time lacked an individual or group of men willing to organize a governing body to administer this code, and this undoubtedly hindered its initial development. The strengthening of the ban in 1905, which prohibited GAA players from taking part in soccer, rugby, hockey or cricket, apparently put paid to the friendly spirit shown between Cavan's GAA and soccer clubs, and it was Gaelic football that grew in strength in this decade, although soccer did continue to be played.[76] While the *Anglo-Celt* did not refrain from publishing accounts of soccer in the early twentieth century, unlike the *Donegal Democrat*, GAA organizers showed more awareness in consistently publicizing their codes, while reports of soccer were more infrequent in publication.

Soccer in Enniskillen grew in strength with the Fermanagh and Western League's development, and this organization has survived to the present day.[77] Its early progress was due in no small part to the work of Enniskillen Celtic, a club said to be 'the pioneers of the game in the district', who, in bringing clubs 'from Belfast and elsewhere' (and making sure these events received sufficient press coverage) were improving their own standard.[78] The club won the North West Junior Cup, the Fermanagh and South Tyrone League and the Charity Cup as St Michael's Hall Celtic in 1905.[79] By 1908, the Fermanagh and Western League was reportedly 'one of the most successful leagues in the north-west', and this was said to be a result of their strict administration of disciplinary measures.[80] Regular reporting of their activities, on and off the soccer field, was a help in raising the public's awareness of the game.

By 1914, competitive soccer in the south and west Ulster areas had grown considerably in strength, with the extension of the above league allowing clubs from Connacht to also compete in this regional body.[81] Clubs in more rural areas in these counties remained in operation, but it was mainly in bigger towns such as

73 Curran, *The development of sport*, pp 127, 152.   74 Ibid., pp 204–5.   75 'History: 1900–1910', http://www.cavangaa.ie/1900_to_1910.html, accessed 24 May 2013.   76 Ibid., and *AC*, 14 Jan. 1905.   77 Ibid. 78 *UH*, 11 Jan. 1908.   79 *AC*, 17 Mar. 1906.   80 *UH*, 11 Jan. 1908.   81 PRONI, Papers of the Irish Football Association. D/4196/A/2 IFA Minute Book 1903–9, Special General Meeting, 23 Mar. 1907, pp 195–6.

Enniskillen, Omagh and Clones that the strongest ones developed, and despite a growth in affiliations to the Fermanagh and Western District, there were only twenty-one clubs registered to this administrative body by the summer of 1907, out of the IFA's total of 304.[82]

The military's relationship with soccer in Ireland still awaits a definitive publication, as does its coverage in the provincial press. This would certainly be useful for future studies of the growth of local soccer and the complexities of nationalism in Ireland. Further analysis would contribute to a better understanding of Irish society's relationship with sport, which like the newspapers that reported it, was central to community life in many towns and villages throughout the country.

82 PRONI, Papers of the Irish Football Association. D/4196/A/2 IFA Minute Book 1903–9, Annual Report, 11 May 1907, pp 195–6.

James W. Upton: activist, editor and forgotten journalist of 1916

ANTHONY KEATING

James W. Upton was a journalist, editor and political activist, who wrote and edited on the regional and national stage during the formative years of the modern Irish state. Upton originally made his name as a Gaelic games journalist, under the pen name 'Vigilant', while pursuing a career in the wine and spirit trade. During 1904 he embarked on a full-time career as a news journalist, employed by both the *Waterford Star* and the *Waterford News*, while continuing to provide Gaelic games articles to a number of national and regional newspapers, including the *Evening Telegraph* and the *Irish Weekly Independent*.[1] Upton, from 1912 until 1916, also wrote for the national *Gaelic Athlete*, published by Joseph Stanley's Dublin-based Gaelic Press. The quality of Upton's writing and the breadth of its distribution soon established him as one of the nationalist journalists who dominated the sporting press in the first quarter of the twentieth century.[2]

Upton's passion and talent for sports reporting was matched by his commitment to the republican cause and to political journalism. He was described in 1936, as 'next to Griffith, the most trenchant of republican journalists',[3] a reputation in no small way established by his work on the *Sinn Féin* newspaper from its opening in 1906 to its closure in 1914. Between 1914 and 1916, Upton also wrote for and edited a number of republican journals, including *Scissors and Paste*, the *Spark* and *Honesty*.[4]

Upton travelled the country to speak at Sinn Féin meetings and trade union protests, becoming valued as a highly effective public speaker and a respected advocate of the Sinn Féin cause. His journalism was to play a supporting role in the defining political event of twentieth-century Irish history: the Easter Rising. His journalistic activism continued during the war of independence and into the era of the Free State. He penned, and provided column space for, critiques of Free State society, its early Cumann na nGaedheal governments and de Valera's first Fianna Fáil administrations. This would ultimately lead to the undermining of Upton's career as an editor when Fianna Fáil attacked *Honesty*

---

1 Upton family papers, Waterford Museum (awaiting cataloguing). 2 Eoghan Corry, *The history of Gaelic Football* (Dublin, 2010), pp 84–5. 3 *IPr*, 15 Apr. 1936. 4 He edited the *Spark* under one of his many pen names, 'Ed Dalton', and *Honesty* under another, 'Gilbert Galbraith'. The latter pen name was ascribed to Joseph Stanley in Tom Reilly, *Joe Stanley: printer to the Rising* (Cork, 2005), p. 26, but papers in possession of the Upton family clearly indicate that these were pen names regularly used by Upton.

following publication of criticism of the party's leadership.[5] Notwithstanding his reputation as a journalist, Upton's name was largely lost to history until the relatively recent past.

This chapter will explore Upton's life and career, with a particular focus upon his contribution as editor of the *Kilkenny Journal* from 1915 to 1922. Upton's tenure as editor saw the newspaper's political focus change from support for the policies of John Redmond's Irish Parliamentary Party (IPP) to support for those of socialist republicanism. Upton was passionate in the belief that the regional press made an important contribution to Irish democracy, and as an editor always focused on the bigger political picture, ensuring that the *Kilkenny Journal*, while provincial, was never parochial.

UPTON'S EARLY CAREER

James W. Upton was born in Ballybricken, Waterford city, on 5 June 1872. An able scholar, he attended Mount Sion Christian Brothers School in Waterford. During his time at Mount Sion, he developed a passionate interest in Gaelic games and nationalism. One of Upton's earliest influences in this regard was the Fenian James O'Conner,[6] who Upton met on several occasions. Gaelic games and nationalism, for Upton, were perfectly seamed. Writing in 1934, he asserted that Gaelic games were responsible for the cultural transmission of Irish identity throughout the centuries of an English occupation that sought to denigrate Irish cultural traditions and, with them, the independent identity of the Irish people.[7] Upton comfortably fitted into that cohort of Gaelic games journalists who W.F. Mandle asserted were 'nationalists unrepentant and unconcealed'.[8]

By the early 1900s Upton was politically active in nationalist circles, and he developed a close friendship with Arthur Griffith. He became a founder member of the first Sinn Féin club in Waterford in 1906, holding office as its secretary and, subsequently, its president. His political activities resulted in him losing his job at the *Waterford Star* in 1914. This was precipitated when, as president of the Waterford Sinn Féin club, he led a campaign to exclude those playing non-Gaelic games from using a local sports ground owned by the Waterford Sports Field Company.[9] A group of local businessmen who objected to the campaign threatened to withdraw advertising from the paper if Upton remained in post and, rather than compromise his employer, Upton resigned.[10] He subsequently took up employment as editor of the *Kilkenny Journal*, a newspaper with which he already

5 Anthony Keating, 'Killing off the competition', *Media History*, 22:1 (2016), pp 85–100. 6 Interview with J.W. Upton's son Seamus Upton, 14 Sept. 2014.   7 Vigilant, 'Athletics in national tradition' in *Golden jubilee souvenir of the Gaelic Athletic Association: a review from 1884–1934* (Dublin, 1934), pp 33–5. 8 William Murphy, 'The GAA during the Irish revolution' in Mike Cronin, William Murphy, William & Paul Rouse (eds), *The Gaelic Athletic Association, 1884–2009* (Dublin, 2009), p. 63.   9 The ground is now known as Parc Breathnach.   10 Interview with Seamus Upton, 15 Sept. 2015.

had a connection, having written its Gaelic games column, 'GAA News' since 1908.[11] Upton took over the editorial reins of the *Journal* from F.L. Gibbons in the spring of 1915 and remained at the newspaper until February 1922. During those seven years, Upton became a highly visible editor and campaigner with regard to housing, trade unionism and republican issues. He was passionate about social and political change, and he viewed the regional press as playing an important role in supporting radical movements. Writing in 1916 he argued that 'the local press has given most substantial aid to all national movements and served to promote national organizations for the advancement of great causes ... The press has proved a most efficient educational agency for the masses.'[12]

When Upton took up the editorship of the *Journal*, it was nationalist in outlook and broadly sympathetic to the aims and tactics of the IPP. The *Journal* supported Redmond's strategy of aiding Britain's war effort to bolster Ireland's progression to home rule, arguing that Ireland should send 'her surplus sons to the Allied races ... who are striving to overthrow the despotism of the kaiser, which is a menace to humanity at large'.[13] The *Journal* declared itself for the 'Irish Party and for what it has done for Ireland'.[14] Its support for the IPP position began to wane during the initial period of Upton's editorship. However, the events of Easter 1916 led to a sea change in its editorial stance that inserted a strident republicanism into its content.

Upton was in Dublin, preparing articles for the *Gaelic Athlete* and editing *Honesty* and the *Spark*, on Friday 24 March 1916 when the Gaelic Press' printing presses were seized by the British authorities. Notwithstanding this seizure, Joseph Stanley and Upton were determined to produce their newspapers. They ultimately realized this ambition by using the printing presses in the basement of Liberty Hall,[15] under the protection of an armed guard provided by the Irish Citizen Army. Writing in the 1930s, Upton recalled these events, recounting with some glee how they had completely dumbfounded the British intelligence service by producing the newspapers under the nose of Dublin Castle.[16]

Stanley and Upton were subsequently attached to the General Post Office garrison, the epicentre of the Easter Rising. Under the direct orders of Pádraig Pearse and James Connolly, they commandeered a small printing works in Halston Street, where they printed and distributed *Irish War News* and two other subsequent handbills during the heat of battle.[17] Following the garrison's surrender, Upton avoided arrest and eventually returned to Kilkenny to continue his editorship and republican agitation. It is unclear when he rejoined the

11 *KJ*, 5 Sept. 1908.   12 *KJ*, 5 Sept. 1916.   13 *KJ*, 26 Sept. 1914.   14 *KJ*, 10 Feb. 1915.   15 The headquarters of the Irish Citizen Army (ICA). Following the outbreak of the First World War a banner reading 'We serve neither king nor kaiser, but Ireland' was hung on its front wall, and the ICA's printing press was housed in the basement.   16 James Upton, 'A history of the Gaelic Athletic Association' (unpublished, 1932), pp 399–400. The only known remaining copy is held in the GAA museum and archive.   17 Reilly, *Joe Stanley: printer to the Rising*, p. 44. Diary of Rosamond Jacob, Monday 15 May 1916. National Library of Ireland, MS 32,582/1–170.

Journal following the Rising. The editorial of 17 May 1916 titled 'The Hour and the Man' suggests that Upton was still absent. Its theme was the futility of the Rising, framing the events in Dublin in a way entirely inconsistent with Upton's view on the heroism of, and the necessary sacrifice offered by, those who took part. By September 1916 the *Journal* had adopted a far more stridently anti-British tone. The 16 September 1916 editorial 'EXPERIMENTUM CRUSIS [*sic*]' attacked the *Irish Times* as the voice of the 'tyrant' of which Ireland had been a 'willing slave' for too long, and for the paper's 'shriek of *vae victus*' over the 'dead and vanquished victims' of the Easter Rising.[18]

During this period Upton used the editorship of the *Journal* to establish the short-lived *Phoenix: a Weekly National Review*, which was published from 9 December 1916 to 24 February 1917. Upton took particular satisfaction in this achievement, reminding his colleagues at the *Journal* during his leaving address in 1922, that they should be proud as they had 'played no mean part ... when Ireland was bleeding and broken after 1916' in producing 'single-handed' the *Phoenix*. Its publication, Upton asserted, played an important role in achieving the first Sinn Féin by-election victory in North Roscommon in 1917;[19] 'some of the best propaganda work came out of this office',[20] he declared.

AFTER THE RISING

In October 1916, the *Journal* carried an article by Major Sir Francis Vane that high-lighted British war crimes in the wake of the Easter Rising, and on 28 October 1916, the editorial 'Hands off the Captives' called for the immediate release of political prisoners. This was followed in short order by an outright attack on Redmond for 'pandering to his own constituency and without virility', in which Upton railed against Redmond for 'persistently preaching from the threadbare gospel of British goodwill that will not achieve anything'.[21]

Throughout 1917, Upton continued his attacks on the IPP regarding what he viewed as British political treachery. He described British Prime Minster H.H. Asquith's promises regarding Ireland as 'twaddle', asserting that David Lloyd George, the secretary of state for war, was a 'Welsh political trafficker' and cas-tigating the 'Liberal friends of Ireland'.[22] Upton urged the Irish people to 'look to a movement that will not talk, but do ... a movement that will educate opinion and consolidate the Irish race into a ... determined unit for the uplifting of their national land'.[23] Always the historian, Upton returned to the subject of Lloyd George's political villainy the following year, when he compared him to 'that

---

18 'Woe to the vanquished'. The phrase serves to remind that those defeated in battle are entirely at the mercy of their conquerors and should not expect – or request – leniency.   19 The North Roscommon by-election of 1917 was held on 3 Feb. 1917. Sinn Féin candidate George Noble Plunkett won it. This was Sinn Féin's first victory in a parliamentary election.   20 *KJ*, 4 Feb. 1922.   21 Ibid., 1 Nov. 1916.   22 Ibid., 3 Mar. 1917.   23 Ibid., 17 Mar. 1917.

other liberal, Cromwell', accusing him of wanting to 'revert to the tactics of Clan Oliver'.[24]

Upton continued in a similar vein throughout the remainder of the war. In February 1918, he attacked the British press and much of the indigenous press, which he referred to as 'West British hirelings',[25] who he said infantilized the Irish people and denigrated their potential for self-determination. Notwithstanding Upton's increasing antagonism to the IPP during 1917–18, he was in correspondence with the local IPP MP, Mathew Keating. The two apparently were discussing trying to arrange a strategic alliance between de Valera, the president of Sinn Féin, and John Dillon, Redmond's greatest rival in the IPP, in an attempt to undermine Redmond's position during the Irish Convention.[26] An undated letter from Keating to Upton, a reply to a now lost letter from Upton to Keating, seems to have explored the possibility of triggering an IPP withdrawal from the Convention, which, in Keating's words, would 'cause alarm over'.[27] However, Keating was doubtful that his faction of the IPP could get support from within his party for a move against Redmond's position without the Convention's collapse, notwithstanding Keating's and Dillon's sympathy with the Sinn Féin strategy. Keating, therefore, suggested to Upton that they facilitate private talks between Dillon and de Valera in preparation for such a collapse. Keating requested that Upton discuss the matter with de Valera and undertook to do likewise with Dillon. In the absence of any other documentary evidence, it is not possible to establish if the 'private conversation' between Dillon and de Valera ever took place as a result of this correspondence.[28] What is clear is that Keating believed Upton, at a minimum, had direct contact with de Valera and provided a point of contact between Sinn Féin and elements in the IPP that were sympathetic to Sinn Féin's strategy.

Upton, upon Redmond's death on 6 March 1918, penned a stinging obituary, referring to him as a politician of empire over Ireland, and accusing him of squandering the best chance of winning Irish freedom during the imperial crisis of 1914. Redmond's political career, Upton asserted, proved the futility of sending Irish representatives to Westminster, given the scorn with which British politicians had treated Redmond after his years of 'faithful service to them'.[29]

Notwithstanding his recent correspondence with Keating, Upton was quick to attack Dillon when he succeeded Redmond as leader of the IPP.[30] Dillon, Upton concluded, was content to 'go on with the same old playacting' that had typified Redmond's politics. He added, scornfully, that Parnell had described Dillon as having the 'pride of a peacock and about half its brains.'[31]

24 Ibid., 13 Apr. 1918. **25** Ibid., 23 Feb. 1918. **26** Dillon, while concerned by de Valera's strategic direction, had a level of respect for de Valera and sympathy for much of the Sinn Féin agenda. See Alvin Jackson, *Home rule: an Irish history, 1800–2000* (New York, 2003), p. 183. **27** Referring to the British Parliament. **28** De Valera and Dillon were to make brief common cause in opposing conscription in 1918. However, they were never to find any greater political accommodation. See F.S.L. Lyons, *John Dillon* (Chicago, 1968), p. 448 **29** *KJ*, 9 Mar. 1918. **30** Jackson, *Home rule*, p. 186. **31** *KJ*, 3 Aug. 1918.

During this period when Upton was at his most vociferous in denouncing Britain and any Irish involvement in its war effort, the *Journal* carried adverts for recruitment into the British army and navy on 17 and 24 of August 1918, respectively. These adverts appeared to be, and were, incongruous with Upton's editorial stance. The explanation for this seeming contradiction can be found in the separation of power and responsibility between the owner and editor of the *Journal*, an issue that will be explored more fully below.

The First World War ended on 11 November 1918 and with it the reason posited by the British government and accepted by the IPP for holding Irish home rule in abeyance. Notwithstanding this, Lloyd George backtracked on his earlier commitment to home rule by announcing that he could not support any settlement 'which would involve the forcible coercion of Ulster', effectively supporting an Orange veto on the process. Upton raged that 'Lloyd George has swallowed his pledges and flung the Irish Party overboard.'[32]

The reaction against the IPP was swift and devastating. The general election in December 1918 saw Sinn Féin win a landslide victory, while the IPP was all but wiped out, reduced from the eighty-four seats it had won in the election of 1910 to just six seats; Dillon was one of the casualties, and the party simply dissolved. Upton's oratory had proved useful to the Sinn Féin electoral machine during the general election. James Lalor, a Sinn Féin election organizer who assisted Kevin O'Higgins' election campaign,[33] recalled how Upton had helped O'Higgins win the seat by agreeing to speak in his support at rallies. Lalor stated that Upton 'proved himself to be a very useful speaker. The crowds at the meetings preferred his speeches of ready wit and satire to those of Mr O'Higgins, who was inclined to labour figures and statistics.'[34] Sinn Féin's sweeping gains heralded the establishment of Dáil Éireann and the adoption of the Declaration of Independence on 21 January 1919 – a day which also witnessed the opening salvo of the war of independence, at Soloheadbeg in Co. Tipperary.

THE WAR OF (EDITORIAL) INDEPENDENCE

The *Journal* was to offer unstinting pro-republican commentary during the conflict. However, Upton's credibility as a republican stalwart was called into question by a rival editor as a result of the *Journal*'s advertising content. This deeply affected Upton, and altered his perception of the traditional separation of advertising content from editorial policy in a way that would remain with him for the rest of his career.

Upton, in March 1919, spoke at a rally in support of workers striking to achieve union recognition at the Kilkenny-based motor company Stratham & Co. During the rally, the spirit of the Red Clydesiders was invoked,[35] and the red flag was waved and

---

32 Ibid., 23 Nov. 1918.   33 Kevin Christopher O'Higgins (7 June 1892–10 July 1927).   34 Bureau of Military History (BMH), Witness Statement (WS) 1,032.   35 Red Clydeside was an era of political radicalism in the city of Glasgow and the surrounding towns on the banks of the River Clyde. Much of the leadership of the movement was associated with the Communist and Independent Labour Party. This period in Clydeside's history lasted from the 1910s until roughly the early 1930s.

sung. A local trade union organizer stated that the *Kilkenny People*, Kilkenny's other nationalist newspaper, had refused to print handbills for the strikers as Stratham advertised with them. Upton made a speech at the rally accusing those other Kilkenny newspapers of carrying adverts for 'blackleg labour' to break the strike.

The editor of the *Kilkenny People*, E.T. Keane, a man with a considerable reputation as a firebrand Sinn Féin activist,[36] took exception to these remarks. Keane's ire was particularly focused upon Upton and the 'proprietoress' of the *Kilkenny Journal*, who he branded as hypocrites. Additionally, Keane drew attention to the use of red flags at the rally – potent symbols of atheistic Bolshevism, at the height of the 'red scare' following the Russian Revolution. Keane asserted that he was a friend to labour, but not a Bolshevik, and that his primary reason for not printing the flyers was that they went beyond details regarding the strike, including content that was illegal, and for which he could be prosecuted as the printer. Keane argued that Upton was fully aware of this as the *Journal*, which had printed the flyers, had been careful to ensure that its name was not on them. He pointed out that his newspaper had been closed down in 1917 under the Defence of the Realm Act for printing Sinn Féin-related electoral material during the by-election campaign of the then imprisoned W.T. Cosgrave. Upton had avoided the same penalty for printing the material through an administrative error by the British authorities, buying time that Upton used to offer an apology and make a commitment not to repeat his transgression, Keane said.[37]

Keane's initial assault was followed by a second body blow to Upton's reputation: he attacked the *Journal* for running adverts to recruit young Irish men into the British military while simultaneously espousing the Sinn Féin cause. Keane asserted that profiteering had been at the heart of the decision to publish the adverts, announcing that he had been offered the same adverts at the premium rate of £5 a column, but had refused rather than see young Irishmen sent to the slaughter.[38]

These rebukes clearly stung Upton, who replied in the following edition of the *Journal* that he took sole responsibility for his speech, thereby distancing the owner of the *Journal* from his political activism, prior to renewing his uncompromising attack on the exploitation of labour by the capitalist class. Assuring his readership that he would always defend his class against those who would exploit workers, Upton sought to neutralize the issue of the red flags, arguing that too much was being made of someone waving a piece of 'red cloth on a stick that signified nothing at the meeting'; however, he passed no comment on the singing of 'The red flag'.[39] Regarding Keane's charge in relation to the adverts, Upton argued that Keane was being unfair – which adverts the paper ran was a decision in the hands of the owner. Probably as a product of this criticism, Upton would become hypersensitive in later years to the type of adverts placed in the journals

---

36 Marie Coleman, 'Keane, Edward Thomas ("E.T.")' in *Dictionary of Irish biography*, dib.cambridge.org, accessed 27 Apr. 2016. 37 *KP*, 29 Mar. 1919. 38 Ibid. 39 *KJ*, 5 Apr. 1919.

that he edited. Indeed, he was to resign from his most successful publication, *Honesty*, in 1931, as a result of a change in advertising policy that he felt would bring the character and credibility of the journal into disrepute. Following his resignation, he established a short-lived journal *Publicity* in 1931, precisely to ensure that he had control over both its journalistic content and its advertising content.[40]

Far from being cowed by Keane's attack, the remainder of 1919 saw the *Journal* increasingly focused upon the cause of the indivisibility of labour and nationalism. During May 1919, a new column appeared in the paper, written by 'Demos', reporting upon labour issues. On 25 June, Upton issued a plea in his editorial in the *Journal* for the unity of nationalism and labour:

> For us, the chief concern must be our own country and to stand by her faithfully in her hour of trial. Labour and nationality must not mean two things now, but must mean what they have always meant – two forces fused for the common good of our brave old motherland.

A political activist to his core, Upton ran for public office in the municipal elections in January 1920, subsequently becoming an alderman for St Canice's Ward, Kilkenny, taking up his seat on a Labour ticket. Additionally, he became a founder member of the Kilkenny Town Tenants' Association, campaigning on the issue of tenants and their rights.

In March 1920 Upton responded to the government of Ireland bill in an editorial titled 'A Calculated Insult', asserting: 'Ireland is a country with an irrefutable case for freedom that is still held in degrading conditions against the express will and wishes of the vast majority of its people.'[41] Reinforcing the indignity of Ireland's plight under British rule, Upton cited a 'French journal' that had observed that 'Ireland is treated worse by the English army of occupation than were Belgium or the north of France by the kaiser's troops.'[42]

For the remainder of the war of independence, Upton campaigned for the release of hunger strikers,[43] kept a watch on British atrocities and corruption, including those perpetrated by the Black and Tans,[44] and encouraged the usurpation of the British justice system in favour of republican courts.[45] He took every opportunity to castigate the British, and every aspect of British rule in Ireland, in excoriating prose. For example, he wrote in an editorial on 9 October 1920: 'Before the eyes of the world today the British government has nothing to recommend it. It is a government in a wild panic with no sense of political honour or dignity, organized and bigoted barbarism as its chief weapon.' Upton's activism as a socialist republican was to lead to plaudits from sections of the community but, unsurprisingly, earned him a 'death warrant' issued by the Black and Tans early in 1921.[46]

40 Keating, 'Killing off the competition'. 41 *KJ*, 31 Mar. 1920. 42 Ibid. 43 Ibid., 17 Apr. 1920. 44 Ibid., 11 Sept.; 25 Sept.; and 24 Nov. 1920, 1 Jan. and 19 Mar. 1921. 45 Ibid., 28 Mar. 1920; 5 June 1920. Mr Seamus Upton informed the author that an old IRA man had informed him that his father had sat on Republican Courts. 46 The original 'death warrant' is in the possession of Waterford Museum.

On 11 July 1921, a truce was declared in the Irish war of independence to facilitate a negotiated settlement between the British government and Dáil Éireann. After some considerable delay, formal talks commenced in October 1921. In the 9 November editorial 'Peace or War?', Upton asserted that Lloyd George would seek the path of least resistance, arguing: 'If liberty is not complete, then liberty cannot be liberty. Neither the Dáil, neither the men negotiating for Ireland today hold a mandate for anything other than freedom.'[47] Doubtless aware of the pressure on the Irish negotiators, Upton on 3 December warned them against the temptation of settling for a two-state solution. However, the 10 December editorial 'The Dawn at Last' heralded the Anglo-Irish treaty as a new dawn after years of struggle in which the Irish Free State would be able to take its destiny in its own hands. The tone of this editorial is so completely out of kilter with Upton's view of events that it seems likely that he was not the author. Upton informed his son Seamus many years later that during the latter stages of the negotiating he was spending time in Scotland, engaged in activities surrounding the negotiations and providing copy to Irish nationalist publications based in Glasgow and Edinburgh.[48] Scotland was very important to the nationalist cause, in terms of the supply of arms, fundraising and providing safe houses for men on the run. Indeed, de Valera later thanked the Scottish people for their assistance in the struggle.[49] While no documentary evidence exists to confirm that Upton was on Sinn Féin business in Scotland, what is known is that he was a longstanding activist who enjoyed close relationships with members of the party leadership. These facts, when considered in tandem with Upton's propoganda activities for Sinn Féin and the letter indicating that Upton had acted as an intermediary between Sinn Féin and elements within the IPP, at the very least, do nothing to undermine Upton's subsequent claim to have been active for the party in Scotland in late 1921. If so, his absence may well explain the incongruence between Upton's position on the treaty and the views expressed in 'The Dawn at Last'.

Upton's position pertaining to the treaty was one of profound disappointment nuanced with political pragmatism. During a meeting of Kilkenny town council, convened to discuss the treaty, Upton's was the only dissenting voice regarding the motion proposed by the mayor that the council wholeheartedly endorse it. Upton tabled an amendment that the council should await clarification from the Dáil regarding the reasons why the mandate afforded to them by 83 per cent of the population of Ireland had been put aside, before the corporation took any decision on whether to support the treaty. Upton argued that the treaty was the result of 'compromising expediency', declaring that all members of the Dáil were equally culpable for the undermining of a 'splendid unity' that had stood against a reign of terror established by the British to 'break the will of

47 *KJ*, 9 Nov. 1921. **48** Interview with Seamus Upton, 15 Sept. 2015. **49** Chris Bambery, *A people's history of Scotland* (London, 2010), pp 172–3.

the people'.[50] However, fearful of division in Sinn Féin, he called for tolerance on all sides of the debate to ensure that the party was not 'stampeded into any semblance of a split'. For Upton, the driving force that made the republic a possibility had been holed below the water line, and the task at hand was to salvage the goal of a thirty-two county republic in the longer term. Upton declared that 'he saw no practical alternative [to ratification] – war was not a practical alternative'. However, he observed:

> the bitter thought for him and men who had fought and worked with him in the past and very recent past was that the republic was not kept in the forefront by the men who had sworn allegiance to it and rallied the country to the letter and spirit of that oath.

He told the meeting:

> I have never belonged to any movement but the movement standing for the absolute independence of Ireland. I stand there still. I respect the men who have done their best for Ireland, they are friends of mine, but I cannot excuse the lowering of the republican colours.

Upton's proposed amendment was rejected, and the council overwhelmingly endorsed the ratification of the treaty. Upton decided to leave Kilkenny. The *Journal* of 4 February 1922 reported his resignation as an alderman, and as editor.

LATER LIFE

Upton's eight years at the *Journal* saw both editor and newspaper evolve a stridently self-confident voice. His increasingly confrontational editorial content is illustrative of his confidence in the power of the *Journal* to promote social and political change. A new political reality was taking root in Ireland, both locally and nationally, altering the political geographies of communities in which local newspapers played important roles in affirming and representing community identity.[51] Accordingly, the regional press became an important conduit for political expression in the increasingly contested political terrain on Ireland's road to independence and beyond.

Upton had shaped the *Journal*, just as it was to shape him. The commercial realities that he experienced at the *Journal* would mould his sense of ethical newspaper production, the pursuance of which would ultimately end his career shortly after the closure in 1931 of *Honesty*, a journal that he had edited since 1925. *Honesty* was a hard-hitting socialist republican journal that did not pull any punches in regard to social and political issues. Additionally, in keeping

50 *KJ*, 4 Feb. 1922.   51 John Horgan, 'The provincial press' in Desmond Bell (ed.), *Is the Irish press independent? Essays on ownership and control of the provincial, national and international press in Ireland* (Dublin, 1986).

with Upton's democratic instincts, it provided a platform for those of divergent political opinions. It was driven out of business when Fianna Fáil, following publication of an article critical of the party's leadership, issued a circular to its membership blackballing the journal. The party found Upton's uncompromising democratic stance politically inconvenient, and *Honesty*'s popularity undermining of de Valera's desire to establish his own newspaper.[52] Following *Honesty*'s demise, Upton became the owner-editor of *Publicity*, which was never to prove financially viable, closing just eight months after its launch in 1931.

Upton struggled as a writer over the following decade. He was commissioned to write an official history of the Gaelic Athletic Association (GAA), but this never saw the light of day due to a dispute between Upton and the GAA's central council over aspects of its content.[53] He continued to occasionally contribute pieces with an historical focus to the *Waterford News* and *Waterford Standard*, and to contribute GAA copy where he could. However, he never regained his former success as a Gaelic games journalist.[54] Upton was eventually forced to take up employment with Waterford City Libraries, where he worked until his final illness. James W. Upton died in Waterford in 1956, aged 84.

52 Keating, 'Killing off the competition'. 53 Anthony Keating, 'A politically inconvenient aspect of history: the unpublished official history of the Gaelic Athletic Association of 1934', *Sport in History*, 37:4 (2017), pp 448–68. 54 One example of this was his article in *Golden Jubilee Souvenir* published in 1932 (cited above).

The story behind the storytellers: Cork newspapermen during the Irish revolutionary period, 1914–22

ALAN McCARTHY

Cork city and county newspapers, and their employees, played particularly important roles in grass-roots political activities from the outbreak of war in Europe in 1914 to the closure of Cork's loyalist newspapers in 1922. Divided along nationalist/loyalist lines, they exacerbated tensions in one of the most politically turbulent areas of the country. They were central to the dissemination of ideas and opinions, and to shaping the public mindset. Those who worked in this largely middle-class, male-dominated industry served as links between the leading political figures and ordinary citizens. In this regard, analysis of the media, particularly the regional media, serves as history from the middle, connecting the 'great man' approach to history, or history from above, with the ordinary rank and file, history from below.

The aim of this chapter is not simply to recount a host of anecdotes about journalists working for newspapers in Cork, but to highlight the crucial roles they played in supporting or opposing the revolutionary movement, which had important ramifications for newspaper reportage at this time. Much like the *philosophes* of the Enlightenment, these pressmen were not staid chroniclers and theorists, but activists who occasionally intruded upon the narrative and so became part of the events that they covered. This was particularly true of Cork. This chapter considers how the political affiliations of staff impacted upon the papers' content, and engages with the rivalries that existed between these newspapers. Though such rivalries obviously added spice to the newspapers' coverage, they also served to highlight the vibrancy of the political scene at this time.

Table 6.1: Cork's newspapers and their political affiliations

Paper	Frequency	Up to 1916	Post-1916	War of Independence	Civil war
Cork Constitution	Daily	Unionist	Unionist	Unionist	Pro-Treaty*
Cork Examiner	Daily	Redmondite	Redmondite	Consitutional Nationalist	Pro-Treaty*
Cork Free Press	Daily**	O'Brienite	O'Brienite	Closed	Closed
Skibbereen Eagle	Weekly	O'Brienite	Redmondite	Loyalist	Pro-Treaty
Southern Star	Weekly	Redmondite	Redmondite	Republican	Pro-Treaty
* When not subject to IRA censorship			*** Until 1915, then weekly*		

I am grateful to everyone who has commented on this work and offered suggestions, particularly Donal Ó Drisceoil, John Borgonovo, Sandra McAvoy and Niall Murray, along with the College of Arts, Celtic Studies and Social Sciences at UCC for supporting this research.

1914–16

Throughout the revolutionary period, Cork's newspapers covered a broad political spectrum and were characterized by their fractious nature. Having briefly flirted with the All-for-Ireland League (AFIL) – a small nationalist party led by Land League veteran William O'Brien that proposed an alternative path to home rule – the *Southern Star* in 1910 resolutely recommitted itself to the Irish Parliamentary Party (IPP) and its leader John Redmond. The *Star* had supported the IPP since the paper's foundation in 1889 by John and Florence O'Sullivan, support that continued under the ownership of a consortium led by Monsignor John O'Leary of Clonakilty, and later under C.T. Kennedy, who purchased the paper in 1916.[1] The newspaper's politics invited frequent exchanges of jibes and diatribes with its arch-rival, the *Skibbereen Eagle*, which enlivened their co-existence. Although coverage in the *Eagle* was often non-partisan, the AFIL found a something of a champion in this organ; its primarily Protestant readership appreciated O'Brien's conciliatory gestures towards unionists. Founded in May 1857 by the Potter family, the *Eagle* became renowned for its biting sarcasm, and known for its oft-celebrated and oft-parodied comment, 'watchful eye on the czar of Russia'.[2] For its part, the *Cork Examiner* scrutinized the AFIL's official organ, the *Cork Free Press*, with similar zeal to which the *Eagle* subjected the czar. The *Examiner* dubbed O'Brien a 'factionist' and critiqued the pompous leading articles he occasionally wrote for the *Free Press*,[3] which owed its existence to the United Irish League's ill-tempered 'Baton Convention' of 1909. At this meeting in the Mansion House in Dublin, O'Brien and his supporters had been prevented from approaching the platform, and informed that no one with a Cork accent would be allowed to speak. In response, O'Brien formed the AFIL, and launched the party's campaign newspaper, the *Cork Accent*, which was later replaced by the *Cork Free Press*.[4] Supporters of the Irish Parliamentary Party in Cork city typically read the *Examiner*, which remained a committed (but unofficial) Redmondite journal and was owned by the Crosbie family. Unionist opinion was represented by the *Cork Constitution* and its weekly edition, the *Cork Weekly News*. Founded in 1825, the newspaper was later taken over by Henry Lawrence Tivy, 'a member of a respected and affluent Cork family', who had prospered as a butter merchant.[5] During the revolutionary period, he co-edited the *Constitution* with William Ludgate and in his spare time bank-rolled Cork Constitution Rugby Club, using the proceeds of a charity game to construct a

---

1 *SSt* centenary supplement (1989), p. 2; publication of seditious articles, NAUK WO 35/69/6.
2 *SE*, 2 Sept. 1899. These comments reflected both the proprietor's flamboyant style and interest in international affairs. For more, see Matthew Potter, 'Keeping an eye on the tsar': Frederick Potter and the *Skibbereen Eagle*' in Kevin Rafter (ed.), *Irish journalism before independence* (Manchester, 2011), pp 49–61.
3 *CE*, 20 May 1910 and 21 June 1915.   4 John O'Donovan, 'Nationalist political conflict in Cork, 1910', *Journal of the Cork Historical and Archaeological Society*, 117 (2012), p. 42.   5 Edmund Van Esbeck, *100 years of Cork Constitution Football Club* (Cork, 1992) p. 16; U116/A/53, p. i, Tivy Family Papers, Cork City and County Archives (CCCA).

memorial on Connaught Avenue, on the south side of Cork city, to those killed fighting for the British army during the Boer War. When the monument fell into disrepair, Tivy, adopting a nom de plume, printed a letter of complaint in the *Constitution*. This became a common method of airing his personal grievances.[6]

Of greater significance than Tivy's vexations was the preoccupation of Cork newspapers with the Great War in Europe, which dominated news coverage at this time. Tivy had a passionate interest in the war effort as his son George was a combatant, while his daughter Eleanor Brianne was a nurse with the Territorial Force. Both George and his older brother Henry Francis served on the staff of the *Constitution* for a number of years and were expected to succeed their father and Ludgate in due course.[7] D.D. Sheehan, editor of the *Southern Star* at the turn of the century, and the cornerstone of the Land and Labour Association, served alongside his own sons on the Western Front. His activities were closely followed by his former paper.[8] William O'Brien was also highly supportive of the war, an influential factor being his wife Sophie Raffalovich, a Russian heiress whose mother resided in Paris.[9] However, O'Brien's support for the war did not stop his radical employee, *Free Press* reporter Tadgh Barry, from distributing anti-re-cruiting pamphlets.[10] The war met with particular approval from the *Eagle*; the paper's editor, Patrick Sheehy, and managing director, Jasper Wolfe, were at the forefront of the recruiting campaign in west Cork.[11]

It was into this pro-war climate that the Easter Rising of 1916 asserted itself, with the idea that a group of radicals and socialists could undermine the efforts of the British military's campaign in Europe appearing abhorrent to both home rule supporters and unionist opinion. The general bewilderment and incre-dulity of the press nationally with which the Rising was greeted was mirrored by the press in Cork.[12] The *Examiner* initially misjudged the Rising to be a 'com-munistic disturbance, rather than a revolutionary movement', with the daily paper – the *Constitution* was the only other daily published in Cork at this time – obviously facing greater pressure to meet publication deadlines at a time when, by its own admission, 'the full facts are not known'.[13] Among the participants in Dublin was the paper's printer, Riobárd 'Bob' Lankford, who was promptly

---

6 Richard Hodges, *Cork and County Cork in the twentieth century*, ed. W.T. Pike (Brighton, 1911), p. 292, pen-portrait of Henry Lawrence Tivy; Donal O'Sullivan, *Sport in Cork: a history* (Dublin, 2010), p. 18. For Tivy's pseudonym adoption, see *Cork Constitution*, 2 Jan. 1919, and John Borgonovo, *The dynamics of war and revolution: Cork City, 1916–1918* (Cork, 2013), p. 110.   7 Irish Distress and Grants Committee (hereafter abbreviated as IDGC): files and minutes, NAUK CO 762/145/10, application of G.L.W. Tivy and CO 762/145/8, application of Henry Francis Tivy. NAUK WO 399/15073, Territorial Force Nurs-ing Service Record of Eleanor Tivy.   8 See *SSt*, 5 Feb., 4 Mar. and 22 Apr. 1916.   9 Joseph V. O'Brien, *William O'Brien and the course of Irish politics, 1881–1918* (Los Angeles, 1976), p. 212.   10 Dublin Castle files: Sinn Féin activists: Timothy (Tadgh) Barry, NAUK WO 35/206/4.   11 IGC, NAUK CO/762/80/12. 12 Michael Laffan, *The resurrection of Ireland: the Sinn Féin Party, 1916–1923* (Cambridge, 1999), p. 47. 13 *CE*, 28 Apr. 1916. See also, Owen Dudley Edwards and Fergus Pyle (eds), *1916: the Easter Rising* (London, 1968), pp 256–8.

dismissed from his post for his role in the insurrection.[14] Of the Cork papers, the *Cork Constitution* and *Weekly News* had the most vitriolic reaction, dismissing the insurgents as 'wreckers' and the Proclamation of the Irish Republic as 'arrant nonsense'.[15] It is noteworthy, of course, that the Tivy family (the *Constitution*'s owners) had also purchased the Dublin *Daily Express* and its sister paper the *Evening Mail* the previous year, and that the premises of both papers were occupied by rebels.[16]

As well as possessing an acidic pen, H.L. Tivy would also fall victim to one. There is no mistaking the similarity between Tivy and the fictional editor of the *Ballybawn Blazer*, 'Miley', in Suzanne Day's satirical novel *The amazing philanthropists*. As well as mirroring Tivy physically, the editor of Ballybawn's unionist paper also shares his marked opposition to the suffragette movement.[17] While Tivy was convinced of his own political positions, the *Cork Free Press* was uncertain about what stance to adopt regarding the Rising. Frank Gallagher, the last editor of the *Free Press*, came into conflict with William O'Brien for wanting to convey moderate approval of the insurrection.[18] It is probable that Gallagher was supported in this by Patrick O'Driscoll, another member of the editorial staff.[19] O'Driscoll, Michael Collins' brother-in-law, had previously owned and edited the Fenian weekly the *West Cork People*. An overlooked figure, O'Driscoll's involvement with the *Free Press* provides further explanation for the O'Brienite journal's support for the rebels.[20] The paper criticized what it regarded as the foolhardy nature of the endeavour, but heaped praise on the courage and conduct of the participants in multiple articles published in May and June 1916. The *Free Press* was one of the first papers in the country to adopt a broadly supportive position with regard to the Rising.[21] The press censor, Lord Decies, subsequently denounced the *Free Press* as 'the worst paper in Ireland'.[22] Forced to become a weekly halfpenny paper in 1915 due to financial constraints, the declining O'Brienite organ's demise was assured by the failure of the AFIL to get its candidate elected in the West Cork by-election of November 1916.[23] The result signalled the final death rattle for the League, and O'Brien shut down the *Free Press* shortly afterwards. The *Skibbereen Eagle*, whose managing director, Jasper

---

14 U156/3, Period 1, p.1. Riobárd Lankford Papers, CCCA.　15 *CWN*, 6 May 1916.　16 Patrick Maume, 'Maunsell, James Poole', *Dictionary of Irish biography*; application of James Francis Walshe, *Daily Express*, Property Losses (Ireland) Committee 1/5644, NAI.　17 Suzanne R. Day, *The amazing philanthropists: being extracts from the letters of Lester Martin, P.L.G.* (London, 1916), pp 18–22. See *CWN*, 3 Jan., 17 Jan. and 2 May 1914 for examples of Tivy's opposition to the suffragette movement.　18 Patrick Maume, *The long gestation: Irish nationalist life, 1891–1918* (Dublin, 1999), p. 181; Patrick Maume, 'A nursery of editors: the *Cork Free Press*, 1910–16', *History Ireland*, 15:2 (Mar.–Apr. 2007), p. 46.　19 *IT*, 7 Sept. 1940. 20 For more on O'Driscoll, see Alan McCarthy, 'The curious incident of the rod in the night-time: Edward Gillman, Patrick O'Driscoll and the *West Cork People*/News & Co. libel case of 1907', *Skibbereen & District Historical Society Journal*, 12 (2016).　21 *CFP*, 6, 13, 20 and 27 May and 3 June 1916.　22 NAUK, WO 35/69/6.　23 Maume, *The long gestation*, p. 172; BMH WS 1,698, Liam de Róiste, 2 Mar. 1915, p. 156. For financial pressures see, for example, AS 83 (1), William O'Brien to Hugh O'Brien Moran, 16 Feb. 1916, pp i–ii, William O'Brien Papers, Special Collections, UCC.

Wolfe, had canvassed for the AFIL in west Cork, briefly found itself as a paper without a party.[24] Reacting to the Rising, the *Eagle* stated that it represented 'a period of bloodshed, rapine and disorder which few cities in the world have ever experienced', calling those who participated in the Dublin disturbances 'misguided'.[25] The following month, those interned at Frongoch and elsewhere were released, and they would soon challenge the IPP's political ascendancy. In early 1918, the restructured Sinn Féin movement purchased the *Southern Star*, guaranteeing itself press support in west Cork.[26]

The turning tide of opinion nationally was expressed, appropriately enough, by not only the Cork newspapers themselves, but also by newspapermen in their extra-journalistic activities. In his 6th Divisional Area Report, General Peter Strickland stated that:

> After the rebellion, the state of the country was quiet and more or less normal for a few months. Towards the end of 1916, and early in 1917, it became clear that the state of quietness of the previous few months was merely transitory. The first case that made this clear was that of the late Thadg [*sic*] Barry, who was tried in January, 1917, by district court martial at Cork for making a violently seditious speech.[27]

Barry, a former sports reporter with the *Cork Free Press*, and later a columnist with the *Southern Star*, was one of a host of active republicans working for Cork newspapers at this time.[28]

1917–19

One of the most significant acts of radicalization in West Cork was Sinn Féin's purchase of the 'practically bankrupt' *Southern Star* in early 1918.[29] Along with heralding a marked increase in press polarization that saw the *Eagle* inching towards loyalism, this acquisition resulted in a host of prominent republican figures becoming attached to the *Star*. Among them were Tadgh Barry, shareholder Michael Collins, Gaelic League organizer Peadar O'Hourihan and future TD Seán Hayes. Seán Buckley, later intelligence officer for the West Cork IRA, was on the board of directors for a time, as was James 'Barney' O'Driscoll. As if to mark the paper's radical departure, new office manager, Seamus O'Brien, was arrested for being in possession of a revolver while travelling by bicycle to Skibbereen shortly after the takeover.[30]

24 U271/A/17, p. 302, De Róiste Diaries, CCCA; O'Donovan, 'Nationalist political conflict', p. 46; IGC, NAUK CO/762/80/12. 25 *SE*, 6 May 1916. 26 Maume, *The long gestation*, pp 189–95; *CE*, 3 and 21 Nov. 1916. 27 General Strickland Papers (p. 363), 'The Irish Rebellion in the 6th Divisional Area from after the 1916 Rebellion to December 1921, compiled by General Staff, 6th Division, Section II', pp 8–9, Imperial War Museum London. 28 Borgonovo, *War and revolution*, p. 51. 29 BMH WS 939, Ernest Blythe, pp 80–1. 30 *CE*, 31 May 1918.

In an effort to avoid arrest, Seán Buckley later relinquished his seat on the *Southern Star*'s board, requesting that Peg Healy – whose brother-in-law, William Keyes McDonnell, was already a director – take his place. Healy's seat at the directors' table was quite unusual for a local/regional newspaper at a time of significant female underrepresentation.[31] Another unusual *Southern Star* characteristic was very high staff turnover owing to the revolutionary activity of the paper's employees, many of whom received unwanted attention from the authorities. Tadgh Barry, arrested again as a consequence of the 'German Plot' of 1918, was one of a number of staff members incarcerated.[32] In November, the OC for the Special Military Area of west Cork bitterly complained that the paper was:

> Under the control of three directors, Peter O'Hourihane [Peadar O'Hourihan], and John [Seán] Buckley, both of whom are in jail, and Jeremiah [James] O'Driscoll who is evading arrest. The editor, John [Seán] Hayes ... was taken prisoner at the GPO, Dublin, in 1916, and was interned ... The paper is financed entirely from Sinn Fein [*sic*] funds, and the present owners are extremists of a bad type.[33]

While individual staff members came and went, editorial continuity was embedded in these papers as their politics were collectively cultivated between staff and readership. So entrenched was the *Eagle*'s hatred of local politician Timothy Sheehy, for example, that obloquies and censures of Sheehy in the paper did not end even when his nephew Patrick Sheehy ascended to the editorial chair.[34] Adherence to core ideas also guided Denis O'Connell, a *Star* reporter who sent west Cork news items to the *Irish Independent*. On one occasion, O'Connell sent a falsified report concerning a Dáil loan meeting in Dunmanway in August 1919, alleging that Michael Collins (then on the run) was in attendance and that James 'Barney' O'Driscoll and Gearóid O'Sullivan (imprisoned in Cork Gaol) had sent cheques, thereby embellishing both the profile and success of the meeting. While the loan-supporting O'Connell sought to mislead the public in the country's most widely circulated paper, when writing for the *Southern Star* he and his colleagues – several of whom were loan agents – leaned towards heavy-handedness, rather than falsehoods.[35] Republican ranks were further swelled by the collapse of the AFIL, which resulted in the transfer of many former O'Brienites, already fringe nationalists, to Sinn Féin. This was exemplified in Skibbereen by the transfer of journalist Geoffrey Wycherley from the *Eagle* to the *Star*.[36]

31 Kathleen Keyes McDonnell, *There is a bridge at Bandon: a personal account of the Irish war of independence* (Cork, 1972), p. 106. 32 This alleged conspiracy between the German empire and Irish republicans was used to justify wide-scale internment of Sinn Féin members in May 1918. 33 *SSt* centenary supplement, pp 29, 61; County Cork (West Riding) Special Military Area Internal Memo to Major General Doran, 7 Nov. 1918, NAUK, WO 35/69/6. 34 *SSt*, 26 Feb. 1916. 35 *II*, 18 Aug. 1919; RIC Crime Special Branch file on Michael Collins, Sinn Féin and Republican Suspect Files, CO 904/196/65, Boole Library, UCC, microfilm. My thanks to Niall Murray for directing me towards this information. Both Seán Buckley and Seán Hayes were Dáil loan agents for the area. See detailed list of documents seized at Sinn Féin HQ, NAUK CO 904/24/3. 36 O'Brien, *The course of Irish politics*, pp 236–9; *SSt*, 1 Dec. 1928; *SSt* centenary supplement, p. 87.

Such movement was more problematical for Protestant O'Brienites. R.B. McDowell informs us that 'From 1918 "unionist" as a political label was being supplemented or superseded by "loyalist," the latter term resonant and implying adherence to high principle, covering not only unionists but those constitutional nationalists who avowedly supported crown authority.'[37] By this definition, rather than relying on the simplistic equation 'Protestant = loyalist', we may define the republican-opposed and government-supporting *Eagle* as loyalist. The O'Brienite/Redmondite divide, framed by the *Cork Free Press* and *Examiner*, and the *Eagle* and *Star* previously, provided a template for heated political division within the new nationalist/loyalist dichotomy. Unquestionably, the goalposts of political affiliation had shifted post-Rising, with the former AFIL paper with primarily Protestant readership deemed to fall on the side of the union, at least within the reductive confines of heightened political anxiety at this time. Such anxiety was justified. The widespread, energetic and committed support for Sinn Féin was given jubilant and exuberant expression, having reached a crescendo in the electoral victory of the party in December 1918. That night revellers blew up the Boer War monument that H.L. Tivy had built in Cork city.[38]

1919–21

Throughout the war of independence Frank Gallagher, formerly of the *Cork Free Press*, played an instrumental role as assistant editor of the *Irish Bulletin*, which gained significant influence on press opinion during the conflict. One of Gallagher's contributors was Alan J. Ellis, a reporter with the *Cork Examiner*. During this period the *Examiner* fell between two stools, failing to reconcile itself to the militarism of the republican movement, while also irritating the crown authorities with its robust critiques of British policy in Ireland.[39] In his later description of the *Examiner* during these pivotal years, Ellis stated that 'the newspaper tried to steer a neutral path in reporting, keeping to facts and leaving the tub-thumping to the editor'.[40] The *Examiner*'s middling approach may be attributed to its city-centre location at this time, with staff witnessing the excesses of Auxiliary police officers on their doorstep, while the city centre itself would be razed to rubble in the infamous 'Burning of Cork'. The paper's staff was not exempt from such excesses either; the Harrington brothers, Michael and George, reporters for the *Examiner* in the city and also brothers of Tim Harrington, the *Irish Independent* editor, were arrested and placed in the Bridewell on fabricated charges.[41] Stephen Dorman, another *Examiner* employee, and an active IRA member, was later killed by crown forces while walking home from

37 R.B. McDowell, *Crisis and decline: the fate of the southern unionists* (Dublin, 1997), p. 83. 38 *CC*, 2 Jan. 1919; Borgonovo, *War and revolution*, p. 110. 39 Alan J. Ellis, *The burning of Cork: an eyewitness account* (Cork, 2004), p. 14. For an example of such a critique see *CE*, 22 Sept. 1919. 40 Ellis, *The burning*, p. 6. 41 Hugh Oram, *The newspaper book: a history of newspapers in Ireland, 1649–1983* (Dublin, 1983), pp 149–51.

work with other *Examiner* employees, owing to his membership of the IRA.[42] Understandably, this environment affected the paper's reporting.

Ellis' account highlights this disconnect between the politics of a staff member and those of the paper he/she worked for. While on hunger strike, Frank Gallagher was overcome with fear of disappointing all those who 'looked up to me ... who read what I wrote and thought I meant it'.[43] It appears that journalists generally sought out papers with which they shared common politics, but were able to reconcile those politics with the practical work of writing copy if they possessed views different to their employers. Prior to his tenure at the *Southern Star*, shortly before Sinn Féin's takeover, Ernest Blythe briefly worked for loyalist newspapers the *Bateman*, of Bangor, Co. Down, and the *North Down Herald*.[44] Similarly, among the *Eagle*'s support staff was Michael O'Sullivan of Skibbereen. O'Sullivan had close ties to the IRA and was dismissed from the *Eagle* as a result.[45] Patrick O'Sullivan, another employee of the *Eagle*, had his application to the Irish Grants Committee for compensation owing to loss of employment rejected as his loyalty to the British government could not be confirmed by the assessment committee.[46]

While the *Constitution* remained unshakeably loyal to the crown, another notable aspect of the paper's reportage was its utter disdain for the labour movement.[47] Prior to his arrest, those inclined towards the left in west Cork could enjoy Tadgh Barry's passionate column in the *Southern Star*, entitled "Neath Shandon's Steeple'. This column, along with pieces Barry contributed to ITGWU's *Voice of Labour*, 'demonstrated his ability to link general questions of theory and ideology with practical union matters', as noted by Donal Ó Drisceoil.[48] Barry also delivered visceral calls to arms within the pages of the *Southern Star*, attacking the 'soul-killers who fatten on the poor work-girls of our city, and build their profits on the weary toil of the underpaid working man'.[49] Barry's death at Ballykinlar internment camp in 1921 resulted in a mass outpouring of grief that surpassed the funerals of former lord mayor Tómas MacCurtain and MacSwiney in terms of size.[50] While the *Eagle* sympathized with the passing of Barry, throughout the Anglo-Irish hostilities the weekly remained vehemently opposed to the republican movement under its editor Patrick Sheehy.[51] This opposition was shared by the paper's shareholders, who, at the time of the *Eagle*'s closure, included Dunmanway solicitor Francis Fitzmaurice, shot dead during the 'Bandon Valley Massacre' of April 1922, Clonakilty J.P. Timothy Canty, and

42 John Borgonovo, *Spies, informers and the Anti-Sinn Féin Society: the intelligence war in Cork city, 1920–1921* (Dublin, 2007), p. 84; Ian Kenneally, *The paper wall: newspapers and propaganda in Ireland, 1919–1921* (Cork, 2008), pp 68–9. 43 Frank Gallagher, *Days of fear* (Cork, 1967), p. 103. 44 P24/1210 (a) and P24/1213, Ernest Blythe Papers, UCD Archives. 45 IGC, NAUK CO 762/80/15. 46 IGC, NAUK CO 762/80/33. 47 See, for example, *CC*, 3 Jan. 1919. 48 Donal Ó Drisceoil, *Tadgh Barry (1880–1921): the story of an Irish revolutionary* (Cork, 2011), p. 17. 49 *SSt*, 9 Feb. 1918. 50 Ó Drisceoil, *Tadgh Barry*, p. 5. 51 *SE*, 26 Nov. 1921; Liam Deasy, *Towards Ireland free: the West Cork Brigade in the war of independence, 1917–1921* (Cork, 1973), p. 51.

Jasper Wolfe, who led the way in preference shares.[52] The animosity between the *Eagle* and the *Southern Star* varied between sarcastic quips and unbridled contempt; on learning of the suppression of the *Freeman's Journal*, the *Star* stated that the *Freeman* 'is not the *Skibbereen Eagle*. It is a great Irish newspaper, with a century of history on its files.'[53] While there was no love lost between pro-prietors and editors, it appears that common membership of the fraternity of journalists ensured a degree of cooperation between reporters of rival papers.[54] Amid this climate of newspaper competition, some rivalries were more intense than others. In his capacity as crown solicitor, Jasper Wolfe defended the crown forces at the inquest into Tomás MacCurtain's death, as well as prosecuting Tadgh Barry and succeeding 'in getting a severe sentence passed' in the process. Wolfe later informed the police 'that if an attack was made on him Barry would be the principal instigator'.[55] The fact that Wolfe would volunteer such infor-mation unrequested goes some way to explain the IRA's conviction that Wolfe – who would have fallen under suspicion regardless, owing to his work as a crown solicitor – was a spy and an informer.[56]

Despite these suspicions, which resulted in Wolfe being kidnapped in October 1921 and July 1922, his solicitors firm was obliged to attend the increasingly popular Sinn Féin courts for monetary reasons (although Wolfe himself, as crown solicitor, could not be present).[57] For republicans, the rise of these courts and reporting about them was hugely significant. The *Southern Star* sought to legitimize these courts with matter-of-fact reporting.[58] In contrast, the *Eagle* patronisingly used inverted commas when reporting on these 'courts'.[59] Neither the *Examiner* nor the *Constitution* paid much attention to them. Rallying behind the provisional government following the cessation of hostilities and the agreement of the Anglo-Irish treaty, the *Constitution* proclaimed in April 1922 that:

> many people are under the impression that Republican courts are now func-tioning for the first time. Such is not the case. They have been working constantly in all parts of Ireland for months before the truce ... The idea prevalent in many instances that their constitution is a haphazard affair is also a mistaken one.[60]

Dáil courts were introduced in attempt to undermine the British legal system, thereby establishing the Irish republic created by the first Dáil as the de facto government.

---

52 IGC, NAUK CO 762/80/17.   53 *FJ*, 18 Dec. 1919.   54 Ellis, *The burning*, p. 9. An exhausted Ellis received a lift home from a 'fellow reporter from the *Cork Constitution*'.   55 NAUK WO 35/206/4; see *SE*, 11 Feb. 1922.   56 Andy Bielenberg, John Borgonovo & James Donnelly Jr., '"Something in the nature of a massacre": the Bandon Valley killings revisited', *Éire-Ireland*, 49:3&4 (Fall/Winter 2014), pp 34–5. 57 Andy Bielenberg, John Borgonovo and Pádraig Óg Ó Ruairc (eds), *The men will talk to me: west Cork interviews by Ernie O'Malley* (Cork, 2015), Interview of Ted O'Sullivan (UCDA P17b/108, pp 1–27), p. 161, n. 98; Jasper Ungoed-Thomas, *Jasper Wolfe of Skibbereen* (Cork, 2008), pp 123–4; Willie Kingston, 'From Victorian boyhood to the Troubles: a Skibbereen memoir', *Skibbereen & District Historical Society Journal*, 1 (2005), pp 30–1.   58 See, for example, *SSt*, 5 Feb. 1921.   59 *SE*, 5 June and 10 July 1920. 60 *CC*, 27 Apr. 1922.

Their operation was coupled with the destruction of crown courthouses and harassment and intimidation of justices of the peace. The manager of the *Skibbereen Eagle*, Edwin Swanton, 'was kidnapped upon 10 July 1921 solely by reason of the fact that he was a justice of the peace who would not resign'. Jasper Wolfe believed that 'The fact that he was on friendly terms with me largely constituted to his kidnapping.'[61] IRA member Stephen O'Brien, however, speculated that Swanton was also 'one of the enemy's murder gang'.[62] Swanton and Wolfe remained in Skibbereen despite their brushes with the IRA. Their attitude was mirrored by their paper, the *Eagle*. Even in the midst of republican agitation and harassment, 'it would not be sold, the directors and shareholders believing that such an act would have been treason to the British empire'.[63]

POST-1921

The declaration of a truce between republicans and crown forces, and the eventual peace treaty, were met with widespread acclaim in the Cork press. However, violence remained a feature of life. In April 1922, west Cork was rocked by the Bandon Valley killings. This violent breakdown in order was indicative of the increasingly unpredictable nature of Irish politics, which reached a bloody climax with the outbreak of the civil war over the terms of the Anglo-Irish treaty. For the most part, Cork papers were united in their call for peace during the drift towards war. In March 1922, the *Southern Star*'s management adopted a resolution to support the treaty editorially.[64] A volte-face was brought about the following month with the return of director Seán Buckley to the fold. As a result, the paper briefly leaned towards the anti-treatyites, indicated by its condescending reference to the 'half-breed' Free State.[65] Although Buckley later stressed moderation and the necessity for unity among 'brother Irishmen',[66] the divisions within the country were exemplified by the split between *Star* director Seán Hales and his brother Tom, who took opposing sides. The *Southern Star*'s board of directors later again resolved to support the treaty, as highlighted in the minutes of its 1922 AGM. Without being critical of republicans, it would at all times 'point out in a clear unmistakable way the advantages of the treaty'.[67]

The treaty also found a resolute supporter in the *Constitution*. Shut down by anti-treatyite harassment in July 1922, in an impassioned final editorial Tivy outlined his hope for:

> the ending of the ruinous warfare which is serving to banish the hopes and destroy the interest of every inhabitant of the country. No matter how prolonged this campaign with its attendant destruction of life and property may be, it must have an end. And it will, when that stage is

61 IGC, NAUK CO 762/27/4.   62 BMH WS 603, Stephen O'Brien, p. 3. Quoted in David Fitzpatrick, *Descendancy: Irish Protestant histories since 1795* (Cambridge, 2014), p. 219   63 IGC, NAUK CO 762/80/12. For more on such harassment, see Ó Drisceoil, ch. 11.   64 *SSt* centenary supplement, p. 62.   65 *SSt*, 22 Apr. 1922.   66 *SSt* centenary supplement, p. 90.   67 Ibid., pp 62, 90.

reached when it becomes necessary to find some formula under which Irishmen of every class can dwell together in unity.[68]

In December 1923, Tivy informed Governor General T.M. Healy that close to £6 million in cash, held in securities and to the credit of suitors within the defunct crown courts, lay untouched: 'This sum, I suggest, should now be under the control of the Irish Free State courts, and if approved by them invested in Irish securities such for instance as a future loan,' Tivy wrote.[69] His generous financial advice shows that the newspaper enterprise, rather than being recalcitrant towards the new political alignment, could have adapted to life in the Free State, much like another ex-unionist paper, the *Irish Times*. Indeed, with treaty-related fissures emerging, the paper opined: 'If the judgment of the electors is to be flouted and the will of the people is to be turned down, there must be an end of democratic government and the substitution thereafter of autocratic rule.'[70]

The *Cork Constitution*'s closure resulted in several resident pressmen in country towns losing their jobs as correspondents for the paper.[71] Irrevocably shaken by his paper's closure, Henry Lawrence Tivy retreated from public life, while his oldest son, Henry Francis, continued as managing director of the *Evening Mail* until 1960 when it was bought by the *Irish Times*. His brothers George and Eric Reginald Tivy ran the family's highly successful wholesale business, News Brothers & Co.[72]

Similar redundancies occurred in west Cork due to the closure of the *Eagle* on 15 July 1922, with the Skibbereen institution stoically announcing that: 'In consequence of conditions arising from the present unsettled state of the country, the directors of the *Eagle* have decided to suspend its publication until further notice.' The *Southern Star* reiterated the *Constitution*'s comments that 'The announcement is much regretted in the town, as, apart from its association with the district, over a long eventful period, a number of persons will be placed on the unemployment list as a result.'[73] The *Examiner* was also in favour of the treaty, but like the *Constitution* was subjected to a rigid censorship imposed by anti-treatyites who occupied the paper's offices during the summer of 1922, before eventually fleeing in August following the amphibious landing of national army troops in Cork.[74] The anti-treatyite cause was espoused by a coterie of propagandists led by Erskine Childers, who based himself in the Victoria Hotel in Cork city, before evacuating alongside his anti-treatyite brothers-in-arms. At this point, Childers was both an anti-treatyite propagandist editing the southern edition of *Poblacht na hÉireann*, and a propaganda figure for pro-treatyites, who denigrated him.[75] Captured by Free State forces in November 1922, Childers was succeeded by Bob Lankford, who,

---

68 *CC*, 22 July 1922.   69 U116/A/35, letter from H.L. Tivy, 12 Dec. 1923, to T.M. Healy, governor general, Tivy Family Papers, CCCA.   70 *CC*, 2 Jan. 1922.   71 Dáil Éireann Debates, vol. 54, no. 9, 18 Dec. 1934. 72 Mark O'Brien, *The Irish Times: a history* (Dublin, 2008), p. 161; Siobhán Jones, 'Southern Irish unionism' (PhD, UCC, 2005), p. 250.   73 *SSt*, 15 July 1922.   74 John Borgonovo, *The battle for Cork: July–August 1922* (Cork, 2011), p. 97.   75 Ibid., p. 48; BMH WS 779, Robert Brennan, p. 573; Andrew Boyle, *The riddle of Erskine Childers* (London, 1977), pp 15, 21.

along with Sean O'Faolain, produced 20,000 copies of *Poblacht na hÉireann* 'on a hillside under war conditions, 15 miles from the nearest town'.[76]

A CONTINUING STORY

Throughout this century-shaping epoch, the regional press played a pivotal role as a moulder of public opinion, and a mirror of it. In Cork, as in the rest of the country, newspapers reflected the turbulent course of Irish political life during this period of upheaval and flux, both within their pages and in the experiences of their staff. Rather than being apolitical recorders of fact and incident, these pressmen pursued their own agendas in their extra-journalistic activities, ranging from wartime recruitment, to electioneering, to IRA involvement. In print they supported or undermined individuals, ideas and institutions, while remaining dynamic, hands-on activists who were integral cogs in the political machine. This provokes questions about the production processes of these newspapers. While a journalist's politics did not necessarily have to align with that of their employer, internal harmony was always preferable at a time of increasingly divergent political outlooks, with division deepening in Cork following the closure of the *Cork Free Press* and collapse of William O'Brien's All-for-Ireland League.

Throughout this tumultuous time, those of a loyalist persuasion could enjoy the *Eagle* and *Constitution*, which served as defiant bastions of loyalist politics. Tivy and his loyalist compatriots in the press remained wholly committed to their political ends in the face of staunch opposition. The corollary of this commitment was, inevitably, heated rivalries between nationalist and loyalist papers in Cork. The *Eagle* and the *Constitution* eventually paid the ultimate price for their editorial policies. In the years that followed the revolutionary decade, the absence of an ex-loyalist/unionist press in the south of the country added a slightly monochromatic tinge to the mainstream media. Nevertheless, a professional respect was maintained within this fraternity of pressmen – a legacy that survives to this day, with the *Southern Star* utilizing the *Eagle* emblem in its masthead. Similarly, a part of the *Constitution* lives on in the *Examiner*; the annual Christmas issue of that paper was in 1933 rechristened the *Holly Bough*, which had been the name of the *Constitution*'s Christmas annual.[77] In the ensuing years many of these pressmen continued to leave an indelible mark on the political landscape of both Cork and Ireland. Others had lodged their final stories. They too deserve to have their stories told.

76 U156/26, p. i, Lankford Papers, CCCA; Seán O'Faolain, *Vive moi!* (London, 1993), pp 159–60.   77 *Cork Constitution*, 2 Dec. 1920. Advertisement for the sale of the *Holly Bough*, 'the Christmas number of the *Cork Weekly News*'.

II

Trends and themes across the Irish regional press

The Irish language in the regional revival press

REGINA UÍ CHOLLATÁIN & AOIFE WHELAN

As a wave of nationalism swept the country in the second half of the nineteenth century, there was an increase in the use and prominence of the Irish language in the press. This chapter will provide an overview of the cultural and ideological impact of Irish-language columns in the regional press during the Gaelic revival period, spanning the late nineteenth and early twentieth centuries. Irish-language columns became particularly prominent in English-medium newspapers in a number of specific regions, and the number of Irish-medium publications increased. The development of the Irish language in the regional press is indicative of the increasing popularity and influence of the Irish-language revival movement throughout the country, along with its related social, cultural, political and economic aspirations.

THE FOUNDATIONS OF IRISH-LANGUAGE JOURNALISM

In the final decade of the nineteenth century, the main Irish dailies sympathetic to Irish nationalism, the *Irish Daily Independent* (later relaunched as the *Irish Independent*) and the *Freeman's Journal*, carried regular features in Irish and declared their support for the native language.[1] By 1897, Donnchadh Pléimionn had become the first paid Irish-language columnist (that we know of), providing a regular Gaelic column for the *Cork Weekly Examiner*.[2] But what prompted this professionalization of Irish-language journalism at the turn of the century? Furthermore, what implications did this have for the journalists and for the nationalist press, particularly for regional titles? Though the first Irish-language journal, *Bolg an tSolair*, was published in Belfast in 1795 by the offices of the radical *Northern Star*, this did not provoke a flurry of similar journals in the native language in the decades that followed.[3] It should be noted, nonetheless, that this initial venture in Irish was conceived in Belfast, home of the United

1 See Aoife Whelan, '"Irish-Ireland" and the *Irish Independent*, 1905–22' in M. O'Brien & K. Rafter (eds), *Independent Newspapers: a history* (Dublin, 2012), pp 67–80; Nollaig Mac Congáil, 'Saothrú na Gaeilge ar nuachtáin náisiúnta Bhéarla na haoise seo caite: sop nó solamar?' in R. Ó Muireadhaigh (eag.), *Féilscríbhinn Anraí Mhic Giolla Chomhaill* (Baile Átha Cliath, 2011), pp 112–91.   2 See 'Pléimionn, Donnchadh (1867–1900)', *Ainm.ie*, http://www.ainm.ie/Bio.aspx?ID=39.   3 See Regina Uí Chollatáin, 'Crossing boundaries and early gleanings of cultural replacement in Irish periodical culture', *Irish Communications Review*, 12 (2010), pp 50–64.

Irishmen, whose revolutionary movement sought to free Ireland from British rule and promoted a particular brand of non-sectarian nationalism.

The next significant development on the Irish-language journalistic landscape came with the establishment of Phillip Barron's *Ancient Ireland* magazine in Waterford in 1835. While the *Dublin Penny Journal* was not solely dedicated to the Irish language, a study of old Dublin journals by Donn Piatt places particular emphasis on its Irish content. The first issue, on 13 June 1832, printed a poem in Irish in Gaelic font on the last page, and by the twentieth edition, Irish was a central feature of the journal.[4] The new series of the *Dublin Penny Journal* from April 1902 did not contain any Irish-language material. The language legacy of these publications, coupled with the ideology of the Young Irelanders, paved the way for revival journalism.[5] Other newspapers and periodicals discussed the preservation of Ireland's native language and literature in the post-Famine period, including Robert Crane's the *Celt*, published in Kilkenny, the *Gael* of Dublin and Richard Dalton's *An Fior-Eirionnach*, founded in Tipperary in 1862.

The advent of the *Nation* newspaper in 1842 was to have a profound effect on the development of the Gaelic column as a journalistic format.[6] In 1858, Canon Ulick J. Bourke began publishing his 'Easy Lessons or Self-Instruction in Irish' in the *Nation*, a series designed to impart a basic knowledge of Irish-language grammar and pronunciation.[7] This series was significant for a number of reasons. First, it represented possibly the first attempt to teach Irish through the popular press, a consequence of the failure of the National School system introduced in 1831 to recognize Irish in its official curriculum. Second, the 'Easy Lessons' column symbolically associated the promotion of the Irish language with the nationalist political rhetoric of the Young Irelanders featured elsewhere in the same newspaper. Morash claims that, 'Like the *Northern Star*, the *Nation* was published not simply to inform, but to forge a national identity.'[8] This was to become a common feature of the Gaelic journalistic milieu in the decades that followed. The Gaelic activist David Comyn, or Dáithí Coimín, who went on to become editor of *Irisleabhar na Gaedhilge* (*Gaelic Journal*), first honed his skills as a columnist with the *Irishman*, the *Shamrock*, *Young Ireland* and the *Teachers' Journal* in the post-Famine period. Comyn appealed to these publications to print '*cúinní Gaeilge*' or Irish-language corners, providing the bulk of the material himself.[9]

4 Donn Piatt, *Cois life fadó agus ábhair eile* (Dublin, 1985), pp 144–6. 5 Regina Uí Chollatáin, 'Newspapers, journals and the Irish revival' in K. Rafter (ed.), *Irish journalism before Independence: more a disease than a profession* (Manchester, 2011), pp 160–73. 6 See James Quinn, *Young Ireland and the writing of Irish history* (Dublin, 2015). 7 See Helen Andrews, 'Bourke, Ulick Joseph', *Dictionary of Irish biography*, http://dib.cambridge.org/viewReadPage.do?articleId=a0812. 8 Christopher Morash, *A history of the media in Ireland* (Cambridge, 2010), pp 80–1. 9 'Coimín, Dáithí (1854–1907)', *Ainm.ie*, http://www.ainm.ie/Bio.aspx?ID=131.

REGIONAL TRENDS

Legg has claimed that 'An important feature of the 1880s was not just the increase in numbers of provincial newspapers, but the increase in the number of newspapers which claimed to have national politics.'[10] Given the fierce competition between regional newspapers with similar political leanings, it is unsurprising that Irish-language columns came to the fore across a number of titles in specific regions during the revival period. This gave rise to geographic clusters of Gaelic journalism published in English-medium newspapers. The sociolinguistic impact of such columns as vehicles for promoting Irish language and culture is important in the study of the revival movement. Interestingly, despite the fact that rural Donegal, Mayo, Galway, Cork, Kerry and the Decies in Waterford were the main Irish-speaking districts, print journalism in the Irish language often emanated from the urban writing tradition in these areas.

DONEGAL AND DERRY

The well-known Gaelic writers Seosamh Mac Grianna and Séamus Ó Grianna both used regional as well as national journalistic platforms. Mac Grianna's writings in the *Derry Journal* and in Dublin's *Evening Press* and *Evening Telegraph* are some of the few examples of Gaeltacht writing in the regional press. While the trend would have been for Gaeltacht writers to publish both literature and journalistic articles in national newspapers (the *Freeman's Journal*, *Irish Independent*, *Irish Press*, *Irish Times*), these Donegal brothers recognized the value of a local forum which crossed community borders. Other contributors of Irish-language material to the *Derry Journal* included Seaghán Mac Meanman, Fionn Mac Cumhaill and Aindrias Ó Baoill.[11]

Some of the regions in which an Irish-speaking district was located produced a local Irish-language literary journal. These literary journals were usually associated with or launched in conjunction with traditional Irish feasts or festivals. In Donegal, the journal *An Crann* (the *Tree*) was launched in Letterkenny in 1916 by the language organization Crann Eithne, founded by Cardinal Patrick O'Donnell.[12] *An Crann* was edited by Séamus Mac Creag and served as a journalistic platform for as many female as male writers in the region.[13] The journal was published periodically until 1924, when another regional title, *An tUltach* (the *Ulsterman*), appeared.[14] The role of the church in the case of *An Crann* provided a communication network for Irish-language enthusiasts in an ecclesiastical context. For example, Cork's Father Peter O'Leary

---

10 Marie-Louise Legg, *Newspapers and nationalism: the Irish provincial press, 1850–1892* (Dublin, 1998), p. 120.   11 See 'Mac Meanman, Seaghán (1886–1962)', *Ainm.ie*, http://www.ainm.ie/Bio.aspx?ID=158; 'Mac Cumhaill, Maghnas (1885–1965)', *Ainm.ie*, http://www.ainm.ie/Bio.aspx?ID=152; 'Ó Baoill, Aindrias (1888–1972)', *Ainm.ie*, http://www.ainm.ie/Bio.aspx?ID=304.   12 See 'Ó Domhnaill, Pádraig (1856–1927)', *Ainm.ie*, http://www.ainm.ie/Bio.aspx?ID=194.   13 See 'Mac Creag, Séamus (1863–1934)', *Ainm.ie*, http://www.ainm.ie/Bio.aspx?ID=319.   14 For *An tUltach* content, see Anraí Mac Giolla Chomhaill (eag.), *Meascra Uladh 3: Leabhar Comórtha An tUltach* (Ulster, 2004).

regularly contributed to the Donegal urban-based *An Crann*, illustrating the benefits of the print forum in overcoming the challenge posed by different regional dialects to promote a shared vision among Gaelic speakers.[15] *An Crann*'s championing of the local Donegal dialect or *'caint na ndaoine'* held great appeal for O'Leary, who strived to promote Munster Irish in his own works.

GALWAY/MAYO

Given the fact that Co. Galway was – and still is – home to a large Irish-speaking Gaeltacht community, it is reasonable to expect that newspapers supporting the native language would prove popular among local readers. However, the impetus for journalistic publishing in Irish sprang not from the heartland of the Gaeltacht itself, but rather from the endeavours of the Catholic hierarchy. By 1870, Canon Ulick J. Bourke, author of the 'Easy Lessons' published in the *Nation*, had been appointed president of St Jarlath's College in Tuam, Co. Galway. Bourke set about establishing a Catholic, independent newspaper that would be 'a popular exponent of national and local opinion'.[16] The *Tuam News and Western Advertiser* was launched in 1870, with Bourke contributing regular articles in Irish and about Irish history. This appears to be the first instance of a regional newspaper printing such material on a regular basis, as acknowledged by Legg:

> The *Nation* printed a column in Gaelic from the mid–1860s, but before 1870 and the *Tuam News* column no provincial paper appears to have published material in Gaelic, and it is debatable whether it would have been profitable, even in those parts of Ireland where it was widely spoken.[17]

John Glynn, a teacher of Irish and mathematics at St Jarlath's, was appointed editor of the Irish-language column in the *Tuam News*. Another important contributor was Eugene O'Growney, who later served as editor of the *Gaelic Journal*, and became a leading figure in the Gaelic revival movement.[18] O'Growney's lament for Canon Bourke upon his death in 1887 was published in the *Tuam News*, and he continued to publish translations of songs and prose, including 'An tAm fadó' ('Auld lang syne').[19] O'Growney drew on his contacts at the *Tuam News* to encourage its manager, Bourke's nephew John MacPhilpin, to reprint his article 'The National Language' (previously published in the *Irish Ecclesiastical Record*) on 14 November 1890, in which he called on the Catholic clergy to support the

15 See John A. Murphy, 'Ó Laoghaire, Peadar (An tAthair Peadar; O'Leary, Peter)', *Dictionary of Irish biography*, http://dib.cambridge.org/viewReadPage.do?articleId=a6390. For *An Crann* content, see Nollaig Mac Congáil, 'An Crann' in Mac Giolla Chomhaill (eag.), *Meascra Uladh 3*, pp 155–86. 16 Legg, *Newspapers and nationalism*, p. 96. 17 Ibid., p. 99. 18 See Lesa Ní Mhunghaile, 'O'Growney, Eugene (Ó Gramhnaigh, Eoghan')', *Dictionary of Irish biography*, http://dib.cambridge.org/viewReadPage.do?articleId=a6774; Regina Uí Chollatáin, 'Deisceabail agus soiscéalta: ceannródaithe athbheochana agus fóram na hiriseoireachta', *Léachtaí Cholm Cille*, 44:1 (2014), pp 22–45. 19 Ní Mhunghaile, 'O'Growney, Eugene'.

Irish-language movement.[20] Some months later, the chair of Irish was reinstated at the Catholic seminary in Maynooth. As O'Growney himself was appointed to the professorship in late 1891, it is important to acknowledge the role of the regional press in promoting his views on the preservation of the Irish language, and the role this journalistic forum played in subsequent strategic appointments and dismissals.[21]

The Irish-language revival entered a new phase in July 1893 with the establishment of Conradh na Gaeilge, or the Gaelic League, by Eoin MacNeill, Douglas Hyde and others. The League aimed to preserve the Irish language as the spoken language of the people of Ireland and to promote a modern literature. Unsurprisingly, print featured prominently as a platform for the promotion of the Gaelic League's language classes, events and campaigns. In a similar vein to Canon Bourke's use of the *Nation* newspaper, O'Growney circulated a series of 'Easy Lessons in Irish' in the *Weekly Freeman* and the *Gaelic Journal* in 1893. These instructional articles were published in book form by the Gaelic League in 1894 under the title *Simple lessons in Irish*. O'Growney's lessons had wide appeal among Gaelic enthusiasts: League records show that by 1897, 32,000 copies of *Simple Lessons* had been sold; by 1901, this had risen to 135,000 copies per year.[22] This practice of using the English-medium mainstream press as a springboard to teach Irish to readers reflects the key role of Irish-language columns in promoting the revival in a pragmatic, rather than purely ideological, manner.

Other titles from the Galway/Mayo region noted for publishing Irish-language material in this period include the *Connacht Sentinel*, *Connacht Tribune*, *Galway Express*, *Mayo News*, the *Mayoman*, *Tuam Herald* and the Irish-language journal *An Connachtach*, established in 1907. The well-known poet and songwriter Séamus Ó Maoildhia, a native Irish speaker from Co. Galway, penned a regular column in the *Connacht Tribune* for over twenty years under the by-line 'Shean-Ghaedhilgeoir'.[23] A connection between the regional and national Irish-language press was forged when Seán Mac Giollarnáth, previously editor of *An Connachtach*, replaced Patrick Pearse as editor of the League newspaper, *An Claidheamh Soluis*, in 1909.[24] Another example of a crossover between the various papers in this region is well-known author Pádraic Ó Conaire, a regular contributor to the *Connacht Sentinel*, *Galway Express* and *An Connachtach*. Ó Conaire's background sets him apart somewhat from polarized stereotypes of the revivalist Irish writer – he was neither a rural native speaker nor an urban, middle-class professional. The son

---

20 Uí Chollatáin, 'Deisceabail agus soiscéalta', pp 39–40. See also Timothy G. McMahon, *Grand opportunity: the Gaelic revival and Irish society, 1893–1910* (Syracuse, 2008), pp 37–9.   **21** See Regina Uí Chollatáin, *An Claidheamh Soluis agus Fáinne an Lae, 1899–1932* (Baile Átha Cliath, 2004), pp 51–5, 99–102.   **22** Pádraig Ó Fearaíl, *The story of Conradh na Gaeilge* (Dublin, 1975), pp 7, 17.   **23** 'Ó Maoildhia, Séamus (1881–1928)', *Ainm.ie*, http://www.ainm.ie/Bio.aspx?ID=91.   **24** Uí Chollatáin, *An Claidheamh Soluis*, p. 116. See also Dorothy Ní Uigín, 'Tréimhseacháin nuabhunaithe Ghaeilge sa chéad 20 bliain den fhichiú haois', *Feasta*, 8 (2009), pp 19–23.

of a publican from Galway city, Ó Conaire had been raised by family members in the Gaeltacht village of Rosmuc, was educated at Rockwell and Blackrock colleges, and had joined the Board of Education in London in 1900 as a copyist and clerk. Like many of his fellow expatriates, Ó Conaire was an active member of the Gaelic League in London. He also began publishing fiction in Irish.[25] Upon returning to Ireland in 1915 (*sans* wife and children), Ó Conaire penned articles for a wide range of regional and national newspapers, and created a journalistic platform from which he highlighted not only the revival of Irish, but also the political, economic and social responsibilities of the government to promote the language accordingly.

Ó Conaire frequently called for further development of a modern literature in Irish. His columns in the regional press reflect his professional interest in fostering new compositions in Irish and supporting aspiring writers, a topic he returned to time and again.[26] Not all of Ó Conaire's columns in the regional press related to the Irish language and its literature – his articles for the *Galway Express* in particular reveal his latent socialism and his discontent with the British government's neglect of the Irish economy. For example, he wrote on 26 June 1920:

> If not for the commitment of the labour movement to freedom, it's likely that no other organization would succeed in Ireland … but what use is freedom, what use is anything if the British army are permitted to bring arms into the country to kill our people?[27]

Even after the establishment of the Irish Free State in 1922, the status of the Irish language was not guaranteed. In a column for the *Connacht Sentinel* in March 1927, Ó Conaire's scathing criticism had switched to the Free State government's failure to sufficiently support the Irish language:

> There are others who are only pretending to help the Irish language. They are mocking us. Many of our executive officers are hidden enemies, false friends who hate the language but are not brave enough to say so out loud.[28]

Ó Conaire's columns raised awareness of the struggle to secure the status of the Irish language in all realms of public life, first under British rule and, subsequently, under the administration of a Dáil he felt could do a lot more.[29]

---

25 'Ó Conaire, Pádraic (1882–1928)', *Ainm.ie*, http://www.ainm.ie/Bio.aspx?ID=186. For Ó Conaire's journalism, see Eibhlín Ní Chionnaith, *Iriseoireacht Uí Chonaire* (Gaillimh, 1989). 26 See *CS*, 22 and 29 Mar. 1927, 27 Sept. 1927, 1 Nov. 1927. 27 'Murach dílse an lucht Oibreachais don tsaoirse ní móide go n-éireodh le haon dream eile in Éirinn … ach cén mhaith an tsaoirse, cén mhaith aon rud dá ligfí don Arm Gallda lón cogaidh a thabhairt isteach sa tír lenár muintir a mharú?' *GE*, 26 June 1920; see also *GE*, 31 July 1920. 28 'Tá cuid eile acu agus nílid ach ag ligean orthu féin go bhfuilid ag cabhrú le Gaeilge. Ag magadh fúinn atáid. Naimhde faoi cheilt agus faoi rún cuid mhaith dár n-ardoifigigh, cairde bréagacha go mb'fhuath leo an teanga ach nach bhfuil sé de mhisneach acu é a rá os ard,' *CS*, 15 Mar. 1927 (translation by authors). See also *CS*, 2 Aug. 1927, 29 Nov. 1927. 29 See *CS*, 15 Feb. 1927, 8 Mar. 1927, 4 Oct. 1927.

This is but one example of the journalistic forum provided by the English-medium press in Connacht to promote and preserve the Irish language.

TIPPERARY

While it is unsurprising that regular Irish-language material was included in regional newspapers aimed at readers in counties Galway and Mayo who were geographically close to Gaeltacht communities, another of the early Gaelic columns could be found in Co. Tipperary's *Cashel Gazette and Weekly Advertiser*, founded by John Davis White in May 1864. White was a strong advocate of antiquities and served for a time as diocesan librarian in Cashel. It is likely that the newspaper's support for the Irish-language revival stemmed from White's lifelong interest in history, literature and local news. The *Gazette*'s first editorial set out the principles the paper adhered to for almost thirty years: to serve all classes of society, not to engage in controversial religious or political topics, to report local news, and to promote local history and literature.[30] It was among the first regional papers to publish regular material in Irish.[31] However, it should be noted that White died in June 1893, just before the foundation of the Gaelic League in Dublin, and his newspaper did not outlive him. A subsequent nationalist newspaper from the same area, Thomas Walsh's *Cashel Sentinel*, which ran from 1885 to 1914, supported home rule and the Gaelic League, indicating that there was a substantial audience for material of this nature in the Cashel region.[32]

In nearby Clonmel, the *Nationalist and Tipperary Advertiser* also published an Irish-language column. Hayes' comprehensive register of Tipperary newspapers traces the *Nationalist*'s origins back to T.P. Gill's *Tipperary Nationalist*, established in Thurles in 1881 as an organ of the Irish Parliamentary Party. This venture lasted only two years, but the printing press was purchased by a company that launched a new *Nationalist* in January 1886, edited by J.G. McSweeney. Subsequent editors included former *Skibbereen Eagle* editor John E. O'Mahony, S.B. Naughton, H. Dillon and James Long. In the 1890s, the *Nationalist* was the leading weekly publication in south Tipperary, according to Hayes, with a circulation of 10,000 within a radius of 70 miles.[33] The inclusion of Irish-language material in the Clonmel *Nationalist*, *Cashel Gazette* and *Cashel Sentinel* is indicative of the rise of the language movement in Munster, outside of the traditional Irish-speaking districts, and represents another geographic cluster of Irish-language journalism.

---

30 J.C. Hayes, 'Guide to Tipperary newspapers (1770–1989)', *Tipperary Historical Journal* (1989), pp 1–16, at p. 4. 31 Legg, *Newspapers and nationalism*, p. 99. See also Fionnuala Carson Williams, 'White, John Davis', *Dictionary of Irish biography*, http://dib.cambridge.org/viewReadPage.do?articleId=a9004; Denis G. Marnane, 'John Davis White of Cashel (1820–1893)', *Tipperary Historical Journal* (1994), pp 97–104. 32 Hayes, 'Guide to Tipperary newspapers', p. 4. 33 Ibid., p. 7.

CORK AND KERRY

Although the emergence of a cluster of regional titles in Co. Tipperary that were sympathetic to and supportive of the rapidly developing language movement in the late nineteenth century secured a place for the Irish language in the public forum, this area was not the heartland of Munster's Irish-language community. A native Irish-speaking population was still thriving in the southern counties of Cork and Kerry. Much like the Connacht titles discussed above, several newspapers in this region published significant amounts of Gaelic journalism around the turn of the twentieth century. The *Kerryman* (founded in 1904) carried regular Irish-language articles from contributors such as Séumas O Súilleabháin, Kevin Danaher, Donncha Ó Céileachair and Seán Ó Ceallaigh ('Sceilg') to name but a few.[34] Some crossover with the national press is evident in the case of the *Kerryman*'s Gaelic columnist 'An Ciarraidheach Malluighthe' ('The Cursed Kerryman'), who also contributed to the *Irish Weekly Independent*.[35] The *Killarney Echo and South Kerry Chronicle*, which ran from 1899 until 1920, was known for its Irish-language content also.

In neighbouring Co. Cork, the daily *Cork Examiner* and its weekly counterpart were to the fore in providing Irish-language material for readers.[36] Father Peter O'Leary was among its earliest contributors; another was 'Torna' (Tadhg Ó Donnchadha).[37] As was the norm for Gaelic columns at this time, the tone and content varied considerably from one contributor to the next. For example, two Irish columns appear in the *Cork Weekly Examiner* of 26 February 1921. The first column, compiled by 'Torna', recounts the traditional song 'An cailín ruadh' ('The red-haired lass). Another column, 'An fear faire' ('The watchman') by 'Lugh Mac Céin', compares Ireland's natural beauty to that of other European countries and criticizes young well-to-do Irish people who travelled throughout the Continent without first exploring more of their own country. Mac Céin laments that Ireland's scenic routes and roads are quiet at present due to '*dlí an "Churfiú"*' ('the curfew law') imposed by the British authorities.[38] In this instance, *Examiner* readers were offered a combination of traditional Irish music and culture, combined with a seemingly light-hearted travel piece that nonetheless quotes Young Irelander Thomas Davis and subtly references the infringement of the war of independence on the inhabitants of Cork. 'Lugh Mac Céin' was a pen name used by Seán Tóibín (actor Niall Tóibín's father), who was attacked by the Black and Tans when they raided the premises of the Irish-language journal *An Lóchrann*, of which Tóibín was manager. Tóibín was employed by the Gaelic League as a travelling organizer or '*timire*' and was an avid collector of

---

34 For further biographical details see *Ainm.ie.*   35 For example, see *Irish Weekly Independent*, 12 Feb. 1921.   36 S.B. Ó hUallacháin, *Pobal an stáit agus an Ghaeilge, 1920–1939* (Baile Átha Cliath, 2010), p. xiii.   37 See 'Ó Laoghaire, Peadar (1839–1920)', *Ainm.ie*, http://www.ainm.ie/Bio.aspx?ID=210; 'Ó Donnchadha, Tadhg (1874–1949)', *Ainm.ie*, http://www.ainm.ie/Bio.aspx?ID=19.   38 *CWE*, 26 Feb. 1921.

traditional stories and songs, a selection of which were published in the *Clare Champion* in 1906.[39]

Another prominent Gaelic League *timire*, Ernest Blythe, had been appointed editor of *Réalt an Deiscirt / Southern Star* in 1918. Blythe, noted for being imprisoned by British forces during his tenure as editor, transformed the paper along Sinn Féin lines, which increased its circulation.[40] Blythe's involvement in the often interconnected spheres of journalism, the language movement and political nationalism serves as a reminder of the considerable influence wielded by the regional press, particularly as the political situation intensified in the wake of 1916. Blythe, who was appointed as Cumann na nGaedheal's first minister for finance in 1923, later recalled: 'In 1906 when I joined the Irish Republican Brotherhood on the invitation of Seán O'Casey, the great majority of its members in Dublin, which was incomparably its strongest centre, had come in through the Gaelic League.'[41]

The expansion of a corpus of Irish-language journalism in the Cork/Kerry region during the revival may seem a natural development considering its large native-speaking population. However, much of the native Irish-speaking community in all Irish-speaking districts was not literate in Gaelic font during this period; though Irish was widely spoken, it was not yet a compulsory subject on the National School curriculum. The regional revival press was instrumental in developing a proficient reading public for material in Irish, thereby fulfilling one of the main aims of the Gaelic League. In many cases, this led to the establishment of local Irish-language journals. *An Lóchrann*, mentioned above, was founded in Kerry in 1907 by Fionán Mac Coluim,[42] who persuaded the owners of the *Kerry People* and *Kerry Evening Star* in Tralee to procure an Irish-language typeset. Mac Coluim and 'An Seabhac' (Pádraig Ó Siochfhradha) then began editing a monthly journal that it was hoped would be 'the Grianán of the buachaillí agus cailíní of Cúige Mumhan who have found their way into the camping ground of Irish-Ireland'.[43] Though it was published somewhat sporadically in the decades that followed, *An Lóchrann* continued in various guises and under different editors until 1931. Tomás Ó Criomhthain and Seán Ó Súilleabháin, both renowned biographers of life on the Blasket Islands, were contributors to *An Lóchrann*, which reinforces the link between literary and journalistic writing as a strong feature of revival writing practices. This was not restricted to Irish language, and the crossover was very evident in English-medium writing practices of this era also.

39 'Tóibín, Seán (1882–1971)', *Ainm.ie*, http://www.ainm.ie/Bio.aspx?ID=174. 40 See 'de Blaghd, Earnán (1889–1975)', *Ainm.ie*, http://www.ainm.ie/Bio.aspx?ID=610. 41 Earnán De Blaghd, 'Hyde in conflict' in S. Ó Tuama, *The Gaelic League idea* (Cork, 1972), cited in Proinnsias Mac Aonghusa, *Ar son na Gaeilge: Conradh na Gaeilge, 1893–1993: stair sheanchais* (Baile Átha Cliath, 1993), p. 118. 42 See 'Mac Coluim, Fionnán (1875–1966)', *Ainm.ie*, http://www.ainm.ie/Bio.aspx?ID=28. For details of *An Lóchrann*'s content, see Art Ó Beoláin, '"An Lóchrann", lampa a lasadh', *Feasta*, 3 (1971), pp 5–9; Aifric Ní Mhuirithe, '*An Lóchrann*: 1907, 1917, 1927, 1931' (MA, UCD, 2012). 43 *An Lóchránn*, cited in Ó Beoláin, 'An Lóchrann', p. 5. See also 'Ó Siochfhradha, Pádraig (1883–1964)', *Ainm.ie*, http://www.ainm.ie/Bio.aspx?ID=783.

WATERFORD AND WEXFORD

Irish-language columns appeared in a host of regional papers in clusters of Gaelic journalism in the south-east: in Waterford, the *Dungarvan Observer*, *Waterford News* and *Waterford Star*; and in Wexford, the *Enniscorthy Echo* and *Enniscorthy Guardian*. Waterford is home to the Gaeltacht community of An Rinn (Ring), and while Irish did not survive as a native language in Co. Wexford, Enniscorthy in particular maintained a strong militaristic tradition dating back to Vinegar Hill in 1798. This sentiment manifested itself politically in 1916 when Enniscorthy was one of the handful of regional towns to ignore Eoin MacNeill's countermanding order instructing the Irish Volunteers not to proceed with planned manoeuvres on Easter Monday.[44]

Yet the *Enniscorthy Echo*'s Gaelic column was not always focused on the political issues of the day. On 26 January 1928, for example, its column 'An Fáinne' opens by praising the afore-mentioned Pádraic Ó Conaire, stating that he was the cleverest Irish writer of the time, with a superb imagination and intellect.[45] The author goes on to compare Ó Conaire's novel *Deoraíocht* (*Exile*) with Victor Hugo's *Les Misérables*, thus moving Ó Conaire's writings out of the realm of the Gaelic canon, and putting them on par with the best of European fiction. Though the column is predominantly literary in this edition, readers are also informed of an upcoming *céilí* dance and a debate in Irish on the motion 'Ladies' fashions versus men's fashions'. The legend of St Brigid is also discussed, as the column appeared just before her feast day, 1 February. These short notes that follow the lengthy literary discussion accurately portray the role of the regional Gaelic column in publicizing social events for Gaelic enthusiasts. They also highlight the Gaelic League's close ties with the Catholic faith, despite the involvement of numerous Protestants in the organization, some of the most famous being Douglas Hyde, the League's first president, and Ernest Blythe.

LOUTH

In the border county of Louth, another cluster of Irish-language journalism can be identified. This relates mainly to material published in the *Dundalk Democrat and People's Journal*, *Dundalk Examiner* and *Drogheda Independent*. The *Dundalk Democrat* was founded in 1849 by the staunch nationalist Joseph A. Cartan and retained a nationalist leaning throughout the revival period. The *Democrat*'s 'Irish Column' often appeared on the paper's front page, alongside a 'Poet's Column' in English. In an era when the majority of newspapers devoted their front pages to advertising, it is remarkable that the *Democrat* afforded its Irish-language material such a prominent position. Its readers clearly had an appetite for literature, as seen in a number of 'Irish Columns' from 1908 that consist of traditional poems, songs and laments. This also provided a platform for

44 *SIn*, 23 Apr. 1916.   45 *EE*, 26 Jan. 1928.

the dissemination of the oral tradition in print format, such as the lament 'Caoineadh ar Athar Eudhmonn Mac Mathghamhna' and 'An cailín ruadh' ('The red-haired lass'), also discussed by Torna in the *Cork Examiner*. Neither of these unsigned columns includes a translation, and both use the traditional Gaelic font.[46] A later example, from February 1913, indicates that the column had developed somewhat. By this time, the verse in Irish, 'An Connachtach' ('The Connachtman'), was accompanied by a glossary of terms and a description of where the columnist (signed 'T. Mac C.') collected the piece.[47]

The *Drogheda Independent* introduced an 'Irish for Beginners' column in 1901 with contributions from a Mr Casey.[48] These articles provided reading material for Gaelic League classes in the locality; the paper's readership spanned counties Louth and Meath. While the League's branch committee in Dunshaughlin praised the *Drogheda Independent* for the inclusion of material in Irish, it later asked that the phonetic spelling be omitted, though its request was largely ignored.[49] This is further evidence of regional press circulation crossing county borders, and of Irish-language columns being used as teaching resources in local classes.

MIDLANDS

In the midlands, the *Leinster Leader* (founded in Naas, Co. Kildare, in 1880) published a regular column in Irish from 1905 to 1914.[50] Under the title 'Irish Ireland', the journalist Brian O'Higgins (also known as 'Brian na Banban') contributed a weekly column mainly in Irish – not to be confused with Eoghan Ó Neachtain's Gaelic column of the same title, which appeared in the *Irish Independent* from 1905–14.[51] The primary objective of O'Higgins' column was to teach the language to his readers through simple stories translated into English, thereby developing a reading public for material in the Irish language. These instructional columns were often bilingual in nature, and were accompanied by material in English discussing the latest develop-ments within the Irish-language movement. For example, O'Higgins' column on 10 March 1906 comprised a short tale, 'An sean-bhuachaill agus an báille' ('The old boy and the bailiff'), with religious and moral overtones that would have resonated with a contemporary readership. The story is translated into English line by line underneath the original text in Irish, indicating the educational objectives of this particular column.[52] An article in English follows, outlining the Gaelic League's latest plans to improve the status of the Irish language in schools across the country.[53]

The pattern of offering readers a traditional text or tale, accompanied by an English translation and followed by an update (in English) of matters relating to the

---

46 See *DD*, 25 Jan. 1908, 1 Feb. 1908.   47 Ibid., 1 Feb. 1913. See also Gearóid Trimble, *The* Dundalk Democrat *agus oidhreacht na Gaeilge in iar-dheisceart Uladh ag casadh an 20ú haois. Catalóg d'ábhar Gaeilge a foilsíodh sa nuachtán ó 1895–1915* (Baile Átha Cliath, 2008).   48 *DrI*, 26 Oct. 1901.   49 Ibid., 15 Feb. 1902, quoted in Daithí Ó Muirí, 'Peadar Ó Muireadhaigh agus bunú na chéad chraoibhe de Chonradh na Gaeilge i gContae na Mí', *Léachtaí Cholm Cille*, 44:1 (2014), pp 73–99.   50 See Clár Spáinneach, '"Irish Ireland": Brian O'Higgins agus an *Leinster Leader*' (MA, UCD, 2004)   51 See Whelan, '"Irish-Ireland" and the *Irish Independent*', pp 67–80.   52 *LeL*, 10 Mar. 1906.   53 Ibid.

Gaelic League and the language-revival movement was often repeated in O'Higgins' column.[54] Like other newspapers of the period, the *Leinster Leader* made great strides in promoting the Irish language, and in creating a readership for material in the native language, but it did so in an Anglophone environment in which O'Higgins' column was presented using an English title and subtitle, an English translation of the primary material and an English-medium description of the latest happenings relevant to the language movement. O'Higgins also contributed to Tom and Michael Daly's *Meath Chronicle*, established in Navan, Co. Meath, in 1897.[55]

Another leading midlands paper, the *Nationalist and South Leinster Times*, first printed in Carlow in 1883, was a staunch supporter of Irish-language journalism and continues to publish a weekly column to this day. Its founder and first editor, Patrick J. Conlon, announced in his first editorial that his paper would function, as its title suggests, as '[a] representative and independent medium, through which a bond, sympathy, union, strength, may be created, perfected, and maintained, for the accomplishment of those objects on which Irishmen have set their hearts'.[56] This was in line with the 'Irish-Ireland' principles promoted by D.P. Moran, editor of the *Leader* newspaper, and shared by the majority of Irish-language enthusiasts in the revival period.[57]

CONCLUSION

For the purposes of this chapter we have chosen to focus mainly on those geographic areas in which clusters of Irish-language journalism emerged, often giving rise to or preceded by a locally produced journal in Irish where a reading public for the native language and its writers had been sufficiently established. This cross-section of Irish-language columns and journals in the regional press demonstrates that the use of Irish was not limited to nationalistic and political trends that were coming to the fore as part of the philosophy of the era in the context of cultural revival.

The question of literacy in creating a reading public in Irish was a common area for debate as early as 1892. With regard to Irish-language print journalism, the added dimension of printing in either the Gaelic or Roman font complicated the literacy issue further. This was noted in the *Gaelic Journal*, in correspondence that examined the retention of the Gaelic font for journalistic purposes. This reply by 'D.O.C.' to a letter from June 1892 shows the value of newspapers using the more familiar Roman font in spreading literacy in Irish: 'Some of the best friends of the Irish print in Roman type, e.g. the *Tuam News*, *Clonmel Nationalist* and *Chicago Citizen*. Would you tell them to stop?'[58] The regional press dimension in the context of Irish-language revival can therefore be interpreted in a much broader context, which is inclusive of the immigrant Irish community abroad.

---

54 See also ibid., 28 Apr. 1906. 55 See Hugh Oram, *The newspaper book: a history of newspapers in Ireland, 1649–1983* (Dublin, 1983), pp 92–3. 56 *CN*, 22 Sept. 1883. 57 See D.P. Moran, *The philosophy of Irish Ireland* (Dublin, 1905). 58 *Gaelic Journal*, June 1892.

The Irish-language regional press in the early twentieth century in many ways represents a development of critical mass in regional Irish-language publishing, leading it to move out of the newspapers into its own dedicated publications and regions, despite differences in reportage, content and even appearance.

A supplementary nationalism: the emergence of the Irish provincial press before independence

CHRISTOPHER DOUGHAN

The latter part of the nineteenth century and the first two decades of the twentieth century marked a denouement, of sorts, in modern Irish history. The goal of self-government, so cherished by generations of Irish nationalists, was finally attained, though the shape it took proved highly unsatisfactory to many Irish republicans and highly problematic for the generations that followed. To a significant extent the period mirrored much of what had gone before over the previous century, with constitutional methods frequently competing with more militant strategies to gain the upper hand within Irish nationalism. These alternating claims had been represented over the previous century by the United Irishmen, Daniel O'Connell and the repeal movement, the Young Irelanders, the nascent home rule movement, the Irish Republican Brotherhood (IRB) and ultimately the Irish Parliamentary Party and Sinn Féin. However, what was quite different about the decades leading up to independence was that it coincided with the advent of the print media as a force of considerable influence. Consequently, Irish nationalists of all hues sought to utilize the medium to their advantage. One of the most notable developments in this respect was the relatively unprecedented expansion of the Irish provincial press. It is a development that has garnered minimal attention from historians and even within the annals of Irish journalistic history it has not been the focus of any sustained study. The official organs of nationalist organizations such as the Gaelic League (*An Claidheamh Soluis*) and Sinn Féin (*Scissors and Paste* and *Nationality*) have at least been profiled by historians such as Virginia E. Glandon and Regina Uí Chollatáin, but provincial publications have rarely been afforded such scrutiny.[1]

Noted individual figures from the provincial press of this era, such as James Daly of the *Connaught Telegraph* and Thomas Stanislaus Cleary of the *Clare Independent*, have received some degree of attention from historians such as

1 See Virginia E. Glandon, *Arthur Griffith and the advanced-nationalist press, Ireland, 1900–1922* (New York, 1985) and Regina Uí Chollatáin, '*An Claidheamh Soluis agus Fáinne an Lae*: the turning of the tide' in Mark O'Brien and Felix M. Larkin (eds), *Periodicals and journalism in twentieth-century Ireland: writing against the grain* (Dublin, 2014), pp 31–46.

Gerard Moran and Oisín Moran, respectively.[2] These texts concentrate primarily on the political activities of Daly and Cleary, though the role of journalist and politician was frequently interchangeable during these years. Equally, certain aspects of the provincial press have been analysed by historians such as Patrick Maume and Michael Wheatley, but these have generally been as part of broader historical works.[3] Despite this lack of attention, provincial newspapers continue to be cited with regularity by many historians. As Maurice Walsh has validly noted, 'historians of modern Ireland enthusiastically use the press as a source', yet there is an 'evident reluctance in Irish historiography to take an interest in the work of journalists'.[4] This imbalance cannot be redressed comprehensively in a work such as this. Nonetheless, this essay provides a concise but detailed overview of the emergence of the provincial press in Ireland in the decades leading up to the foundation of the Irish Free State in 1922.

In this respect, it outlines some of the most distinctive characteristics of this section of the Irish print media during this period. This includes the extent to which it was often dominated by individual personalities. In many instances, it was the editor or proprietor who was the primary driving force behind the newspaper. Frequently, the profile of such an editor or proprietor (in many cases it was a dual role) was heightened due to a simultaneous political or parliamentary career. In addition, their profiles were raised further, as this chapter illustrates, by the remarkably lengthy periods many of these senior press figures spent at the heads of their particular newspapers. This chapter also details how prolonged periods of family ownership became a distinguishing feature of the provincial press in Ireland. Furthermore, it describes how this was accompanied by a markedly Catholic dimension. The close ties that developed between the provincial press and organizations such as the GAA and the Gaelic League are also briefly documented. Finally, I will examine how the rise of Sinn Féin, in the aftermath of the 1916 Rising, impacted on the provincial press.

In the context of this chapter the provincial press refers to nationalist papers based outside of Dublin, Belfast and Cork, which accounted for the greater part of the provincial print media. The predominance of nationalist titles resulted from the launch of many such publications during the last two decades of the nineteenth century and the opening decade of the twentieth century. This hitherto unparalleled growth can be primarily attributed to the considerable increase in the levels of literacy in the country from around 1850 onwards. This

---

2 See Gerard Moran, 'Agrarian radical or tenant reformer: James Daly, a reappraisal' and Oisín Moran, 'Thomas Stanislaus Cleary (1851–98): Land League leader and campaigning newspaper editor' in Brian Casey (ed.), *Defying the law of the land: agrarian radicals in Irish history* (Dublin, 2013), pp 80–9, 100–13. 3 See Patrick Maume, *The long gestation: Irish nationalist life, 1891–1928* (Dublin, 1999) and Michael Wheatley, *Nationalism and the Irish Party: provincial Ireland, 1910–1916* (Oxford, 2005). 4 Maurice Walsh, *The news from Ireland: foreign correspondents and the Irish revolution* (London, 2008), p. 6.

was due in no small part to the advent of a Catholic secondary-school structure.[5]
As a consequence, these increased literacy levels were most marked among the
nationalist population.

In light of this significant development it is not surprising that it was only
in the latter half of the nineteenth century that Irish newspapers began to specifically identify themselves as nationalist. Prior to this they had generally been
classified as either Tory or Liberal. Marie-Louise Legg traced the genesis of this
change to 1876 with the establishment of the *Western News* in Ballinasloe, the *Celt*
in Waterford, and the *People's Advocate* in Monaghan.[6] Other sources have noted
the *Ballina National Times* and the *Galway Press* as being among the earliest
identifiably nationalist papers in the provinces.[7] Very few of these titles displayed
any significant degree of longevity, with the possible exception of the *Western
News*, which remained in publication until 1926. Nonetheless, this apparent lack
of staying power was not to be a portent of what was to follow.

The ensuing decades witnessed the launch of outright nationalist titles on a
scale previously unknown. The durability of these newspapers is illustrated by
the fact that most of them have lasted well into the twenty-first century. Among
others, these included titles that are now considered stalwarts of the provincial
print media in Ireland, such as the *Leinster Leader* (established in 1880), *Midland
Tribune* (1881), *Western People* (1883), *Limerick Leader* (1889), *Clonmel Nationalist*
(1890), *Mayo News* (1892), *Kilkenny People* (1893), *Meath Chronicle* (1897),
Fermanagh Herald (1902), *Clare Champion* (1903), *Kerryman* (1904), *Connacht
Tribune* (1909) and *Donegal Democrat* (1919). Additionally, many other nationalist organs were launched during this period that did not display the remarkable
longevity of the aforementioned newspapers, but still lasted for close on fifty
years or more. Some of the most pertinent examples were the *Galway Observer*
(1881–1966), *Wexford Free Press* (1888–1966) and *Frontier Sentinel*, based in
Newry (1904–1972). To further bolster the increasingly nationalist dimension to
the Irish provincial press, many newspapers that had been launched well before
the 1880s had developed clearly nationalist sympathies by the late nineteenth
century. These included such familiar names as the *Derry Journal*, the *Anglo-Celt*
in Cavan, *Dundalk Democrat*, *Connaught Telegraph*, *Sligo Champion*, *Tuam Herald*
and *Wexford People*.

One of the features central to this development was the extent to which individual
personalities became synonymous with specific newspapers. This particular

5 Mark O'Brien, 'Journalism in Ireland: the evolution of a discipline' in Kevin Rafter (ed.), *Irish
journalism before independence: more a disease than a profession* (Manchester, 2011), p. 18. 6 Marie-Louise Legg,
Newspapers and nationalism: the Irish provincial press, 1850–1892 (Dublin, 1998), p. 80. 7 *WP, 125th Anniversary, 1883–2008* (18 Nov. 2008); *FJ*, 8 July 1922; *CT*, 15 July 1922; *TH*, 22 July 1922; the anniversary
edition of the *Western People* traces the launch of a specifically nationalist newspaper as far back as 1864,
with the launch of the *Ballina National Times*. In a similar vein, the *Galway Press*, which appears to have
been published for a short period in the early 1870s, is described in the obituary of one nineteenth-century
Irish journalist as being 'the first home rule paper founded in Ireland'.

characteristic was best illustrated by the significant number of newspapermen whose profile was notably enhanced by their election to parliament. The most prominent examples of such personalities were figures such as Jasper Tully (*Roscommon Herald*), John Patrick (J.P.) Hayden (*Westmeath Examiner*), Patrick Aloysius (P.A.) McHugh (*Sligo Champion*) and James Patrick (J.P.) Farrell (*Longford Leader*).

Of this sample group of provincial journalists, Tully has possibly received the greatest amount of attention, and indeed he was arguably one of the most colourful characters to emerge from the Irish provincial press during this era. Tully controlled the *Roscommon Herald* (which was founded by his father, George, in 1858) from 1881 until shortly before his death in 1938. He was elected as an MP of the Irish Parliamentary Party for South Leitrim in 1892, a seat he held until 1906. Tully's relationship with the party was often fractious and he ultimately became 'an unremitting enemy of the Irish Party'.[8] In 1917, he stood as an independent candidate in the North Roscommon by-election, but finished in a distant third position, as Count Plunkett achieved Sinn Féin's first significant electoral success.[9] J.P. Hayden, who founded the *Westmeath Examiner* in 1882, also served as an MP of the Irish Parliamentary Party. He was elected to Westminster for the South Roscommon constituency in 1897 and held the seat until 1918. Hayden remained as editor-proprietor of the *Westmeath Examiner* for an extraordinary seventy-two years, his tenure only ceasing upon his death in 1954.[10]

P.A. McHugh, who acquired the *Sligo Champion* in 1886, also pursued a career in politics. Two years after the acquisition of the paper, he became mayor of Sligo, and he subsequently served as an Irish Parliamentary Party MP, first for North Leitrim from 1895 to 1906 and then for North Sligo from 1906 to 1909.[11] McHugh did not match the exceptional longevity of J.P. Hayden; he died in 1909 at the relatively young age of 51. Nonetheless, the esteem in which he was held in the region is illustrated by the fact that a memorial in his honour was unveiled outside Sligo town hall only seven years after his death.[12] In Co. Longford, the *Longford Leader* was established in 1897 by J.P. Farrell. The previous year Farrell had been elected as the Irish Parliamentary Party MP for West Cavan and from 1900 until 1918 he served as MP for North Longford. Similar to so many of his parliamentary colleagues he lost his seat in the face of the Sinn Féin landslide at

8 Michael Wheatley, *Nationalism and the Irish Party: provincial Ireland, 1910–1916* (Oxford, 2005), pp 15–19; *Roscommon Herald: Centenary Supplement* (5 Dec. 1959); Wheatley also describes Tully as 'obsessive, quarrelsome, and litigious', while the centenary supplement of the *Roscommon Herald* acknowledged that he was the '*enfant terrible*' of the Irish Parliamentary Party.   9 Cyril Mattimoe, *North Roscommon: its people and past* (Boyle, 1992), pp 190–1.   10 Jeremiah Sheehan, *Worthies of Westmeath: a biographical dictionary with brief lives of famous Westmeath people* (Moate, 1987), pp 54–5; *Westmeath Examiner*, 2 Oct. 1982; *Irish Times*, 11 Feb. 1992, 2 Mar. 2000; Hayden went blind in his later years and everything had to be read to him by Nicholas Nally, who succeeded him as editor. Nally remained as editor until 1999, meaning that, quite remarkably, the paper had only two editors for the first 117 years of its existence.   11 *Sligo Champion: Sesquicentenary Issue, 1836–1986* (5 Dec. 1986); Padraig Deignan, *The Protestant community in Sligo, 1914–49* (Dublin, 2010), p. 45.   12 Owen McGee, 'McHugh, Patrick Aloysius' in James McGuire and James Quinn (eds), *Dictionary of Irish biography* (Cambridge, 2009).

the 1918 general election.[13] These direct links to the Irish Parliamentary Party were also in existence at other provincial newspapers. The *Leinster Leader* was acquired in 1886 by James Laurence (J.L.) Carew and James Leahy, both parliamentary representatives for Kildare. However, the paper was primarily associated with Carew; it served as his political mouthpiece until his death in 1903.[14]

There were some notable exceptions to this tendency for provincial papers to be inextricably associated with a single personality. Among these were the *Mayo News*, which was established in 1892 by brothers William and Patrick Joseph (P.J.) Doris, and the *Kerryman*, which was launched in 1904 by the triumvirate of Maurice Griffin plus cousins Daniel and Thomas Nolan.[15] Nonetheless, the prevailing trend during this period, which can be traced back to the 1880s, was for senior newspapermen to be solely linked to one title over a long period of time. This was probably best exemplified by the remarkably lengthy tenures of so many provincial editors. J.P. Hayden's prolonged occupancy of the editorial chair at the *Westmeath Examiner* was the most striking example of this phenomenon, yet it was representative of a broader trend within the provincial print media. Indeed the instances of such prolonged editorial tenures were so frequent that they rendered the thirty-year terms of newspapermen such as Thomas J.W. Kenny (*Connacht Tribune*) and Patrick A. MacManus (*Fermanagh Herald*) almost unremarkable.[16] At the Castlebar-based *Connaught Telegraph*, Thomas H. Gillespie occupied the editorial chair from 1899 until 1939.[17] James Pike edited the *Midland Tribune* in Co. Offaly from 1912 to 1948, while Patrick Quilty was editor of the *Meath Chronicle* from 1919 until 1960.[18] These editorial terms were exceeded by Michael A. Casey and Con Cregan, who served for over half a century as editors of the *Drogheda Independent* and *Limerick Leader*, respectively.[19] Others to occupy the editorial chair for fifty years or more included Edward Thomas (E.T.) Keane (*Kilkenny People*) and William Myles (*Tipperary Star*), while Patrick Dunne remained as editor-proprietor of the *Leitrim Observer* for almost sixty years.[20]

The regularity of editorial reigns lasting four decades or more was accompanied by extended periods of family ownership at many provincial newspapers. The *Tuam Herald* in Co. Galway provides one of the most appropriate examples of this characteristic. Throughout almost the entirety of its existence since its

13 *75 years of Longford: the Longford Leader, 1897–1972* (29 Sept. 1972).   **14** *Leinster Leader: Centenary Supplement* (15 Nov. 1980).   **15** *Mayo News: Centenary Supplement* (2 Mar. 1994); *The Kerryman 1904–2004* (5 Aug. 2004); *KM*, 8 Feb. 1908, 7 Apr. 1928; William Doris was elected MP for West Mayo in 1910, which was around the time a lifelong rift developed between the two brothers. While William remained faithful to the Irish Parliamentary Party, P.J. Doris began to embrace the more separatist policies of Sinn Féin, which resulted in the *Mayo News* ultimately being regarded as a Sinn Féin organ. Maurice Griffin of the *Kerryman* joined Sinn Féin well before it started to gain any significant electoral support and, accordingly, the paper was considered sympathetic to the party from a relatively early stage.   **16** *CT*, 11 May 1940; *CS*, 14 May 1940; *IT*, 18 May 1940; *FH*, 29 Dec. 1934; *IR*, 20 Dec. 1934; *UH*, 22 Dec. 1934. **17** *CTe*, 8 Apr. 1939; *Connaught Telegraph: Commemorative Issue* (Apr. 1996).   **18** *MT*, 7 Feb. 1948; *MC*, 3 Dec. 1960.   **19** *DrI*, 25 Mar. 1938; *LL*, 2 July 1966.   **20** *KP*, 19 May 1945; *TS*, 25 Sept. 1976; *LO*, 30 Sept. 1968.

establishment in 1837 the paper has been owned by only two families, the Kellys and the Burkes.[21] The *Anglo-Celt* in Cavan exemplifies this particular trait to an even greater extent. Upon celebrating its 150th anniversary in 1996 the paper proudly noted that it had passed through four generations of ownership by the O'Hanlon family since 1863.[22] Lengthy and unbroken terms of family ownership were equally visible at several other provincial newspapers. The acquisition of the *Midland Tribune* by John Powell in 1888 signalled the commencement of close on a century of family ownership.[23] One of the most notable aspects of the centenary of the *Clare Champion* in 2003 was the fact that it had remained under the control of the Galvin family since its foundation.[24] The *Meath Chronicle* was founded in 1897 by brothers Tom and Michael Daly, but was purchased by James Davis in 1917, which marked the beginning of a family proprietorship lasting almost one hundred years.[25]

While individual families played leading roles in the Irish regional press, so too did many Catholic clergy, who were directly involved in the establishment of newspapers. This had been evident from as early as the 1880s, with the launch of titles such as the *Leinster Leader, Midland Tribune, Western People, Drogheda Independent* and *Southern Star*. The establishment of the *Leinster Leader* in 1880 followed the establishment of a limited liability company, several of whose initial shareholders were drawn from the ranks of parish priests and curates in Cos. Kildare and Carlow.[26] At the start of the 1880s the only paper serving Co. Offaly was the unionist *King's County Chronicle*. This may have been one of the major factors that prompted three Catholic priests, Robert Little, Denis Sheehan and Patrick Brennan, to launch the *Midland Tribune* in 1881, and thus provide the county with a nationalist organ.[27] The origins of the *Western People* in Ballina, Co. Mayo, were not entirely dissimilar. The paper was launched in 1883 following a meeting at St Muredach's cathedral in the town, organized by Fr Anthony Finnerty with the aim of establishing a newspaper that would reflect the town's Catholic ethos.[28] The genesis of the *Drogheda Independent* in Co. Louth can be traced to an Augustinian priest, Fr James Anderson, who founded the Drogheda Independent Club in 1881 with the intention of promoting nationalist ideals in the town. This led to the formation of the newspaper three years later.[29] Two years after the establishment of the *Southern Star* in Skibbereen, Co. Cork, the paper was purchased by a consortium headed by Monsignor John O'Leary of Clonakilty. The consortium was comprised of ten shareholders, two of whom – Michael Cunningham and Daniel O'Brien – were also priests.[30]

21 *Tuam Herald: 150th Anniversary Supplement* (21 May 1988); *TH*, 10 May 2012. 22 *Anglo-Celt: Souvenir Supplement 1846–1996* (30 May 1996). 23 *Midland Tribune: 1881–1981 – 100 Years of a Family Newspaper* (7 Nov. 1981). 24 *CCh*, 28 Mar. 2003. 25 *One Hundred Years of Life and Times in North Leinster: a Meath Chronicle Centenary Publication* (30 Aug. 1997). 26 *Leinster Leader: Centenary Supplement* (15 Nov. 1980). 27 *Midland Tribune: 1881–1981* (7 Nov. 1981). 28 *Western People, 125th Anniversary, 1883–2008* (18 Nov. 2008). 29 *Drogheda Independent: Centenary Supplement* (11 May 1984). 30 *Southern Star, 1889–1989: Centenary Supplement* (11 Nov. 1989).

This highly prominent Catholic dimension to the provincial press was augmented by the devout Catholicism of many editors and proprietors. Several of the aforementioned newspapermen were noted for their staunch Catholic faith, including P.J. Doris, Con Cregan, Tom Daly and Michael A. Casey.[31] This characteristic was widely shared across many provincial publications. The obituary of Josephine Maguire, who inherited the *Clare Champion* from her brother only a few months after its establishment in 1903, noted her determination that the paper should be 'a most staunchly Catholic journal' conveying 'a most staunchly Catholic tone in every article that appeared in its weekly issue'.[32] This loyal sense of Catholicism was shared by many editors and proprietors across the provincial press, though it was understandably less pronounced in Ulster. Among those included in this particular cohort of senior pressmen were Thomas F. McGahon (*Dundalk Democrat*), Edward Walsh (*Munster Express*), Cornelius O'Mahony (*Waterford Star*), R.J. Kelly (*Tuam Herald*), Michael Lynch (*Ulster Herald*), John McAdam (*Donegal Vindicator*) and brothers John F. and Edward T. O'Hanlon of the *Anglo-Celt*.[33]

Many of these newspapermen (for it was almost solely men that occupied the upper echelons of the Irish provincial press) were enthusiastic supporters of cultural nationalist movements such as the Gaelic League, but perhaps most notably the GAA. Indeed, it was far from uncommon for editors or proprietors to be active members of both organizations. Terence de Vere, editor-proprietor of the *Western People*, was one of the founders of the Ballina Stephenites club in the town.[34] Cecil A. Stephens, co-founder and proprietor of the *Donegal Democrat*, was secretary of the Ballyshannon branch of the Gaelic League and also had strong GAA connections, while fellow co-founder and editor of the paper John Downey was similarly a Gaelic League enthusiast in addition to playing hurling for the Aodh Ruadh GAA club in Ballyshannon.[35] In a similar vein James Reddy of the *Nationalist and Leinster Times* in Carlow was an enthusiastic Gaelic League member in addition to serving as secretary to the Carlow county board of the GAA.[36] J.J. McCarroll of the *Derry Journal* was also an ardent supporter of both the Gaelic League and the GAA, while Brandon J. Long of the *Clonmel Nationalist* was noted as a lifelong supporter of Gaelic games.[37]

These ties with organizations such as the Gaelic League and the GAA, allied to the close links between the Irish Parliamentary Party and many local papers, meant that by the second decade of the twentieth century the provincial press had assumed a highly prominent position within Irish nationalism. It is scarcely surprising that the Sinn Féin party, the newly emergent Irish nationalist force, should seek to exert its influence in such a key sector of the print media. As early as 1907, Sinn Féin had attempted to wield such influence when it spent £250 in

---

31 *MN*, 27 Feb. 1937; *LL*, 2 July 1966; *DrI*, 25 Mar. 1938; *One Hundred Years of Life and Times in North Leinster* (30 Aug. 1997)   32 *CCh*, 20 Feb. 1937.   33 *DD*, 25 Jan. 1941; *ME*, 12 July 1946; *WS*, 7 Nov. 1941; *TH*, 5 Sept. 1931; *UH*, 20 Apr. 1935; *DV*, 13 June 1925; *AC*, 24 May 1947, 29 Dec. 1956.   34 *WP*, 12 Apr. 1941.   35 *DoD*, 24 May 1947, 15 Jan. 1971.   36 *CN*, 8 Apr. 1944.   37 *DJ*, 3 Mar. 1937; *ClN*, 20 Apr. 1938.

establishing the *Leitrim Guardian* in Manorhamilton.[38] As the party's popularity soared in the wake of the 1916 Rising it issued instructions to its membership to bring pressure to bear 'on the local press to secure support for the policy of Sinn Féin'.[39] The party instructed local branches to send 'deputations to the editor or proprietor before whom the prospect of support or its opposite should be intelligently and candidly put' and that 'articles and letters on Sinn Féin should be sent to the press, and their insertion demanded if necessary'.[40]

The party's rapidly increasing electoral strength at this time coincided with its takeover of a number of provincial newspapers. In September 1917, the *Galway Express*, previously a unionist organ, was purchased for £535 by Sinn Féin interests in the city.[41] Similarly, a group of Sinn Féin supporters in Sligo purchased the *Sligo Nationalist* in April 1920 and renamed it the *Connachtman* or *Connachtach*.[42] The *Southern Star* was Sinn Féin's most noteworthy newspaper acquisition. The paper was purchased for £570 in December 1917, with Michael Collins being the most significant name among the group that constituted the new ownership. Ernest Blythe was editor for a brief period following the takeover, while three future TDs – Seán Buckley, Seán Hales and Seán Hayes – were also members of the group that bought the *Southern Star*.[43]

By the time Sinn Féin had begun to acquire its own mouthpieces within the provincial press, Irish newspapers were dealing with circumstances that had not previously been experienced. Strict military censorship had been introduced at the start of First World War under the Defence of the Realm Act. Nevertheless, it was only in the aftermath of Easter 1916 that the forcible closure of provincial newspapers became a serious issue. The threat of suppression became an even more pressing matter for the provincial press as the situation in Ireland grew increasingly hostile from early 1919 onwards. Press censorship reports for this period indicate that the principal aim of the measure was to stem the increasing popularity of Sinn Féin. This was effectively admitted by the chief press censor, Lord Decies, in August 1918 when he was happy to report 'that the restrictions of censorship are proving an increasing embarrassment to the seditious activities of Sinn Féin'.[44]

The desire of the British authorities to muzzle any pro-Sinn Féin sentiment within the provincial press was clearly evident in the immediate aftermath of Easter 1916 when several provincial editors and proprietors with perceived republican links were arrested and imprisoned. The most prominent of these

---

38 Richard P. Davis, *Arthur Griffith and non-violent Sinn Féin* (Dublin, 1974), p. 43; Ciarán Ó Duibhir, *Sinn Féin: the first election, 1908* (Manorhamilton, 1993), p. 85; Lawrence William White, 'Dolan, Charles Joseph' in McGuire and Quinn (eds), *Dictionary of Irish biography*. 39 Official instructions for the organization of Sinn Féin clubs, 16 May 1917 (BMH, Mary Alden Childers collection, CD6/6/3). 40 How to form Sinn Féin clubs, CD6/9/4. 41 *FJ*, 21 Sept. 1917; *II*, 22 Sept. 1917. 42 Michael Farry, *The Irish revolution, 1912–1923: Sligo* (Dublin, 2012), p. 78. 43 *II*, 26 Dec. 1917; *Southern Star 1889–1989: Centenary Supplement* (11 Nov. 1989); Peter Hart, *Mick: the real Michael Collins* (London, 2005), p. 121. 44 Press Censorship Report, Aug. 1918 (Colonial Office, UK National Archives, CO904/167/1).

were P.J. Doris of the *Mayo News* and William Sears of the *Enniscorthy Echo*.[45] Indeed the *Enniscorthy Echo* remained out of publication between April 1916 and February 1917, as the majority of the paper's staff was arrested and detained following the Easter Rising.[46] As popular support for Sinn Féin rose dramatically, the Office of the Press Censor (OPC) in Dublin increasingly concerned itself with blocking press reports of speeches made at Sinn Féin meetings and rallies. During this time the titles that endured the lengthiest periods of suppression were the *Southern Star*, *Clare Champion*, *Waterford News* and *Kilkenny People*. Most of these newspaper closures took place while the OPC was still in operation. However, the nature of the shutdown of several newspapers after this office closed in September 1919 was considerably more aggravated.

The offices of the *Galway Express* were destroyed by crown forces in September 1920 during what the *Connacht Tribune* described as the 'city's night of horror'. This resulted from an incident at the city's railway station that led to the deaths of an English policeman, Edward Cromm, and local man, Seán Mulvoy.[47] The *Galway Express* briefly reappeared later that year but ceased publication shortly afterwards. About a month after this attack in Galway the *Westmeath Independent* was subjected to similar treatment. The paper, which had come to be regarded as a pro-Sinn Féin organ, was actually subjected to two attacks by crown forces during October 1920, the second of which forced the paper to suspend operations. The *Westmeath Independent* remained out of publication until February 1922.[48] In November 1920 Patrick Dunne, editor-proprietor of the *Leitrim Observer* in Carrick-on-Shannon, was held at gunpoint, along with his sister Eliza, as the paper's plant and machinery were destroyed by crown forces.[49] Dunne, a strong supporter of Sinn Féin, was arrested several days later and detained at Ballykinlar Camp in Co. Down. The *Leitrim Observer* only resumed publication in January 1923.[50] The *Kerryman* in Tralee was subjected to similar treatment in April 1921. During the course of a series of reprisals in the town, the offices and printing works of the paper were destroyed by crown forces. The reprisals followed the IRA killing of Major John Alastair McKinnon at the golf links outside Tralee.[51] The *Kerryman* did not resume publication until August 1923.

45 *MN*, 6 Mar. 1937; *II*, 25 Mar. 1929; *EE*, 30 Mar. 1929.   **46** *EE*, 17 May 1952.   **47** *CT*, 11 Sept. 1920; Tomás Kenny, *Galway: politics and society, 1910–23* (Dublin, 2011), p. 32.   **48** Hugh Oram, *The newspaper book: a history of newspapers in Ireland, 1649–1983* (Dublin, 1983), pp 143–4; *OI*, 22 Apr. 1922; *Westmeath Independent: 150th Anniversary Special Supplement* (July 1996); Wheatley, *Nationalism and the Irish Party*, p. 241. The *Westmeath Independent* was owned by Church of Ireland member Thomas Chapman, and had been launched in 1846 as a distinctly Protestant organ. However, Chapman, who acquired the paper in 1883, supported the Land League and the Irish Parliamentary Party; he transferred his allegiance to Sinn Féin after the 1916 Rising and subsequently became president of the local branch of the party. **49** *IT*, 11 Nov. 1920.   **50** *Leitrim Observer: 1890–1990: One Hundred Years of History in the Making* (28 Nov. 1990).   **51** *II*, 21 Apr. 1921, 21 Apr. 1938; *The Kerryman 1904–2004* (5 Aug. 2004). Following the death of Major McKinnon, the British military visited the paper's offices to demand that the evening issue, the *Liberator*, be printed in ruled black mourning columns as a mark of respect for McKinnon. The publishers refused and decided not to print any edition on that day.

The attacks on these newspapers effectively brought to an end a rather remarkable period in the history of the Irish provincial press. It was one in which nationalist papers swiftly became the predominant force in this key section of the Irish print media and, fittingly, the end of this period coincided with the attainment of Irish self-government. During this time, the provincial press was characterized by a number of clearly distinctive features. The extremely close relationship between one individual and their own particular newspaper was possibly the most visible of these features. This was principally due to the presence of a highly dominant figure at the head of the paper who also had a parallel political career or who remained as editor or proprietor (or both) for several decades. In many cases it was a combination of both of these factors.

Many of these editors and proprietors were also devoutly Catholic, which accounted for the decidedly religious profile of the provincial press at this time. One of the other discernible characteristics of such newspapermen was their firm allegiance to the main forces of cultural nationalism, most notably the GAA. The large numbers of senior figures of the provincial press who were highly supportive or actively involved in the organization was a clear illustration of this. The other most striking features of the provincial press was (and arguably still is) the extent of family ownership. This is exemplified by the fact that many of the most familiar provincial titles have passed through several generations of family ownership.

There is much to indicate that the emergent provincial press of the late nineteenth and early twentieth centuries greatly shaped the nature of society in the Irish Free State and beyond. The Catholic church and the GAA, institutions that have been referred to as pillars of Irish society, are clearly indebted to the provincial press for the level of loyalty and support they enjoyed over the course of a century or more. It can also be asserted with much validity that the provincial press contributed to the highly conservative nature of Irish society that emerged following independence and fed into what Tom Garvin describes as an 'institutional continuity' that existed alongside 'a conservative, if democratic, nationalist elite' upon the foundation of the Free State.[52] In this regard, the high degree of family proprietorship of provincial newspapers, prolonged editorial reigns, and the steadfast Catholic faith of many senior press figures can only have assisted in creating a sense of stability, possibly bordering on stagnation, which reinforced the conservatism of the new state. This could occasionally manifest itself in a highly negative manner. This was evident in its meek acceptance of censorship regulations, most notably the 1929 Censorship of Publications Act, which highlighted 'Irish journalism's general compliance with the church-driven censorship agenda'.[53] It was further demonstrated by its failure to adequately

52 Tom Garvin, *Preventing the future: why was Ireland so poor for so long?* (Dublin, 2004), p. 26.
53 Anthony Keating, 'Censorship: the cornerstone of Catholic Ireland', *Journal of Church and State* (Nov. 2013), pp 14–19.

report sexual crime in the early years of the Free State, for fear of offending the Catholic hierarchy or 'contaminating the Free State's Celtic Catholic identity'.[54] However, even if its role in such matters is rather questionable, it only serves to illustrate that the Irish provincial press that began to take shape in the early 1880s undoubtedly grew to assume a crucial, if largely unrecognized role, in Irish society for many decades to come.

---

54 Anthony Keating, 'Sexual crime in the Irish Free State, 1922–33: its nature, extent and reporting', *Irish Studies Review*, 20:2 (May 2012), p. 148.

Keeping an eye on … : sourcing and covering international news in the Irish regional press, *c.*1892–1949

JAMES T. O'DONNELL

On 5 September 1898, the *Skibbereen Eagle*,[1] a small weekly newspaper in west Cork, declared that it would be keeping an eye on Tsar Nicholas II of Russia and his imperialist expansionism. As Matthew Potter has noted, in the 1890s the *Eagle*'s editor-proprietor, Frederick Peel Eldon Potter, had begun 'to use the issue of imperialism to cleverly tap into the zeitgeist' of the day.[2] Though Potter and the *Eagle*'s proclamation might be regarded as the most famous example of an Irish regional newspaper concerning itself with international events – the paper even received a reference in James Joyce's *Ulysses* as J.J. O'Molloy's 'watchful friend'[3] – this was by no means unique. For example, when peace terms were agreed at the end of the South African War (1899–1902) between the Boer republics of the Orange Free State and Transvaal, and the British empire, the *Clare Man* commented that:

> After two years and a half of the most barbarous, cowardly and iniquitous war ever waged on a civilized people, England has agreed to peace terms favourable in a large measure to the brave Boers. [...] The Dutch language will be allowed in the schools and in courts of law. [...] These terms show that victory is not all on the side of the British as the jingoes would fain make out … England in her greed for gold and territory has been taught a severe lesson.[4]

The South African War had provided a focus for advanced nationalists in Ireland and their supporting press. The Irish Transvaal Committee, of which the Irish Parliamentary Party MP for East Clare, Willie Redmond, was a member, was established to promote a pro-Boer, anti-imperial, sentiment. This committee in turn formed a nucleus around which Arthur Griffith founded Cumann na nGael, which in turn formed the basis for Sinn Féin.[5] In this context, the *Clare Man*'s reference to the Dutch language, and its criticism of British jingoism and imperialism, can be seen as a reference to Ireland's position within the British empire and the treatment of the Irish language. As in this example, the coverage of international events in the Irish

1 More properly the *Eagle and County Cork Advertiser*, but better known to posterity as the *Skibbereen Eagle*: 'We will still keep our eye on the Emperor of Russia [...]'. 2 Matthew Potter, 'Keeping an eye on the tsar: Frederick Potter and the *Skibbereen Eagle*' in Kevin Rafter (ed.), *Irish journalism before independence: more a disease than a profession* (Manchester, 2011), p. 53. 3 James Joyce, *Ulysses* (London, 2000), p. 176. 4 *ClM*, 7 June 1902. 5 Donal P. McCracken, *Forgotten protest: Ireland and the Anglo-Boer War* (Belfast, 2003), p. 73.

regional press, and comment offered on them, was often used as a method to reflect and consider Ireland's own position.

As Marie-Louise Legg has noted, in 'the last two decades of the nineteenth century the provincial press brought their readers increasingly into contact with the rest of Ireland, politically and economically'.[6] Through their coverage of foreign news, these newspapers also brought their readers into contact with international events. The development of an increasingly literate public associating with nationalist objectives, with disposable income to purchase newspapers,[7] provided for a mass readership of newspapers catered to by increased production.[8] And this growing Irish regional press of the late nineteenth and early twentieth centuries was increasingly nationalist, a development driven at least in part by market conditions.

But how did Potter at the *Eagle* and his contemporaries in the Irish regional press expect to be able to keep an eye on international events? How did they expect to get the news that would allow them to inform their readers of these developments, in a period when even the larger, daily Irish newspapers did not generally deploy their own staff reporters overseas? Just as the introduction of the rotary printing press in the 1860s had allowed for economies of scale and mass production of newspapers, the development of the international and domestic telegraph networks provided for a 'quantum leap in the collection and distribution of news'.[9] By the late nineteenth century, most regional newspapers regularly carried at least part of a column of international news provided by news agencies utilizing the telegraph network. As Donal Lowry has noted, when the South African War broke out, 'all national and local newspapers of any significance were largely dependent for coverage of the war on identical reports syndicated from international news agencies'.[10] The technological developments that facilitated this structure of distribution frequently enabled local newspapers to publish international news before the London newspapers, utilizing the postal network, had even arrived.[11]

That is not to say that regional newspapers did not rely on more traditional methods to gather information on international events. The *Clare Journal*, for example, offered a payment of 2*s.* 6*d.* for any letters received from Clare soldiers serving in the South African War that it published.[12] In a similar vein, during the Spanish civil war (1936–9) the *Kerryman* printed a letter received in Tralee in 1937 reporting that 'Brig. Gen. E. Horan, Bridge St., was wounded in Spain'.[13]

6 Marie-Louise Legg, *Newspapers and nationalism: the Irish provincial press, 1850–1892* (Dublin, 1998), p. 147.   7 Legg, *Newspapers and nationalism*, p. 128; Diarmaid Ferriter, *The transformation of Ireland* (New York, 2005), p. 33; John Horgan, *Irish media: a critical history* (London, 2001), p. 174.   8 Legg, *Newspapers and nationalism*, p. 120; L.M. Cullen, *Eason and Son: a history* (Dublin, 1989), p. 5.   9 Joel H. Wiener, 'Get the news! Get the news! – speed in transatlantic journalism, 1830–1914' in Joel H. Wiener and Mark Hampton (eds), *Anglo-American media interactions, 1850–2000* (Basingstoke, 2007), p. 60.   10 Donal Lowry, 'Nationalist and unionist responses to the British empire in the age of the South African War, 1899–1902' in Simon J. Potter (ed.), *Newspapers and empire in Britain and Ireland* (Dublin, 2004), p. 161.   11 Legg, *Newspapers and nationalism*, p. 132.   12 *CJ*, 8 Jan. 1900.   13 *KM*, 1 May 1937.

The printing of correspondence, both solicited and unsolicited, provided a mechanism by which newspapers could provide a focus and local context to their coverage of international news.

However, the news agencies provided immediacy and coverage of a range of international topics that these less regular and slower methods could not supply. The newspapers could then shape this raw telegraphed news through comment and the construction of headlines. The telegraph network and the coverage of international news it provided was an important part of the 'communications revolution' that contributed to the economic and political development of the Irish regional press.[14]

THE DEVELOPMENT OF NEWS AGENCIES AND INTERNATIONAL NEWS SUPPLY STRUCTURES

The reliance of Irish newspapers on news agencies to cover international events has been noted elsewhere, but little concerted attention has been paid to how this phenomenon worked.[15] Through their use of news-agency material, Irish newspapers were connected to, and part of, a global business network where news was a tradable commodity.

By the end of the nineteenth century, the international news market was dominated by four main agencies: Havas in France, Reuters in Britain, Wolff in Germany and, from 1898, the Associated Press (AP) in America. These agencies formed the 'News Ring', whereby the business of international news gathering and distribution was cartelized, and the globe divided up into areas of exclusive pre-eminence. Further, only 'the cartel agency assigned a certain territory was to conclude contracts with a [domestic] agency in that area'.[16] These agreements secured the domestic agency exclusive rights to the international agency's news, and that of its fellow cartel members. It also enforced a reciprocal exclusivity on the outward flow of news from the domestic agency operating in such a way as 'to ensure the hegemony of the cartel and the subordination of other agencies', as Terhi Rantanen has written.[17] From the 1860s the international telegraph cable industry had been undergoing a similar process and by this time cartels 'ruled the global cable business'.[18]

Within this cartel structure Ireland was part of Reuters' territory, as was much of the British empire. The domestic agency Reuters contracted with in Britain and Ireland for reciprocal supply was the Press Association (PA). Both

---

14 Ferriter, *The transformation of Ireland*, p. 33.   15 See, for example, Lowry, 'Nationalist and unionist responses', p. 161; Fearghal McGarry, 'Irish newspapers and the Spanish civil war', *Irish Historical Studies*, 33:129 (May 2002), pp 68–90, at p. 76; Donal Ó Drisceoil, *Censorship in Ireland, 1939–45: neutrality, politics and society* (Cork, 1996), p. 117.   16 Terhi Rantanen, 'Foreign dependence and domestic monopoly: the European news cartel and the US Associated Presses, 1861–1932', *Media History*, 12:1 (2006), p. 21.   17 Ibid.   18 Dwayne Winseck and Robert M. Pike, 'The global media and the empire of liberal internationalism: circa 1910–30', *Media History*, 15:1 (2009), p. 32.

Reuters and the PA were based in London, as were the competitor agencies of the Exchange Telegraph Company (ETC) and Central News Agency. From 1922 the British United Press (BUP), a Canadian-registered subsidiary of the United Press in America that was also based in London, entered the market, though its service was not taken up enthusiastically by Irish newspapers. In 1926 the PA purchased a majority shareholding in Reuters, and in 1937 the PA and ETC bought a joint controlling share in their competitor Central, closing down its international news service. These organizational developments can be seen against a wider background of mergers and acquisitions in the international cable and news market from the 1920s that 'transformed the global communications business in a few short years'.[19] In 1934 the 'News Ring' collapsed following agitation for greater competition from AP and was replaced with a series of bipartite agreements. As far as Ireland was concerned, little changed though.

As a result of these commercial structures, Irish newspapers were largely reliant on a handful of London-based news agencies for their international news. Dominant among these was the PA, which distributed Reuters as well as AP, Havas and Wolff. During the First World War, connections with Wolff were terminated, after which it was largely confined to Germany; Havas inherited most of Europe. In 1933, Wolff was merged with the German Telegraph Union, nationalized under Nazi control and renamed the Deutsches Nachrichtenbüro (DNB), whereupon reciprocal supply agreements were once again severed.[20] Following the fall of France in 1940, Havas came under the control of the Vichy regime.[21] After the Second World War, following the gradual relaxation of the Allies' press controls in Germany, the Deutsche Presse Agentur (DPA) agency was formed in 1949 from a merger of the three Allies-controlled agencies in the western zones, which Reuters cooperated with.[22] Reuters refused, however, to cooperate with Havas' post-war successor Agence France-Presse (AFP) when it accepted a large government subsidy, posing a threat to its independence, in Reuters' eyes.[23]

Following the collapse of the 'News Ring' in 1934, as mentioned above, AP had declined to compete in Britain and Ireland and concluded a reciprocal supply agreement with the PA and Reuters, leaving these two London-based agencies to dominate their home market. The reason for this decision was the value AP placed on the British and Irish news it received as part of the reciprocal supply agreement from the PA for use in its own international news service. In 1933, De Witt McKenzie, AP's executive assistant in charge of foreign affairs, wrote in a confidential memorandum considering whether to compete in the British and Irish market that the PA service 'covers all domestic news and undoubtedly is

---

19 Ibid., p. 44.   20 Jürgen Wilke, 'The struggle for control of domestic news agencies (2)' in Oliver Boyd-Barrett and Terhi Rantanen (eds), *The globalization of news* (London, 1998), p. 50.   21 Graham Storey, *Reuters' century, 1851–1951* (London, 1951), pp 212–13.   22 Donald Read, *The power of news: the history of Reuters* (2nd ed. Oxford, 1999), p. 310.   23 Ibid., p. 309.

the best thing of its kind abroad'.[24] By adopting a competitive posture AP would lose the PA service for inclusion in its own service elsewhere, which it could not adequately replace. As a result, in the post-war world there was greater competition in the international news market, but the Irish newspapers remained primarily reliant on the London-based PA-Reuters service for their coverage of international events. This situation continued until well after the end of the Second World War. Attempts were made to set up a national news agency in Ireland, but the short-lived Irish News Agency (1950–7) faced strong resistance from vested interests in the established Irish print media and elsewhere.[25]

INTERNATIONAL NEWS SUPPLY STRUCTURES IN IRELAND AND THEIR DEVELOPMENT

The above might create the impression of an Irish media passively dominated by international commerce and a globalized market. The truth is, however, somewhat more complex. As mentioned above, the PA was the primary conduit for international news in Ireland. It and Reuters (effectively the same service) were certainly the most frequently cited sources in regional newspapers' foreign news columns. But it is informative to examine the genesis of the PA and the role of Irish newspapers in its development.

In 1869, the government in Westminster nationalized the telegraph network in Britain and Ireland under the control of the Post Office. The responsible legislation was the Electric Telegraph Act. One of the stated aims of the act was 'Free trade in the collection of news for the press, of which collection the telegraph companies had hitherto had a monopoly, with low rates for the transmission of such news, no matter by what or by how many agencies it might be collected'.[26] Up to this point the telegraph network had developed alongside the burgeoning railway network in the nineteenth century. The transmission of information was controlled by private companies that in 1858 had created a cartel structure under the joint Intelligence Department of the Electric and Magnetic Companies.[27] As well as having no recourse to alternative telegraphic news due to this structure, dissatisfaction with the service was common among newspapers because, at least in part, 'the prime purpose of the telegraph was to convey commercial news' and other forms of news were something of an afterthought.[28]

The first moves among the newspapers to organize a collective system of newsgathering and distribution to counter the telegraph companies' cartel

24 18 Dec. 1933, AP Corporate Archives, New York, AP 02.1 Box 32/10, records of General Manager Kent Cooper, Subseries 2: Foreign Bureaus 1924–39. **25** John Horgan, 'Government propaganda and the Irish News Agency', *Irish Communications Review*, 3 (1993), 31–42. **26** House of Commons Parliamentary Papers. *Telegraphs: report by Mr Scudamore on the re-organization of the telegraph system of the United Kingdom*, pp 1–2; 1871 (304) XXXVII.703. **27** Roger Neil Barton, 'New media: the birth of telegraphic news in Britain, 1847–68', *Media History*, 16:1 (2010), p. 393. **28** Ibid., pp 384, 386.

structure came in 1865. After an unsuccessful appeal to the Electric and Magnetic Companies following an increase in rates, the president of the Provincial Newspaper Society (PNS), a Mr Fisher of the *Waterford Mail*, unsuccessfully proposed the creation of a limited liability company to negotiate a centralized agreement.[29] The momentum for collective organization of news supply did not pick up again until 1867, when the postmaster general first officially indicated the intention to purchase the telegraph networks. The PNS, as the provincial press' trade organization, made representations. Suspicions were raised, however, that the larger dailies were planning to exclude the smaller non-dailies from a potential new organization to gather and distribute news over the nationalized telegraph network, when a circular letter was issued on 30 March 1868. The signatories to this letter included a number leading provincial newspapers, including the *Edinburgh Scotsman, Glasgow Herald, Manchester Guardian* and *Sheffield Independent*. It invited proprietors of daily provincial newspapers to a meeting in Manchester to discuss the formation of a company to organize the collection and distribution of news.[30] The PNS issued a counter circular to all members, declaring the dailies' plans 'contrary to the spirit of the agreement of 1865', and sought a meeting with the chairman of the dailies' grouping, J.E. Taylor of the *Manchester Guardian*.[31]

On 29 June 1868, a meeting of proprietors of daily provincial newspapers was held at the United Hotel, Haymarket, London. Among the thirty present were nine from Ireland: Thomas Crosbie, *Cork Examiner*; F.D. Finlay, *Northern Whig*, Belfast; a Mr Coulter and Thomas Potts, both *Saunders's Newsletter*, Dublin; Sir John Gray MP and J.W. Gray, both of the *Freeman's Journal*, Dublin; H. Maunsell, *Dublin Evening Mail*; David A. Nagle, *Daily Herald*, Cork; and J. Robinson, *Dublin Daily Express*. The stated aims of this meeting were the formation of 'a cooperative association of proprietors of provincial newspapers ... [for] ... collecting and supplying news'. It was intended that 'all provincial newspaper proprietors ... [including the non-dailies] ... be invited to join'.[32] The product of this meeting was the PA, the articles of association of which were issued on 6 November 1868, forming a company structured along cooperative lines, with the provincial newspapers of Britain and Ireland, both daily and non-daily, as its shareholding members.[33] Among the original shareholders were eighteen Irish newspapers holding 14 per cent of the issued share capital. These were the *Belfast News Letter, Cork Constitution, Cork Examiner, Kerry Evening Post, Londonderry*

29 Ibid., p. 394; H. Whorlow, *The provincial newspaper society, 1836–1886* (London, 1886), p. 75. Barton dates this price increase to 1865 whereas Whorlow places it in 1864. The salient year is, however, undoubtedly 1865. The PNS had been established in 1836 as a representative trade and lobby body for the non-London-based newspapers of Britain and Ireland. Prior to the this point it had, in particular, worked for the reform of libel laws and the removal of stamp duty.   30 Circular, 30 Mar. 1868, Guildhall Library Manuscripts Collection, London (GL) MS 35356.   31 Whorlow, *The provincial newspaper society*, p. 81. 32 Minutes of meeting, 29 June 1868, GL MS 35357.   33 Memorandum and articles of association of the Press Association Limited, 6 Nov. 1868, GL MS 35355.

Guardian, *Londonderry Journal*, *Londonderry Standard*, *Londonderry Sentinel*, *Morning News*, Belfast, *Northern Whig*, Belfast, *Tralee Chronicle* and *Waterford Mail*. In addition, the Dublin-based *Daily Express*, *Dublin Evening Mail*, *Dublin Evening Standard*, *Freeman's Journal*, *Irish Times* and *Saunders's Newsletter* were among the PA's original shareholders.[34] By the turn of the century the number of Irish shareholders had fallen to thirteen located in Belfast, Cork, Dublin and Derry, and holding just under 11 per cent of the issued share capital.[35] Irish shareholding in the PA would thereafter remain relatively steady at around 10 per cent

This shareholding indicates the involvement and support of Irish newspapers in the formation of the PA: it was as much their organization as their British contemporaries'. In the first three decades of the PA's operation, its board members included F.D. Finlay of the *Northern Whig* (1871), J.A. Henderson of the *Belfast News Letter* (1873–4), J. Robinson of the *Daily Express* (1875–8) and Edmund Dwyer Gray of the *Freeman's Journal* (1880–4). Irish representation continued at the highest level of the PA from this point into the twentieth century. Thomas Crosbie of the *Cork Examiner* was a board member from 1888 to 1891 and again from 1894 to 1898. His son, George Crosbie, was on the board 1907–16, serving as chairman in 1911–12. Charles W. Henderson of the *Belfast News Letter* was appointed to the board in 1917, served as chairman in 1921–2, and stepped down in 1930. Charles Henderson's son James served on the PA board from 1935 to 1951 and was chairman in 1940–1.[36]

In addition to these board-level representatives, Irish shareholding members of the PA regularly attended general meetings, though these were primarily the larger dailies from Belfast and Cork, as well as Dublin. A number also provided financial support for the PA's 1926 acquisition of a controlling interest in Reuters, mentioned above, through the investment in a series of interest-bearing notes. These were the *Belfast News Letter*, *Belfast Telegraph*, *Cork Examiner* and *Londonderry Sentinel*, as well as the Dublin-based *Dublin Express and Mail*, *Irish Times* and *Irish Independent*.[37]

The Irish newspapers, then, were centrally involved in the founding, development and organization of their dominant source of international news: the London-based PA, also distributing Reuters news and that of the other major international news agencies. The PA's pricing model was based on an annual subscription, adjusted according to the differing financial resources and news requirements of daily and non-daily newspapers, levying a pro-rata charge 'according to the number of days on which the news [was] supplied'.[38] It was not a requirement for newspapers to be shareholding members, though membership did bestow a 10 per cent discount on subscription fees. In addition to international

34 PA share ledger – first issue, 1868–70, GL MS 35386/1.   **35** PA returns to Companies House, 1906, GL MS 35383/2.   **36** Reports of PA General Meetings, 1870–1955, GL MS 35365/1–15.   **37** Ledger, 'The Press Association Limited: list of a series of 800 twelve-year notes of £100 each', GL MS 35610. **38** PA Tariff, 1885, GL MS 35460/2.

and domestic news the PA offered a variety of services, including reports from London and overseas newspapers, parliamentary reports, sporting information and market intelligence. It is tempting to think that this latter service was the basis for Cork butter merchant H.L. Tivy's statement in 1881 that 'I saved a good many of my customers last season from the loss which in the end, unfortunately, overtook others, being enabled to do so by a close acquaintance with the state of the markets across the channel.'[39] Tivy was proprietor of the *Cork Constitution*, as well as the Dublin *Daily Express* and *Evening Mail*.

Details of newspapers' annual subscriptions to the PA's services do not survive, though the citation of the agency and its services in the columns of the Ireland's regional newspapers indicates its wide use. What do survive are records of orders for exceptional service not covered in subscriptions. These provide an interesting indication of the pattern of usage, particularly for the smaller, non-shareholding newspapers. Between 1899 and 1914 there are thirteen non-Dublin-based Irish newspapers listed in the PA's non-members order books (see table 9.1).

Table 9.1: Irish newspapers listed in the PA non-members order book, 1899–1914[40]

Clare Journal, Ennis	*Limerick Chronicle*	*Waterford Mail*
Cork Free Press	*Limerick Leader*	*Waterford News*
Kerry Evening Star	*Limerick Weekly Echo*	*Waterford Star*
Kerry News	*Londonderry Indepedent*	
and Weekly Reporter	*and Sporting News*	
Kerry People	*Newry Reporter*	

This number declines somewhat during the First World War, to eleven (see table 9.2). This may be due to war news being carried in the subscription service. Also significant would have been the effect of censorship under the Defence of the Realm Act and the operations of the official press bureau. The role of the bureau was to distribute official reports from the Admiralty and War Office and examine telegrams sent and received by the newspapers. The PA noted in its annual report for 1914 that 'special correspondents have not been allowed to accompany the various armies; and all cablegrams received about the war from abroad have been severely censored'.[41] These harsh restrictions on war news were subsequently eased, and the PA was able to report the following year that 'censorship is not nearly so severe as it was during the early months of the war [...]. The Admiralty and War Office have allowed correspondents to be attached to the forces in various parts of the world.'[42] During this period the authorities

39 Letter from Henry L. Tivy & Co., Butter Merchants, Oct. 1881, Tivy Family Papers, Cork City and County Archives, U116/A/53.   40 PA Non-Members Order Book, GL MS 35468/1.   41 PA Annual Report and Statement of Accounts for 1914, in report of PA AGM 1915, GL MS 35365/9.   42 Ibid. For an examination of Irish correspondents visiting troops during the First World War, see Mark O'Brien, '"With the Irish in France": the national press and recruitment in Ireland, 1914–1916', *Media History*, 22:2 (May 2016), pp 159–73.

Table 9.2: Irish newspapers listed in the PA non-members order book, 1914–16

Clare Journal, Ennis	*Kerry Press*, Tralee	*Omagh Herald*
Clonmel Chronicle	*Limerick Chronicle*	*Waterford News*
Cork Free Press	*Limerick Leader*	*Waterford Standard*
Kerry News, Tralee	*Munster News*	

Table 9.3: Irish newspapers listed in the PA non-members order book, 1928–36[43]

Clonmel Chronicle	*Kerry Champion*, Tralee	*Star*, Dublin
Clonmel Nationalist	*Kerry Express*, Tralee	*Star*, Waterford
(from 1931)	*Kerry Liberator*, Tralee	*Sunday Independent*, Dublin
Connacht Sentinel, Galway	*Kerry News*, Tralee	*Tipperary Man*, Thurles
Evening News, Waterford	*Kilkenny Post*	*Tipperary Star*, Thurles
Evening Telegraph and	*Limerick Chronicle*	*Tribune*, Galway
Evening Press, Dublin	*Limerick Echo*	*Wexford People*
Galway Observer	*Limerick Leader*	
Irish Press, Dublin	*Munster News*, Limerick	

Table 9.4: Irish newspapers listed in the PA non-members order book, 1936–9

Connacht Observer, Galway	*Liberator*, Tralee	*Waterford Evening News*
Connacht Sentinel, Galway	*Limerick Chronicle*	*Waterford Star*
Irish Press, Dublin	*Limerick Echo*	
Kerry Champion, Tralee	*Limerick Leader*	
Kerry Express, Tralee	*Sunday Independent*, Dublin	
Kerry News, Tralee	(until Jan. 1939)	
Kilkenny Post	*Tipperary Star*, Thurles	

were keeping a close eye on Irish newspapers, compiling detailed records of their political allegiances, place and frequency of publication, and circulation.[44]

Taking the non-members' orders as an indication of the use of news agencies by the regional press in Ireland, the interwar period saw a surge in activity with twenty-three titles listed between 1928–36 (see table 9.3), decreasing to fifteen between 1936 and 1939 (see table 9.4).

There was a marked decline in the pattern of usage in 1939–40, with only eight Irish newspapers listed in the non-members order books (see table 9.5). This can, again, most reasonably be attributed to the outbreak of the Second World War. War news was included in the PA's subscription services, but censorship again became an important factor. In Dublin the neutral Irish state imposed 'the most intensive

43 PA Non-Members Order Book, 1928–36, GL MS 35468/2; PA Non-Members Order Book, 1936–40, GL MS 35468/3. **44** List of Irish newspapers during the Great War, NAUK, NATS 1/261; list of national and local Irish newspapers from 1917, containing details of their political affiliation and circulation numbers, National Archives of Ireland (NAI), CSO/RP/1918/15619/19.

period of censorship' in its history.[45] Newspapers were not prevented from using news agency material, but they were required to publish their sources clearly,[46] and in order not to give even the slightest hint of contravening Irish neutrality, the censor required an 'almost pathological even-handedness' in the reporting of both Allied and Axis news.[47] In Northern Ireland, censorship aimed at supporting the British war effort was implemented by the press office established within the Northern Ireland Cabinet Office. From May 1940, this became the regional office of the Ministry of Information.[48] During the Second World War, the PA had resident Ministry of Information staff in its newsroom in London to oversee the news despatched. Between March and September 1944, corresponding with the period of the build up to D-Day and its aftermath, additional staff were placed in the PA newsroom with the specific purpose of operating a special censorship regime on news sent to the whole of Ireland.[49]

Table 9.5: Irish newspapers listed in the PA Non-Members Order Book, 1939–40[50]

Connacht Observer, Galway	*Kilkenny Post*	*Waterford Evening News*
Irish Press, Dublin	*Liberator*, Tralee	*Waterford Star*
Kerry News, Tralee	*Limerick Echo*	

In 1940, the PA changed its pricing model to a comprehensive annual subscription, and the practice of exceptional orders represented in the order books ceased.

The consumption of news-agency material by the regional Irish newspapers is consistent with the development of 'a recognizable pattern of mass readership' from the 1920s.[51] However, improved communication-and-distribution infra-structure provided for a marked growth in the readership of 'national' dailies outside of Dublin. These increasingly became the main sources of interna-tional news for the Irish public. In addition, the post-war era saw an increase in the broadcast output of Radio Éireann. Originally transmitting as 2RN from 1926, the Irish national broadcaster's international news output in the inter-war period largely consisted of rebroadcasting information received from other radio stations, such as the BBC and Vatican Radio.[52] This changed in 1946, when Radio Éireann signed its first agreement for an international news service jointly supplied by the ETC, PA and Reuters.[53] This service was to provide 'complete world cover including Great Britain and British racing results'.[54]

45 Donal Ó Drisceoil, *Censorship in Ireland, 1939–1945: neutrality, politics and society* (Cork, 1996), p. 284. 46 Ibid., p. 117.   47 Horgan, *Irish media*, p. 46.   48 John W. Blake, *Northern Ireland in the Second World War* (Belfast, 2000), pp 173–8.   49 For an examination of the news agencies and censorship in Ireland during the Second World War, see James T. O'Donnell, 'Content, comment and censorship: a case study comparing coverage of Dunkirk and D-Day in Irish newspapers', *Media History*, 23:3–4 (Aug.–Nov. 2017), pp 345–59.   50 PA Non-Members Order Book, 1936–40, GL MS 35468/3.   51 Cullen, *Eason and Son*, p. 168.   52 John Horgan, *Broadcasting and public life: RTÉ news and current affairs, 1926–1997* (Dublin, 2004), p. 4; Ó Drisceoil, *Censorship in Ireland*, p. 100.   53 PA Annual Report and Statement of Accounts for 1946, in Report of PA AGM, 1947, GL MS 35365/14.
54 PA General Manager's Report Book, 14 Feb. 1946, GL MS 35363/3.

As the Irish public turned to national print and broadcast media for their national and international news, the regional press turned their focus to covering more localized events. This did not prevent them from addressing international events occasionally though. In May 1949 commenting on India's move towards a republic the *Connacht Tribune* noted that the British commonwealth might soon contain four republics: India, Ceylon, Pakistan and South Africa. It continued:

> Ireland is in factual association with the commonwealth but acknowledges no political link whatsoever. Ireland, in point of fact, has paved the way for all that has happened and Mr de Valera's 'Document No. 2' of 1921 is written large on India's acceptance of freedom.[55]

At the same time, reflecting on the recent declaration of the Republic of Ireland and criticizing the Ireland bill in Westminster said to be necessary because Ireland was a republic, the *Leinster Express* noted: 'Our British neighbours are glad to have settled up with India and Pakistan about their commonwealth membership.'[56] As before, while they were commenting on international events these regional Irish newspapers were using them as a prism through which to consider Ireland's own position.

CONCLUSION

From the late nineteenth century, Irish regional newspapers played an important role in informing an increasingly literate and politically engaged public of national and international events. In the latter case, these were often used to reflect on Ireland's own condition and concerns, but in order to do this the newspapers needed access to a regular and reliable sources of information. News agencies were the key conduit for this information, facilitated by technical and commercial developments. The news agencies the Irish newspapers relied on were predominantly London-based, but to describe them as wholly British would be a distortion of the true picture, and the resistance the INA faced from the Irish media should be noted. The dominant and most important news agency from an Irish perspective was the PA, also distributing the Reuters service. Irish newspapers were centrally involved in the creation and development of this agency, indeed the first suggestion to form an organization along the lines of the PA had come from a Waterford newspaperman. It is true that the larger dailies were the most actively involved in corporate structures of the PA, but it was newspapers from Belfast and Cork, not Dublin, that represented Ireland at board level. In the post-war era, broadcast media and daily newspapers – rather than the less frequently published regional titles – came to dominate international news coverage. But while their coverage of international events declined, the regional newspapers' interest in them did not

55 *CT*, 7 May 1949. 56 *LE*, 7 May 1949.

altogether disappear, even if their coverage and comment was often used to reflect specifically Irish concerns.

The mood of the nation: Ireland's response to Redmond's call to war in 1914, as reported in the regional press

ELAINE CALLINAN

On 3 August 1914, the eve of Britain's declaration of war on Germany, Sir Edward Grey, the foreign secretary, announced in the House of Commons that war was imminent, as it was 'clear that the peace of Europe cannot be preserved'. John Redmond, leader of the Irish Parliamentary Party, immediately began formulating an appropriate Irish response. He turned to two trusted colleagues – the Roscommon South MP John Hayden and the MP for Liverpool, T.P. O'Connor (John Dillon and Joseph Devlin were in Ireland) – and told them that he was thinking of making a short statement.[1] Hayden supported the idea, but O'Connor cautioned against it, as he believed Ireland was still politically sensitive due to the Bachelor's Walk killings. He was referring to the incident on 26 July 1914 in which the King's Own Scottish Borderers had opened fire on a jeering crowd in Bachelor's Walk in Dublin as Irish Volunteers marched into the city centre after the landing of rifles and ammunition at Howth Harbour earlier in the day.[2]

Redmond's indecision was perhaps alleviated when Andrew Bonar Law, leader of the Conservative and Unionist Party, instantly announced the opposition's unhesitating support for Britain's war effort. Moreover, the day before, the *Irish Times* had reported on Edward Carson's declaration that a large body of Ulster Volunteers would give their services for home defence, and would 'hold themselves at the disposal of the government'.[3] It was now or never for Redmond, so he stood and announced that the government could withdraw its troops from Ireland as the coasts of Ireland would be 'defended from foreign invasion by her armed sons, and for this purpose armed nationalist Catholics in the South will be only too glad to join arms with the armed Protestant Ulstermen in the North'.[4]

Redmond explained that his aspiration in combining the Volunteer forces was to produce a result 'which will be good not merely for the empire, but good for the future welfare and integrity of the Irish nation'.[5] The occasional cheers and

---

1 Patrick Maume, *The long gestation: Irish nationalist life, 1891–1918* (Dublin, 1999), p. 147.   2 Ronan Fanning, *Fatal path: British government and Irish revolution, 1910–1922* (London, 2013), p. 128.   3 *IT*, 1 and 3 Aug. 1914; see also *CN*, 1 Aug. 1914, for example.   4 *Hansard*, House of Commons (HC) Parliamentary Debates (PD), 5th Series, vol. lxv, c. 1809–29: speeches of Grey, Bonar Law and Redmond.   5 HC, PD, 5th Series, vol. lxv, c. 1829: John Redmond; *IT*, 4 Aug. 1914: John Redmond; Thomas Hennessy, *Dividing Ireland: World War I and partition* (London and New York, 1998), pp 46–7.

shouts of approval from all sides of the House as he spoke, and the subsequent standing ovation from members (aside from Carson) demonstrated that he had certainly won parliamentary support.[6] However, had Redmond wisely seized this opportunity to suggest a consolidation of the Ulster and Irish Volunteer movements, or had he placed himself and the party in a perilous position just as Ireland was about to attain home rule?

To answer this and ascertain the mood of the nation this chapter will examine reports, commentary and reaction to Redmond's main speeches in 1914. The influence of the regional press in shaping and reflecting opinion will be explored, although it is important to note that many newspapers were biased in favour of constitutional nationalism. For instance, the *Longford Leader* was owned by the Irish Party MP J.P. Farrell and the *Sligo Champion* was owned by P.A. McHugh MP. Most newspapers were unsympathetic to radical nationalist opinion. The larger dailies such as the *Irish Times* and *Belfast News Letter* were the preserves of unionist opinion, and the *Freeman's Journal* began life as an Irish Party organ.[7] By selecting a wide array of regional newspapers from across the four provinces, this work aims to capture a range of opinion.[8]

The regional press in Ireland at the beginning of August 1914 appeared largely uninterested in the impending European conflict. Opinion and reports were almost exclusively dedicated to the home rule crisis, the Howth gunrunning, and the Bachelor's Walk incident.[9] Britain's declaration of war instantly altered this, and media coverage across the British Isles shifted to wartime happenings. Therefore, Redmond's decision to feature in the war announcement immediately enhanced his prestige. He had expressed Ireland's support early, and he had done so before Carson had a chance to make a House of Commons statement.[10] Redmond had correctly presumed that the offer of Irish support for the war effort would elicit a positive response from MPs, and even from the most ardent unionists. Unionists could hardly criticize him for his desire to support Britain in her hour of need, given that patriotism to the union had often been at the heart of their protests against home rule. In this few minutes of speech-making, Redmond managed to address a broad audience spectrum to demonstrate that Ireland could collaborate with the empire at times of dire need.

The Great War was a unique conflict, so Redmond could not rely on emulating the oratorical skills or deeds of predecessors like Charles Stewart

6 Stephen Gwynn, *John Redmond's last years* (London, 1919), pp 132–3.   7 Unionists also bought and read other publications, such as the *Morning Mail, Daily Irish Telegraph* and *Irish Post* to name a few. Despite gallant efforts by Dillon to hold onto the *Freeman's Journal*, it was sold in 1919; Felix M. Larkin, '"A great daily organ": the *Freeman's Journal*, 1763–1924', *History Ireland*, 3:14 (May/June 2006).   8 For further information on nationalist newspapers, their editors and the people who bought and read them, see Marie-Louise Legg, *Newspapers and nationalism: the Irish provincial press, 1850–1892* (Dublin, 1998) and Hugh Oram, *The newspapers book: a history of newspapers in Ireland, 1649–1983* (Dublin, 1983).   9 Michael Wheatley, *Nationalism and the Irish Party: provincial Ireland, 1910–1916* (Oxford, 2005), pp 198–9.   10 In the *Times* of 1 Aug. 1914, Carson had declared that a large body of the Ulster Volunteers would give their services for home defence and that many would be willing to fight anywhere they were asked. See also the *IT*, 3 Aug. 1914.

Parnell or Daniel O'Connell. Furthermore, no nationalist leader before had had to call for active support for Britain in a war, and no predecessor had attained a binding promise of Irish self-government.[11] In this crucial hour Redmond had to verbalize Ireland's support for the empire and maintain the battle for home rule, and do so in a practical way. Through his repeated use of the word 'democracy', he expressed sympathy and anxiety, stating that Ireland 'would desire to save the democracy of this country [Britain] from the horrors of war'.[12]

J.J. Lee highlights that Redmond's objectives for participation in the war were: to secure the operation of home rule, woo British opinion ahead of a likely 1915 general election, unite nationalists and unionists in shared wartime comradeship, and secure better arms and training for the National Volunteers.[13] Redmond's ultimate agenda remained unchanged. For him, the war made England's difficulty Ireland's opportunity, as the anticipated *sine qua non* of his support for Britain in the war effort was the attainment of home rule for all Ireland.[14] To achieve this, he offered Irish Volunteers for the defence of Ireland's coastline; however, he also clearly stated that Ireland 'would make every possible sacrifice' for the purpose of saving the democracy of Britain. It could be suggested that even at this stage he was considering the possibility of Irish Volunteers enlisting in the British army to serve overseas – an offer he expanded on in his speech to Volunteers at Maryborough in Queen's County later that month,[15] and at Woodenbridge in Co. Wicklow in September.[16]

Nationalists' attitudes to Redmond's Commons speech were expressed in many of the regional newspapers. The *Nationalist and Leinster Times* reported on the 'approval of Mr Redmond's speech'. It accepted that Ireland's destiny was intertwined with the British empire, commenting that Redmond's speech had done more for a 'really united Ireland' than any of his predecessors in national leadership. This newspaper also carried the record of Carlow county council's 'hearty approval of Mr Redmond's statesmanlike speech in the House of Commons', and assured Redmond that 'Carlow people of all creeds and classes are prepared to support his proposed assistance for the defence of Ireland'.[17] The *Drogheda Independent* saw Redmond's offer as the practical manifestation of the 'union of hearts' and the beginning of Young Irelander Thomas Davis' dream that a 'union of Orange and Green' would portray to the world a 'vision

11 Joseph P. Finnan, *John Redmond and Irish unity, 1912–1918* (Syracuse, 2004), p. 85.   12 HC, PD, 5th Series, vol. lxv, cc. 1828–9: John Redmond.   13 J.J. Lee, *Ireland, 1912–1985: politics and society* (Cambridge, 1989), p. 21. There was no general election in 1915. The next election held after 1910 was in 1918.   14 Keith Jeffery, *Ireland and the Great War* (Cambridge, 2000), p. 14.   15 *Weekly Irish Times*, 22 Aug. 1914: full text of Redmond's speech at Maryborough (now Portlaoise, Co. Laois).   16 This work has quoted from: Gerard Reid, *Great Irish voices* (Dublin, 1999), pp 40–1: House of Commons speech; and F.X. Martin, *The Irish Volunteers, 1913–1915: recollections and documents* (Dublin, 1963), p. 148. McConnel points out that when Redmond met Kitchener three days later he was already considering how Irishmen might serve overseas: James McConnel, 'Recruiting sergeants for John Bull? Irish nationalist MPs and enlistment during the early months of the Great War', *War in History*, 14:4 (2007), pp 408–28. 17 *CN*, 8 Aug. 1914.

of a united Ireland'.[18] The *Clare Champion* hoped that Irish unionists and nationalists had it within their power not only to change Ireland, but to win by 'National unity a greater measure of Irish self-government'.[19] The *Cork Examiner* believed unionists could be convinced that 'when they rely on Ireland's honour they can rest assured that she will keep her compact'. They accepted that it was unreasonable to suggest that unionists would become home rulers or that political differences would cease, but hoped that Irishmen working together to defend her shores might ultimately regenerate Ireland and work together for the greater good under an Irish parliament.[20] Also, the *Limerick Leader* called Redmond's speech a 'master stroke of tact, patriotism and statesmanship', believing it would make home rule inevitable, with North–South unity likely in the near future.[21]

In the unionist press, opinion was expressed in letters to the editor of the *Irish Times*. Bryan Cooper, an ex-unionist MP for South County Dublin,[22] stated: 'I am this day joining the National Volunteers and I urge every unionist who is physically fit, to do the same.' Lord Bessborough and Lord Monteagle also urged support for the Volunteer movement.[23] The *Leitrim Gazette/Advertiser* commented that after Redmond's speech the Irish question 'no longer exists in the face of the European difficulty'.[24] The *Kilkenny Moderator* described Redmond's attitude as 'phenomenal' – 'there was in fact, but one mind and one heart in regard to England in her present conflict with Germany ... The Irishman is earnest, determined, enthusiastic ... fanatically loyal to England in this gigantic struggle.'[25] For many unionists in the southern provinces of Ireland Redmond's speech alleviated their fears and proved that the Irish Party was sincere in all its professions of loyalty to the empire.

However, it is incorrect to suggest that all Ireland supported Redmond's position or believed in his words. The *Belfast News Letter* reported on rumours of a political agreement between the government and Redmond, with home rule receiving the royal assent. This prompted a repeated request to unionists to use everything in their power to resist the bill becoming law. They cautioned that if the Irish National Volunteers became armed they would retain these arms for use after the war was over.[26] There were also dissenting voices within Irish nationalism, with Sinn Féin warning that a victorious England in the war would be more powerful, and therefore Ireland's claim for home rule might be dismissed.[27] Overall though, the response to Redmond's House of Commons speech was enthusiastic, positive and supportive.

Later that month, Redmond presented the colours to 3,000 Irish Volunteers gathered at the GAA grounds in Maryborough, Queen's County. Here he reiterated the pledge offered in the Commons for the defence of Ireland, stating that Volunteers north and south would stand 'shoulder to shoulder' to 'defend

18 *DrI*, 8 Aug. 1914.   19 *CCh*, 8 Aug. 1914.   20 *CE*, 4 and 5 Aug. 1914.   21 *LL*, 5 Aug. 1914. 22 Cooper lost his seat in the Dec. 1910 general election.   23 *IT*, 8 Aug. 1914.   24 *LG*, 6 Aug. 1914.   25 *KMo*, 15 and 20 Aug. 1914.   26 *BNL*, 4 Aug. 1914.   27 *SF*, 8 Aug. 1914.

the good order and peace of Ireland, and defend her shores against foreign foe'.[28] His primary motive for suggesting the combining of Volunteer organizations was to forge comradeship between Ulster and Irish National Volunteers to neutralize the sectarian divides that existed between many unionists and nationalists, to create what he called 'a free and united Ireland – united North and South, Catholic and Protestant'. For a short period of time it appeared that Redmond's aspirations for unity settled the aggressive and sectarian rift that had developed, and averted the threat of civil war.

In the Maryborough speech there are clear signs that Redmond was contemplating Volunteer service at the frontline of the war. Evidence lies in his comments about a press account of the Inniskilling Fusiliers being escorted by the Ulster and Irish Volunteers from Enniskillen to 'the seat of war', when he prayed to God that this 'may be an omen for the future'.[29] He could have simply been hoping for future continued cooperation between Irish and Ulster Volunteers for the movement of troops on Irish soil; or, he could have been hoping that these forces would ultimately take their own place at the seat of war to advance the cause of home rule by building camaraderie on the battlefield. The latter seems more likely, which is supported by his remarks that the ideal of the Volunteers is 'at any cost and any sacrifice to create a united nation'. More importantly, however, Redmond did not want to actively recruit enlistment for the war effort until Ireland's demands for home rule were secured. He certainly encouraged Irishmen to contemplate enlisting by flattering them, stating that they were the 'sons of the greatest fighting race in the history of the world'.[30] The language and terminology of Redmond's speech to the Volunteers at Maryborough was rousing and motivating, and it was employed to persuade them to discharge their duty as Irishmen in the Great War for the cause of home rule.

The home rule bill became law on 18 September, although a suspensory bill postponed its enactment for the duration of the war, and an amendment clause for Ulster was added. 'Cheers loud and prolonged' followed in the House of Commons, and in Ireland Redmond received widespread praise for the passing of the bill.[31] For instance, the *Anglo-Celt* reported on T.J. Hanna's statement that he had been 'directed by Mr John E. Redmond to acknowledge receipt of Cavan Council's resolution congratulating him and the Irish Party relative to the passing of the home rule bill'.[32]

Two days later, on 20 September, Redmond – while driving with his wife to his Irish home in Aughavannagh, Co. Wicklow – detoured to a Volunteer meeting in Woodenbridge. He stressed again that the primary duty of Ireland's 'manhood' was to defend the shores of Ireland from foreign invasion. But,

---

28 *Weekly Irish Times*, 22 Aug. 1914: Redmond at Maryborough. 29 See *Strabane Chronicle*, 15 Aug. 1914 for the account of the Inniskilling Fusiliers, with the headline 'Unite to send off Inniskillings', although Redmond only refers to reading an 'account' in the 'public press'. See *IT*, 16 Aug. 1914 for Redmond's Maryborough speech. 30 *IT*, 16 Aug. 1914: Redmond at Maryborough. 31 See *UH*, 26 Sept. 1914 for House of Commons reaction to the passing of the home rule bill. 32 *AC*, 7 Nov. 1914.

Redmond went a step further and stated that it was the duty of the Volunteers 'to account yourselves as men not only in Ireland itself, but wherever the firing line extends'.[33] In broadening the Volunteers' mandate, Redmond verbalized his previous intimations in the Commons and at Maryborough. His hope was to create a universal sentiment of 'Irishness' that would be forged through common sacrifice on the battlefields of Europe. Ireland's moral duty to support the war would, he believed, bring political benefits, as he stated in December 1914: 'if ... we seized the opportunity to stab her [Britain] in the back, the home rule settlement would not be worth an hour's purchase ... I believe that Ireland would have been dishonoured before the world if she took such a course as this.'[34]

Earlier in September 1914, Prime Minister Herbert H. Asquith had visited Dublin and further substantiated Redmond's war effort. This visit was extensively reported on in the regional newspapers. The *Southern Star* commented that the prime minister was received with 'loud and prolonged cheering', the *Kerry News* remarked on the 'crowded attendance' in the Mansion House and the *Anglo-Celt* reported on 'a scene of immense enthusiasm'.[35] In petitioning for recruits, Asquith appealed on the grounds that Irishmen did not want to see the Belgian towns and villages 'devastated by marauders' and her fields 'drenched with the blood of her soldiers', and that Ireland and England's common foe was Germany. Asquith also stated that the Irish Volunteers were to be a 'permanent, integral, and characteristic part of the defence forces of the crown'.[36] These words certainly implied a distinctive Irish brigade or corps, particularly because of his use of the word 'characteristic', suggesting the Irish Volunteers would be visibly distinctive. At Woodenbridge, Redmond had claimed the right for Ireland to have an expeditionary force that would be kept together as an Irish unit in order to 'gain national credit for their deeds, and feel like other communities of the empire'. Carson had managed to create a distinctive division for unionists – the 36th Ulster Division. Despite Redmond's appeals for comradery and unity, there was an underlying fear that the unionist side would gain advantage because of political volatility due to the war. However, Redmond did not succeed in his appeal for a distinctive Irish brigade because Lord Kitchener, secretary of state for war, maintained that the creation of such a force would lead directly to civil war, and perhaps to revolution.[37]

In the latter months of 1914 Redmond found an eloquent war voice which he used to encourage Irishmen to enlist. However, he continued to maintain that enlistment was a matter of one's own conscience and a matter of free will.[38] Other Irish Party

33 Martin, *The Irish Volunteers*, p. 148: Redmond's speech to Volunteers at Woodenbridge.   34 National Library of Ireland (NLI), Redmond Papers (RP), MS 15,524: Redmond to Fitzpatrick, 16 Dec. 1914. 35 *KN*, 28 Sept. 1914; *SSt*, 3 Oct. 1914; *AC*, 3 Oct. 1914. Reports of Asquith in Dublin appear in other regional newspapers, such as: *SSt*, 3 Oct. 1914; *FH*, 3 Oct. 1914; *TH*, 10 Oct. 1914; and *MC*, 3 Oct. 1914. 36 *IT*, 3 Oct. 1914: report of Asquith's speech.   37 NLI, RP, MS 15,215/2/A: T.P. O'Connor to John Redmond, 19 Feb. 1915. The 10th and 16th Divisions were primarily Irish, although the Irish designation denoted the recruiting area, but the division had no distinguishing nationalist characteristic.   38 *IT*, 26 Oct. 1914: Redmond in Belfast.

MPs supported this claim, for instance William O'Malley, MP for Galway, pointed out that 'there would be no compulsion on any man to join the army; unlike Germany ... conscription did not prevail'.[39] Redmond honed in on German atrocities in Belgium to raise empathy with the plight of a small Catholic nation. 'It is true ... our cities have not been sacked; it is true our cathedrals and our universities have not been burned to the ground,' he said, claiming this was due to the 'brave men – thank God, many of them gallant Irishmen – who are day and night risking and giving their lives to defend our property, our liberty and our honour'.[40] His stated compassion with and identification to the plight of Belgium clearly captivated the Irish people. Regional newspapers, such as the *Anglo-Celt*, reported on fundraising endeavours set up in various counties to provide finance 'for the Belgian refugees who are coming to town'.[41] Fundraising was discussed at a meeting in Monaghan, and the Cavan Urban Council agreed to take 20 Belgian refugees.[42] The *Nationalist and Leinster Times* stated that Belgian refugees began arriving in Carlow by train in 1915, and a large number of people lined the platform to give the visitors a 'most enthusiastic reception'. A moving report in this newspaper commented that, 'realizing all the sufferings they had endured, and thinking of their homes and hearths which had been foully desecrated ... [they] broke down completely, weeping bitterly'.[43] Belgium's suffering at the hands of the Germans became material for seven-inch, two-column wartime recruitment advertisements, which intensified in late 1914 and early 1915, in nearly all regional newspapers. The emotive appeal 'Is Ireland to Share Belgium's Fate?', with straplines that generated fear and concern, encouraged the 'men of Ireland' to enlist for 'defeating the Germans in Belgium': 'Read what the Germans have done to the churches, priests, women and children of Belgium.'[44]

At Woodenbridge, Redmond's encouragement of the Volunteers to enlist and fight 'wherever the firing line extends' caused alarm among members of the original committee of the Irish Volunteers. They issued a manifesto declaring that Redmond had announced a policy that was 'fundamentally at variance with their own published and accepted aims and objects'.[45] This manifesto stated that 'Ireland cannot, with honour or safety, take part in foreign quarrels otherwise than through the free action of a national government of her own.' They repudiated the claim of any man to offer up 'the blood and the lives of the sons of Irishmen and Irishwomen on the service of the British empire while the national government ... is not allowed to exist'.[46] This difference of opinion caused a split in the Irish Volunteer movement. Prior to the split the numbers enrolled in the Volunteers totalled approximately 188,000, and of this 13,000 adhered to

---

39 *CT*, 17 Oct. 1914: speech of William O'Malley, MP; McConnel, 'Recruiting sergeants for John Bull?', p. 412.   40 See *UH*, 3 Oct. 1914, for full speech.   41 *AC*, 31 Oct. 1914.   42 Ibid.   43 *CN*, 9 Jan. 1915.   44 For examples, see *NG*, 13 Mar. 1915 and *CTe*, 6 Mar. 1915.   45 Martin, *The Irish Volunteers*, pp 152–5.   46 F.S.L. Lyons, *Ireland since the Famine* (London, 1971), p. 341. The circular issued by the Provisional Committee HQ opposing Redmond's call also rejected Redmond's entitlement to 'any place in the administration and guidance of the Irish Volunteer organization': Galway County Council Archives, City Corps correspondence, GS13/02, 24 Sept. 1914.

the original Provisional Committee.[47] In other words, the vast majority declared in favour of Redmond. While there was much praise of Redmond and while many Volunteers supported him, in reality only about one in ten of the National Volunteers actually signed up for military service in 1914–15. Redmond was quick to point out that this overlooked the fact of high emigration from Ireland which left the country with fewer men of fighting age, and the fact that Ireland's rural agricultural society was less able to discharge young men for military service.[48] The 13,000 who joined Eoin MacNeill's faction is not an inconsequential number, however it is small by comparison to the 175,000 who remained with the National Volunteers. MacNeill offered no realistic political alternative to home rule, patent in his article 'The north began' for *An Claidheamh Soluis* in November 1913, where his main point was that 'Feudalism in Ireland is doating as well as decaying'. His ultimate solution was that the empire either make terms with Ireland or let Ireland go her own way – a mission, it could be argued, that Redmond was already in the process of trying to achieve.[49]

The initial response to the Woodenbridge speech across most of the regional media (which included unionists and nationalists) was largely positive. An example is the *Nationalist and Leinster Times*, which reported on various Volunteer meetings held throughout Cos. Carlow, Kildare, Wexford and Wicklow and Queen's County, where statements of support were published, such as:

> Carlow District Council SUPPORTS IRISH LEADER'S ATTITUDE: We again desire to record the fact that this county never wavered in allegiance to him [Redmond], nor doubted the success of his able leadership. We are in a position to say that in all Carlow, there is not one follower of the factionist manifesto which would subject the National Volunteers to irresponsible nobodies.

Similar headlines were: 'Boys of Wexford for Redmond'; 'Castledermot Company of the Irish Volunteers at a meeting decided to support Mr Redmond'; and 'Erill in Queen's County gives loyal adherence to Mr Redmond'.[50] The *Connacht Tribune* on 17 October 1914, upon the announcement that home rule was to be placed on the statute book, condemned the 'action of the minority of the Provisional Committee, and we pledge our loyal support to Mr John E. Redmond'. In Oughterard, Co. Galway, the 'strong denunciation of the recent antics of an insignificant section of Irish factionists' was placed on record.[51]

Redmond's Woodenbridge speech directly appealed for Volunteers to serve abroad, where his aspiration was that after sharing 'the bloody sacrament of

47 Lee, *Ireland, 1912–1985*, p. 22: Lee provides these figures (188,000 to 13,000) in favour of Redmond. There are variations in these figures by different authorities on the subject, however the overall ratios are similar. 48 According to House of Commons 1914 emigration statistics (CD 7883) the total number that emigrated in 1914 was 20,583 (males and females). This was a decrease of 10,653 when compared against 1913 records. It does not include seasonal migration. 49 Martin, *The Irish Volunteers*, pp 57–61. 50 *CN*, 10 Oct. 1914; *CT*, 17 Oct. 1914. 51 *CT*, 17 Oct. 1914.

the battlefield', unionists and nationalists would avoid the exclusion of Ulster (or parts thereof) from the home rule bill by consent. This aspiration cannot be entirely dismissed, given that many prominent southern unionists joined the National Volunteers or shared recruiting platforms with nationalists. Yet, leading and prominent Ulster unionists remained determined in their opinion that home rule would never be accepted. Sir George Richardson, general of the Ulster Volunteers, stated in the *Daily Chronicle* that 'when the war was over and their [the army and navy] ranks were reinforced by some 12,000 men thoroughly well-trained and with vast field experience, they would return to the attack and relegate home rule to the devil'.[52] Therefore, regardless of battlefield sacrifices, it was unlikely that home rule would appeal to ardent unionists in Ulster after the war either.

It could also be argued that Redmond seriously miscalculated when he encouraged the Irish Volunteers to support the war effort 'wherever the firing line extends', by promoting foreign service prior to bargaining for a specific Irish Brigade or obtaining distinctive insignia for National Volunteer divisions in the Great War. Stephen Gwynn attributes blame to the petty bureaucracy of the War Office, who caused the most comprehensive damage to Redmond's vision of an Irish army in France and Flanders.[53] While Redmond's Woodenbridge speech caused a split in the Volunteer movement, his words proved inspiring among those who remained, and influenced positive reports in the print media. The *Westmeath Independent* maintained that 'the best way for Irishmen to woo Ulster and defend Ireland's rights after the war, was to 'play their part well now'.[54] The *Sligo Champion* stated that recruiting was vital for the successful implementation of home rule.[55] Popular opinion had largely taken Redmond's side in 1914 and early 1915.

The anticipated short war extended into a prolonged war, and the initial high praise for Redmond and the Irish Party declined substantially as the party faced formidable challenges. Newspaper reports on the heavy death toll at the Western Front led to diminished recruitment and provided fodder for anti-war and anti-recruitment campaigns. Reports from the War Office in December 1915 stated that 119,923 had been killed and 338,758 wounded, and that 69,546 were missing.[56]

The issue of conscription dogged the Irish Party throughout the war years, even though spokesmen rejected rumours that it would impact on Ireland. Redmond persistently maintained that 'the enforcement of conscription in Ireland is an impossibility'.[57] The introduction of the military services bill for Britain in the House of Commons in early January 1916 led to renewed protests from nationalists. Nationalists in the House of Commons voted against the bill and finally convinced the government to exempt Ireland. However, in 1918 the British coalition government, under David Lloyd George, extended the military services

---

52 NLI, RP, MS 15,215/2/1, NLI, *DC*, 26 Oct. 1914.   53 Gwynn, *John Redmond's last years*, p. 162. 54 *WI*, 26 Sept. 1914.   55 *SC*, 26 Sept. 1914; see also Wheatley, *Nationalism and the Irish Party*, p. 208. 56 Finnan, *John Redmond and Irish unity*, p. 109.   57 NLI, RP, MS 15,165, NLI: Redmond to Asquith, 15 Nov. 1915.

bill to Ireland, connecting it to a new home rule settlement. This had the effect of alienating both nationalists and unionists.[58] On 21 April 1918 an anti-conscription pledge was taken throughout Ireland, and a few days later at a conference of all nationalist leaders in Dublin, the words of this pledge were ratified. Conscription became the catalyst for the mobilization of nationalist Ireland to resist the imposition of an unacceptable edict by the British government. The Irish Party at times struggled to defend the indefensible, such as their continued support for recruitment while simultaneously opposing conscription.

The 1916 Easter Rising and subsequent executions and arrests of over 3,000 people caused difficulties for the Irish Party. However, this Rising did not occur until late April 1916, yet enlistment into the army by Irishmen (nationalist and unionist) had begun to decline rapidly as early as February 1916. While no political party could claim the legacy of the Easter Rising, it led to the reorganization of Sinn Féin, particularly during the by-elections of 1917 and 1918.[59] The Irish Party now faced a strong challenge from an organized nationalist party with separatist tendencies. During the war years, Sinn Féin and others opposed to the Irish Party engaged in anti-war activity that largely comprised speech-making and articles against recruitment. This increased in 1918 with the conscription crisis. As early as 1915 Augustine Birrell, chief secretary for Ireland, warned Redmond that 'the revolutionary propaganda grows in strength and ... in confidence'.[60]

In 1914 (and through much of 1915 and 1916) after Redmond's House of Commons speech and his Maryborough and Woodenbridge addresses to Volunteers, the majority of regional press reports attest to the Irish Party's political supremacy and demonstrate that Redmond went unchallenged in most parts of southern Ireland.[61] The enlistment figures of 50,107 at the start of the war in 1914 (up to February 1915)[62] provide some indication that Redmond's recruitment call inspired many to enlist.[63] Michael Wheatley claims that 'all Irish opinion backed Redmond, who had offered the hand of friendship to England in her greatest difficulty'.[64] Reports and commentary in Ireland's regional press substantiate this statement and verify Redmond's popular appeal in his support of Britain in the Great War at that time. The regional press dedicated many column inches to detailed news of the Great War; they reflected opinion and sentiment in

---

58 Alan J. Ward, 'Lloyd George and the 1918 Irish conscription crisis', *Historical Journal*, 27:1 (1974), p. 111.   59 Sinn Féin in the early war years largely comprised Arthur Griffith's followers and was a small political party, but, as the war years progressed, the name came to represent any Irish nationalist opposed to the Irish Party and home rule.   60 NLI, RP, MS 15,169/5735: Birrell to Redmond, 19 Dec. 1915. 61 David Fitzpatrick, *Politics and Irish life, 1913–1921: provincial experience of war and revolution* (Cork, 1977), p. 90.   62 Jeffery, *Ireland and the Great War*, p. 7, table 1.   63 Jeffery suggests that a total of 140,460 Irish recruits were raised during the war, which is lower than David Fitzpatrick's figure of 210,000. Jeffery states that Fitzpatrick's 'careful and reliable' total includes the 58,000 existing Irish regulars and reservists in 1914 and several thousand officers: Jeffery, *Ireland and the Great War*, pp 5–6; David Fitzpatrick, 'Militarism in Ireland, 1900–1922' in Thomas Bartlett and Keith Jeffery, *A military history of Ireland* (Cambridge, 1997), pp 386–8.   64 Wheatley, *Nationalism and the Irish Party*, p. 202.

their editorials and letters to the editor, and attested to the favourable resolutions of local county councils.

The regional press clearly demonstrates that the mood of the nation was solidly behind Redmond's call to support the Great War effort in 1914. However, the rising death toll, conscription, ambiguities over the suspension of home rule, the rise of Sinn Féin, the aftermath of the Easter Rising, labour unrest, the Spanish flu epidemic, and the death of John Redmond in 1918 altered the mood in subsequent years. Ireland's regional press continued to observe, interpret and exemplify these changes.

'Sledge-hammers and blue pencils': censorship, suppression and the Irish regional press, 1916–23

DONAL Ó DRISCEOIL

The years of the First World War, the war of independence and civil war were turbulent for the commercial press in Ireland, especially in the regions. In addition to the inconvenience of newsprint shortages and disruption to transport and communications, Irish regional newspapers, like the rest of the Irish press, were subjected to a variety of forms of interference and control from a number of different sources from the outbreak of war in 1914 to the end of the civil war in 1923. They were targeted by the British press censor, the IRA, the Black and Tans and Auxiliaries, the British army, the national army, the provisional/Free State government and the anti-treaty IRA, all of whom by their actions were acknowledging the influential role of these publications. Dozens of regional titles were suppressed or attacked in this period, while all were affected by censorship, official and unofficial, at each phase.

DORA

The Defence of the Realm Act (DORA), passed by the British parliament at the outbreak of war in August 1914, gave wide-ranging draconian powers to the state, formalized in an extensive set of Defence of the Realm Regulations (DRR) 'for securing the public safety and defence of the realm'; these included the power to severely restrict freedom of expression. The main regulations in this regard related to the protection of military information, and the prohibition of material deemed prejudicial to recruitment or intended or likely to cause disaffection with the king. Wartime press censorship was implemented by the press bureau in London, and the Irish press was subjected to identical war-related control as its British counterpart. Censorship of the British press was primarily war-related, though it seeped into the political realm also, with powers being used against dissidents, such as conscientious objectors and radical labour.[1] This politicization of censorship was facilitated by the vagueness of terminology in

1 See, for example, D. Hopkin, 'Domestic censorship in the First World War', *Journal of Contemporary History*, 5:4 (1970), pp 151–69, and B. Millman, 'HMG and the war against dissent, 1914–18', *Journal of Contemporary History*, 40:3, pp 413–40.

DORA, such as 'likely to cause disaffection', and would be far more evident in Ireland after 1916, when Ireland-specific press censorship was established.

The vast majority of regional papers, in common with their metropolitan counterparts, reflected either the constitutional nationalist consensus or a solid unionist position. Following the outbreak of war, almost all editorially supported the British war effort, with the nationalist titles backing Irish Parliamentary Party leader John Redmond's pro-war/recruitment policy, some more enthusiastically than others. War reportage, meanwhile, was dependent on press-agency reports filtered through the British censorship system, all of which made action against the regional papers unnecessary. The *Meath Chronicle* was the only mainstream paper identified by the new undersecretary for Ireland, Mathew Nathan, following his appointment in October 1914, as meriting 'special consideration'; the other publications he highlighted were Arthur Griffith's *Sinn Féin*, the *Irish Volunteer*, Terence MacSwiney's *Fianna Fáil*, James Connolly's *Irish Worker* and the IRB's *Irish Freedom*.[2] The *Chronicle* remained committed to constitutional nationalism; its criticism of Redmond's commitment of the Volunteers to the British war effort was the probable reason for its coming to notice. When the authorities eventually acted against 'seditious' publications in December 1914, however, neither the *Meath Chronicle* nor any other commercial newspaper was targeted. Sporadic action against republican journals continued up until the Easter Rising, after which the landscape underwent a transformation.

The first regional newspaper to be suppressed in this period was the *Enniscorthy Echo*, which was shut down by the authorities immediately following the 1916 Rising and remained out of circulation until February 1917. The *Echo* was the most republican of all the regional papers; its editor and proprietor William Sears was a Sinn Féiner, and many of his staff, such as Bob Brennan and Sean Etchingham, were prominent Wexford republicans. It was Sears who proposed the establishment of the *Irish Volunteer*, which was first published in February 1914, printed by the *Echo* and edited by one of its staff, Laurence de Lacy. Enniscorthy rose in 1916, and the Volunteers (led by the *Echo*'s Bob Brennan) held the town for five days, before agreeing to surrender on 1 May. Sears and several members of his *Echo* staff were among those arrested and interned in the aftermath.[3]

DECIES

In the immediate aftermath of the Easter Rising the British military commander in Ireland, General Sir John G. Maxwell, blamed a distorted portrayal in the press for the negative public reaction to his repressive policies. Annoyed by the increasing appearance of what he saw as 'subversive' opinions in the Irish press, many of which were reprinted from mainstream American newspapers, he demanded a strengthening

2 L. Ó Broin, *Dublin Castle and the 1916 Rising* (New York, 1971), pp 22–5, 37–40. 3 See *The 1916 Rising and County Wexford: an educational resource* (Wexford, 2016), pp 8, 32.

of press control.[4] An Irish system of press censorship, separate from but complementary to the press bureau's operation in London, was established. The well-known sporting peer Lord Decies, a press officer on his staff, was appointed at the end of May 1916 to head it up.[5] On 1 June Maxwell wrote to Irish editors informing them that they were to submit copies of their published papers to army headquarters for examination, and the press censor warned them about publishing the following types of material lest they breach the Defence of the Realm Regulations (DRR) and expose themselves to suppression: resolutions and speeches of corporations, county councils, urban councils and boards of guardians; letters from soldiers connected with 'the late Rising' in Dublin; extracts from American newspapers or private letters to the press from America; criticisms 'of a violent nature', in the form of letters from individuals, related to the Rising; letters from detainees; 'indiscretions' made by other papers, either in the foreign or home press.[6]

When the *Kilkenny People* failed to submit a published copy in the first week of censorship, it was immediately warned via the local RIC that unless it complied, it would be forced to submit full proofs *before* publication (an intolerable burden for a regional paper), and that failure to do that would result in suppression. Its proprietor and editor, E.T. Keane, a former Parnellite who was embracing republicanism, had been warned in a letter from Maxwell on 28 May that his 'Voice of the People' editorial on 20 May was 'written with the intention of inciting the people against the military authorities', making the paper liable to suppression under DORA, and instructing him to submit proofs to the district inspector (DI) of the RIC in Kilkenny. Keane published the letter from Maxwell, whom he described as 'the military dictator who rules Ireland', on 3 June, leaving blank spaces in lieu of his reply and further correspondence, which had been refused publication by the DI. 'If the "Voice of the People" cannot speak free and untrammelled', declared Keane, 'it will not speak in the accents of slavery'. The editorial of 10 June again contained blanks that highlighted censorship, and Keane further annoyed the authorities by publishing in pamphlet form the correspondence that he had been prohibited from publishing in his paper. Local censorship by the RIC now ceased and the paper operated henceforth under Decies' new regime, testing the latter's self-proclaimed 'moderation' to its limits.[7]

Gradually, the Office of the Press Censor (OPC) began to issue specific directions to the press about what not to publish, such as the notice sent in August 1916 forbidding reports of a Listowel board of guardians' resolution condemning the execution of Roger Casement. The *Liberator* of Tralee, sister paper of the *Kerryman* (one of the earliest of the regional papers to come out in explicit support of the rebels), published the resolution with comments

---

4 C. Townshend, *Easter 1916: the Irish rebellion* (London 2005), p. 308. 5 For a detailed examination of the Irish press censorship in this period, see D. Ó Drisceoil, 'Keeping disloyalty within bounds? British media control in Ireland, 1914–29', *Irish Historical Studies*, 38:149 (May 2012), pp 52–69. 6 Decies to all editors, 5 June 1916, Office of the Press Censor (OPC) 3/128, National Archives of Ireland (NAI). 7 *Kilkenny People*, 3 and 10 June 1916; RIC DI, Kilkenny to Decies, 11 June 1916, OPC 1/20, NAI.

under the heading 'Ireland's Greatest Martyr', without reference to the OPC. The attorney general recommended warning the editor, which was done. In the meantime, on 19 August the paper published a letter – which had not been submitted to the OPC – on the prison treatment of Kerry rebel Austin Stack headed 'Atrocious and Barbarous'. When this was reproduced by the *Kerryman*, the papers' printing plant was seized on 29 August, the first punitive action of its kind by the authorities since the establishment of the system. The paper was out of circulation until the plant was restored on 21 September, following the signing of a bond by the publishers promising not to reoffend.[8]

THE OPC'S 'ADVICE'

More generalized instructions were also issued in the early months that had the effect of strengthening self-censorship and overall censorship control. The seizure of the *Kerryman*'s plant was a reminder to all editors and proprietors of the potential consequences of not following the OPC's 'advice'. The *Midland Reporter*, published in Boyle, Co. Roscommon, had a narrow escape in September when Decies argued successfully against Maxwell that the paper should not be suppressed for reprinting 'Tales of Rebellion' from the *New York Times*; a severe warning was issued to the *Midland Reporter* instead – and also the following week to the *Roscommon Herald*, which published the same piece.[9] The *Cork Free Press*, which traditionally represented the views of the anti-Redmond constitutional nationalist All-for-Ireland League but was edited by republican Frank Gallagher and had a number of other republicans on its staff, was sailing close to the wind and also narrowly escaped suppression in September.[10] In general, however, the shift in public opinion away from constitutionalism and towards militant separatism was not yet reflected in the regional press. A military intelligence report from the south of the country in October 1916 noted that the press remained generally 'friendly', despite active opposition to the threat of conscription, with only the *Kilkenny People* and the *Cork Free Press* being identified as hostile. The former was noted as having 'a very large circulation among the lower classes, and I consider it one of the main causes of unrest and disaffection in that district'. The hostility of the *Cork Free Press* was put down partly to the separatist politics of a number of its staff, and partly to the paper's popularity among advanced nationalists, to which it had to cater. In a condescending assessment, the writer summarized the importance of the regional press:

> Owing to the fact that the standard of education is very low, the press has great influence in the country districts, the views of the people being

8 Correspondence regarding the *Kerryman* and *Liberator*, 13 Aug. to 21 Sept. 1916, OPC 2/89, NAI.
9 Correspondence regarding the *Midland Reporter* and *Roscommon Herald*, Sept. 1916, OPC 1/30, NAI.
10 Correspondence regarding the *Cork Free Press*, CO 904/160, Sept. 1916, NAUK.

drawn from the local paper, the priest and the national school master. Anything that appears in print is quoted as truth ...[11]

The press censorship regime moved from military to civilian control in November 1916, but maintained the same policy and approach. In discussions with his superiors, Decies successfully argued for the continuation of his moderate or liberal censorship regime. This was not only because 'Sinn Féin thrives upon repression' and under a subtle censorship 'Sinn Féin policy, comment and argument ... reaches the public in a diluted form', but also because that way, international – especially American – opinion could be given the impression that expression in Ireland was relatively free.[12] The hope was that Ireland would be pacified to allow Britain to concentrate on the war, the crisis of British governance would pass, 'disloyalty' and 'extremism' would be corralled, and the transition to some form of home rule would occur. The OPC's light-touch regulation did require occasional repressive actions to underpin it; on 13 November 1916, for example, the plant and type of the *Southern Star* in Skibbereen, Co. Cork, were seized by order of Maxwell, putting the paper out of circulation until 16 December, because of an editorial on 4 November that railed against Dublin Castle's penalization of members of the Dublin Metropolitan Police who had joined the Catholic organization the Ancient Order of Hibernians, while membership of the (Protestant) Freemasons was allowed; this, according to the *Star*, showed the authorities to be 'anti-Irish and alien', with a 'glaring and ill-concealed contempt' for the Irish people and the Catholic church.[13]

The OPC regularly issued circulars to the press relating to specific events, reminding editors to submit matters – relating to recruitment, Irish Volunteer drilling, republican speeches, prisoners and so on – that might 'offend' against the DRR. Summarizing what he regarded as 'seditious matter' for the editor of the *Tipperary Star* in mid-1917, Decies explained that reference to the Sinn Féin movement or republican songs (so long as extracts were not given) or republican flags was not 'prima facie objectionable'; but where language was reproduced, such as in reports of speeches, that 'justifies the late rebellion, advocates the principle of rebellion in Ireland, or incites to unlawful acts', these were clearly precluded by the DRR.[14] Such references were frequently excised from reports in regional newspapers, as were allusions to Britain's fortunes in the war. Editors also had to be reminded not to publish numbers of battalions and regiments, the names of commanders or orders or addresses by commanders in the field, and to submit any letters received from Irish soldiers on the front.[15]

---

11 Military Intelligence reports from the Southern District, 2 and 30 Oct. 1916, CO 904/157, NAUK. 12 Press Censorship Monthly Report (PCMR), Aug. 1918, CO 904/166, NAUK, and Decies to Chief Secretary's Office, 6 Aug. 1918, OPC 6/1, NAI. 13 *SSt*, 4 Nov. 1916. 14 Decies to editor, *Tipperary Star*, 24 July 1917, OPC 2/99, NAI. 15 PCMR, Aug. 1917.

A 'CERTAIN LATITUDE'

The released 1916 commander Éamon de Valera ran for Sinn Féin in the East Clare by-election in July 1917. A 'certain latitude' was given to the publication of his 'inflammatory' speeches in the hope that 'their violence would alarm moderate opinion' and create a 're-action against extremist policy', but to no avail – he swept to victory. This policy was then dropped, and reports of Sinn Féin election speeches were heavily censored.[16] The *Kilkenny People* celebrated de Valera's victory and was suppressed on 18 July. The suppression removed a key press supporter of the Sinn Féin candidate W.T. Cosgrave in the upcoming Kilkenny by-election on 10 August 1917. Cosgrave won the seat comfortably nonetheless, and anger at the suppression may have bolstered Sinn Féin support. From the OPC's perspective, however, the effect of the *Kilkenny People* ban was to greatly increase the number of proofs submitted by regional newspapers. Police intelligence reports from the south of the country also noted the 'chastening effect' the suppression had on other local editors.[17] The paper remained out of circulation for twelve weeks, returning on 13 October, in its own words, 'bloody, but unbowed'.

In the meantime, the death of republican prisoner Thomas Ashe in Mountjoy Jail in September 1917 as a result of force-feeding created a major problem for Decies and his staff, as well as for the Dublin Castle regime more generally. Ashe's death became a huge cause célèbre in Ireland, and the press was warned to take the 'greatest care' regarding the case, to submit all letters and publish nothing 'likely to cause disaffection'. The Catholic bishop of Killaloe, Dr Fogarty, sent a condemnatory letter to the press, which concluded: 'The world sees already in these hideous atrocities what the triumph of "English culture" means for small nationalities.' The OPC told the press not to publish it, but the *Freeman's Journal* and the *Clare Champion* both defied the order. The authorities were reluctant to act against the *Freeman's Journal*, the prominent press voice of moderate nationalism (and could hardly justify singling out the *Champion*), while also being anxious not to be seen to censor a bishop.[18] Decies sought a clear reassertion of the OPC's power from his superiors, but none was forthcoming as Chief Secretary Henry Duke's Irish policy continued to drift. On Duke's initiative, there was a brief relaxation of censorship in October 1917. This 'temporary licence for seditious utterances' also backfired. There was confusion and annoyance in the press, and regional papers took the opportunity to feature more material on Sinn Féin and the Volunteers, with reports of drilling, marches and speeches. Decies believed that, if left unchecked, this would rapidly develop into the publication of 'military orders to rebel forces'. He re-asserted his control in November, and issued a warning to all editors that they were to publish no

16 Decies to attorney general, 17 July 1917 and to Duke, 24 July 1917, OPC 3/147 and 1/6, NAI; PCMR, Aug. 1917.   17 PCMR, Aug. 1917; Military Intelligence report from Southern District, 31 Aug. 1917, CO 904/157, NAUK.   18 Circulars and correspondence regarding Ashe, OPC 9/171 and 10/22, Sept.– Oct. 1917, NAI; PCMR, Sept. 1917.

such reports unless the events discussed therein were the subject matter of a prosecution. Such censorship was justified, he told Duke, because this publicity disclosed the 'most unsettled, dangerous condition in the country' and was likely, as well as causing disaffection, to be of use to the enemy, Germany.[19]

The move had the desired effect of removing reports of republican displays from the press, but republican momentum continued to gather across the country. Regional newspapers tended to follow their readers in shifting their sympathies towards Sinn Féin and the Volunteers; many began to feature syndicated 'Sinn Féin Notes' from late 1917, and some papers, like the *Galway Express* and the *Southern Star*, had been taken over by republicans by early 1918. By the end of 1917, one army intelligence report for the south and west reported that the 'Local press has been, as a whole, captured by Sinn Fein – that is, it produces what will be acceptable to its readers.' (This reflected the pattern during and after the Land War, the last example of mass politicization in rural Ireland, when twenty-four regional papers switched allegiance to explicit nationalism in the 1878–90 period.[20]) According to the authorities, even papers that held the Redmondite line editorially still 'gave Sinn Féin the utmost publicity'. 'The attitude of the local nationalist press', according to an intelligence report of November 1917, '... is to write milk and water editorials against Sinn Féin, while advertising it without stint in their news columns'.[21]

ENDGAME

The problem for the Decies policy of diluting the Sinn Féin message was that the earlier stream of publicity in relation to republicanism had become a flood. The political temperature was rising in early 1918 as the prospect of conscription being imposed on Ireland loomed and the food crisis worsened. Cattle drives and land seizures alarmed the authorities, and Clare was declared a special military area in February. The *Galway Express, Connacht Tribune, Weekly Observer* and *Westmeath Independent* had all been 'severely warned' and threatened with suppression in December 1917 and January 1918. Duke's administration seemed to be losing control, and Sinn Féin and the Volunteers grew in strength and confidence, along with the Irish Transport and General Workers' Union and the wider labour movement. The chief secretary wanted censorship eased or even abolished in the hope that moderate Sinn Féiners would be alarmed and alienated from the 'extreme section'. Decies argued that the result would be 'chaos', with the press 'flooded with seditious matter, which would be extremely difficult to handle with prosecutions'. Duke then suggested that 'a collected mass of the outrageous utterances of professed rebels should be published all at once with appropriate ridicule and condemnation in order to inform Great Britain, disgust

19 PCMR, Nov. 1917; Decies to Duke, 26 Nov. 1917, OPC 5/47, NAI. 20 Marie-Louise Legg, *Newspapers and nationalism: the Irish provincial press, 1850–1892* (Dublin, 1998), p. 128. 21 Military Intelligence reports from Southern District, 31 Oct. and 30 Nov. 1917, CO 904/157, NAUK.

people of common sense, frighten the timid and possibly enlist the condemnation of the church'.[22] Such was the desperation within Dublin Castle.

It was in this atmosphere that the British announced the extension of conscription to Ireland in April 1918. There was an enormous backlash that united nationalist Ireland. Detailed plans for resistance were drawn up, hundreds of thousands signed an anti-conscription pledge, and the country was brought to a halt by a general strike. The OPC's task was hopeless, given the depth and breadth of the opposition. In general, it attempted to keep out the more blatant appeals to armed resistance, and made life a little more difficult by denying newspaper space to notices to union members about the general strike and appeals for contributions to the National Defence Fund.[23] Five regional papers sympathetic to Sinn Féin – the *Weekly Observer* (Newcastlewest), the *Clare Champion*, the *Mayo News*, the *Westmeath Independent* and the *King's County Independent* – were all temporarily suppressed in March and April. The opposition to conscription was ultimately successful, and Sinn Féin gained most of the political kudos. Largely as a result, Duke resigned in May 1918. Lord French was appointed viceroy/lord lieutenant and supreme commander of the British army in Ireland and took a more hard-line approach, but was persuaded to allow Decies to continue his conciliatory censorship hand in hand with the wave of repression he initiated. In July, Sinn Féin, the Irish Volunteers, Cumann na mBan and the Gaelic League were banned and a licensing system for public gatherings was introduced, effectively pushing the separatist movement underground. Across the summer and early autumn of 1918 republican pamphlets, leaflets, picture postcards and ballads were seized from printers and newsagents. The *Southern Star* was suppressed on 24 August, and remained out of circulation until March 1919.[24]

The war ended in November 1918, but the Irish censorship regime remained in place, with the December general election looming. Deletions were made to Sinn Féin's 'Manifesto to the Irish People' when it was submitted by the press,[25] and on the eve of the election the machinery of the *Meath Chronicle*, where Sinn Féin election material was being printed, was dismantled by the military.[26] Sinn Féin won a substantial majority of the Irish seats and the elected members who were not imprisoned or on the run assembled on 21 January 1919 for the first meeting of the secessionist parliament, Dáil Éireann. The press was instructed not to publish the Democratic Programme, the Declaration of Independence or speeches proposing and seconding the Declaration. The Message to the Free Nations and the constitution of the Dáil were passed for publication, as well as some minor speeches.[27] The Dáil tried to use the regional press to assert its claim to be the sovereign authority, leading to a ban on the widely featured 'Sinn Féin

22 PCMR, Jan. 1918.   23 PCMR, Apr. 1918.   24 Correspondence regarding the *Southern Star*, Aug. 1918–Apr. 1919, OPC 5/47, NAI.   25 Ibid., Dec. 1918; Decies to undersecretary, 19 Nov. 1918, and chief secretary to Decies, 27 Nov. 1918, OPC 5/47, NAI. For the redacted manifesto, see D. Macardle, *The Irish republic* (Dublin, 1951), pp 921–2.   26 *II*, 4 Dec. 1918.   27 Decies to Press Bureau, 22 Jan. 1919, OPC 8/49 ('new'), NAI.

Notes' in February 1919. Also censored were references to Éamon de Valera as 'president' and to the existence of the 'Republic'.[28] Decies resigned on 28 April 1919 and was replaced by Major Bryan Cooper. His main duties, as he outlined them in a memo, were removing 'offending passages' from reports of seditious speeches, stopping inflammatory letters to the daily press and removing 'violent passages' from accounts of attacks on the police or military. The *Waterford News* was suppressed in May 1919 and the last newspaper to be banned before the end of censorship was the *Kilkenny People* on 12 August, following its publication, in deliberate defiance of the OPC, of extracts from a speech by Count Plunkett.[29] The *People* did not reappear until 13 September.

'LAWLESS CENSORSHIP'

Irish censorship was lifted on the last day of August 1919. On 12 September the Dáil was declared illegal and the Dáil loan to fund the revolutionary government was declared seditious. Advertising its prospectus opened the press to suppression in the new, post-censorship landscape and twenty-five papers in all were suppressed in September and October 1919 for publicizing the loan, including thirteen regional titles. The republican media went underground, and the first edition of the secretly published and highly effective *Irish Bulletin* was produced in November 1919. The *Times* of London condemned the 'dragooning of the Irish press', and gave prominence to a protest letter from Cooper, the recent Censor, which condemned the new policy, especially the suppression of provincial newspapers, 'which only tends to inflame and exasperate moderate opinion in Ireland'.[30] Cooper's warnings were ignored. The experiment of utilizing the indirect power of censorship to keep 'disloyalty' within bounds was deemed to have failed, and was replaced with the direct power of repression and coercion.

According to Secretary to the Treasury Warren Fisher, from the second half of 1919 the authorities drew no distinction between the gunmen, Sinn Féin and the majority of the population who supported the republican agenda: 'they decided that the Irish problem would be settled if the majority of the people in Ireland were forbidden to think, discuss, talk, write or speak the political views they favoured'.[31] What the *Irish Bulletin* dubbed 'lawless censorship' was carried out by the British forces across the country. Key enforcers were the Black and Tans and the Auxiliaries, sent to Ireland to supplement the beleaguered RIC between March and June 1920. Sixteen provincial titles – the *Munster News*, *Leitrim Observer*, *Nenagh Guardian*, *Kerry News*, *Liberator* (Tralee), *Weekly Observer* (Newcastlewest), *Galway Express*, *Kerry Sentinel*, *Westmeath Independent*, *Southern Star*, *Enniscorthy Echo*, *Kerryman*, *Kerry Weekly Reporter*,

28 PCMR, Feb. 1919; chief secretary to Decies, 22 Feb. 1919 and Decies to undersecretary, 11 Aug. 1919, OPC 5/47, NAI.   29 Correspondence, Aug. 1919, OPC 11/136, NAI.   30 *Times*, 27 Sept. 1919.   31 Quoted in E. O'Halpin, *Decline of the union: British government in Ireland, 1892–1920* (Dublin, 1987), p. 190.

Offaly Independent, An Stoc and *Tipperary Star* – were put out of circulation in late 1920 and early 1921, their offices and printing works having been attacked or destroyed either in direct reprisals following the publication of material about the activities of the crown forces, or as part of generalized attacks on towns. The works of the *Kerry News* and *Kerry Weekly Reporter* were destroyed in August 1920, putting them out of circulation until 1924. The *Liberator* of Tralee was gone from April 1921 until August 1923. The burning of the Athlone printing works of the *Westmeath Independent* in November 1920 put more than 100 people out of work and silenced the paper until February 1922. As the *Offaly Independent* and *An Stoc* in Galway were also printed in Athlone, these were also put out of circulation.[32] In July 1920, during an attack on the offices of the *Munster News* in Limerick, the sister of the owner died from injuries received after having jumped from the burning building.[33]

The overall result was restrained and understated coverage of the behaviour of the crown forces in the surviving weeklies, and a decreasing tendency to feature 'Sinn Féin Notes' and Dáil-sourced news. In the eight counties declared to be under martial law in December 1920 and January 1921,[34] the local press was censored by the British forces and compelled to insert matter unfavourable to Sinn Féin and the IRA. In March and April 1921, for example, the *Enniscorthy Echo* was forced to publish extracts from the unionist *Irish Times* (described by the *Irish Bulletin* as 'practically the organ of the English government in Ireland') and the RIC's propagandist *Weekly Summary*, while newspaper correspondents in Cork in the same months were warned by the military not to send reports 'which seem in any way to reflect on the conduct of the crown forces'. They were warned also against 'describing such matters as the execution of rebels in a way which could be considered sympathetic to the victims', and threatened with expulsion if they did so.[35]

British intimidation of journalists and suppression of newspapers was a generous aid to republican propaganda. The republican side did not always endear itself to the profession, however. Papers were seized and actions taken against pressmen and papers by the IRA, but in general, as Ian Kenneally states, 'republican assaults on press freedom did not reach anywhere near the level of those practised by the Irish administration and crown forces'.[36] The main targets of IRA actions were the Dublin-based *Irish Independent* and *Freeman's Journal*, but in September 1920 the IRA attacked the *Dundalk Democrat* and in December the IRA caused extensive damage to the printing presses of the *Cork Examiner*, which had editorially supported Bishop Cohalan's pastoral condemning IRA ambushes. While the paper only missed one day's publication, according to one

32 Thanks to Ian Kenneally for additional information. See also I. Kenneally, *The paper wall: newspapers and propaganda in Ireland, 1919–1921* (Cork, 2008), p. 16. 33 *KE*, 17 July 1920. 34 Cork, Kerry, Limerick, Tipperary, Clare, Kilkenny, Waterford and Wexford.o 35 Kenneally, *Paper wall*, p. 127 and M. Walsh, *The news from Ireland: foreign correspondents and the Irish revolution* (London, 2008), p. 123. 36 Kenneally, *Paper wall*, p. 66.

of the raiding party the attack 'had a salutary effect on the proprietors of the newspaper in question'; another noted that 'as a result of our action, the paper considerably modified its anti-Irish tone'.[37]

TREATY AND CIVIL WAR

Following the truce between the British and the IRA in July 1921, the Irish press was freer from interference than at any time since before the outbreak of the war in 1914; a brief interlude of politico-military non-interference with newspapers complemented the temporary sense of relief and guarded optimism that prevailed in the country in general. However, the signing of the Anglo-Irish treaty on 6 December 1921 and the subsequent split in the ranks of the republican movement disturbed the slumbering beast of censorship and suppression once again. Of all the metropolitan and regional newspapers, only the *Connachtman* in Sligo, the *Donegal Vindicator* and the *Waterford News* took an explicit anti-treaty position in December 1921/January 1922, followed later by the *Kerry Leader*, which began publication in March 1922. While proprietorial/editorial political preferences, a reading of the popular mood and a pragmatic desire in the newspaper industry for a maintenance of 'normality' (relatively free-flowing circulation and a restored advertising revenue stream) played their part in creating this consensus, there may also have been a more direct material dimension, as suggested by the anti-treaty *Donegal Vindicator* when it pointed out that newspapers championing the republic had been warned they would be deprived of the support of the 'moneyed people'.[38]

Dorothy Macardle, in her later account of the Irish revolution, sums up republican feelings about the Irish media consensus: 'All warnings against the treaty, all caution as to the dangers latent in it, all opposition to partition, even, seemed flung to the winds. Every effort of the press was concentrated in stampeding the people into a panic-stricken terror of rejection, a blind clamour for surrender, for peace at any price'.[39] The fact that almost all of the mainstream Irish press in the twenty-six counties was pro-treaty to varying degrees gave a clear advantage to the treaty's proponents and led frustrated anti-treatyites to resort to intimidation and 'sledge-hammer censorship' in response. This reflected poorly on the democratic claims of republicans and allowed their opponents to characterize them as lawless and dictatorial, and to cast themselves as a democratic bulwark against 'anarchy', and champions of the liberty of the press (which, conveniently, happened to be overwhelmingly pro-treaty).

The day after the Dáil had voted by a small margin to approve the treaty, the IRA in Cork compelled the *Cork Examiner* to publish a republican proclamation against the settlement, which appeared on 9 January. On 14 January the editors

---

37 *IT*, 27 Dec. 1920; *CE*, 28 Dec. 1920; *CTe*, 1 Jan 1921; *FJ*, 3 Jan. 1921; BMH WS 1,675, Joseph O'Shea and BMH WS 1,547, Michael Murphy. 38 5 May 1922, cited in M. Laffan, *The resurrection of Ireland: the Sinn Féin Party, 1916–1923* (Cambridge, 2005), p. 383. 39 Macardle, *Irish Republic*, p. 624.

of Tipperary's *Nationalist* (Clonmel) and the *Clonmel Chronicle* refused the 'request' of the local IRA commanding officer to publish the same proclamation. On 19 January the printing presses were badly damaged at the *Nationalist*, and when the *Chronicle* protested, copies of that paper were seized.[40] Harassment and intimidation continued in various parts of the country over the following two months. It peaked with the destruction of the *Freeman's Journal* presses on 30 March. On 10 April the anti-treaty IRA executive sent a message to editors notifying them that 'publication of any matters relative to the Irish Republican Army is prohibited unless passed by the Publicity Department, IRA'. Failure to comply led to attacks on papers and the seizure of others. This was part of a general pattern whereby pro-treaty meetings were broken up, and clashes between both sides intensified. In Sligo a pro-treaty rally to be addressed by Arthur Griffith was scheduled for Easter Sunday, 16 April, despite an anti-treaty IRA ban on public gatherings in the region. The anti-treatyites failed to stop the meeting, but they did destroy copies of the following week's issue of the pro-treaty *Sligo Champion* containing its report on the meeting. The proprietor then issued a large poster that was put up around the town headed 'Irish Black and Tans Raid the Champion'.[41] On 29 April the local IRA closed the Clonmel *Nationalist* following the editor's refusal to submit to republican censorship. It was unable to publish for two weeks, and the provisional government agreed to pay half the wages of the laid-off staff of seventeen.[42]

In the initial territorial or conventional phase of the civil war (from the end of June to mid-August 1922) the Free State-censored Dublin newspapers were mainly kept out of, or could not reach, areas in the control of the republicans. Local and regional newspapers in republican-held areas either gradually went out of business – some temporarily, like the *Tipperaryman*, others permanently, like the *Cork County Eagle* (Skibbereen) – due to the disruption of supplies and communications, or refusal to submit to republican censorship, while those that continued to publish were censored by the anti-treatyites and compelled to carry republican war news and general propaganda supplied by the republican publicity department. In classic war-propagandist style, this emphasized or exaggerated republican victories; challenged Free State military claims and highlighted the enemy's atrocious behaviour; tried to boost republican morale in the face of Free State military supremacy and advance; mourned and praised fallen republican leaders; characterized the treaty regime as the product of a *coup d'état;* and repeatedly stressed the apostasy, Britishness and venality of the 'Anglo–Free State' 'regime' or 'junta'. In the first days of the civil war, a team of republican censors moved into the Cork city-centre offices of the *Cork Examiner*, *Evening Echo*, *Weekly Examiner* and the unionist daily, the *Cork Constitution*.

---

40 *IT*, 17–18 Jan. and 9 May 1922; *CC*, 19–20 Jan. 1922.   41 *FJ*, 22 Apr. 1922; Michael Farry, *The aftermath of revolution: Sligo, 1921–23* (Dublin, 2000), p. 61.   42 Correspondence between the *Nationalist* proprietors and the Ministry of Home Affairs, 1–25 Apr. 1922, JUS H5/200, NAI; *IT*, 29 Apr. 1922.

Republican propaganda and opinion pieces, as well as news, were integrated into the papers' general content. The previous week the *Limerick Leader*, *Limerick Echo*, *Munster News* and *Limerick Chronicle* had ceased publication rather than submit to republican censorship.

All newspapers publishing in the areas under the provisional government/ national army's control were subjected to a press censorship regime headed by Piaras Beaslaí. His instructions to staff coloured the coverage of the civil war in those regional newspapers that were able to continue in business in the midst of the disruption caused by the conflict. As well as conventional censorship rules relating to sensitive military information, directions centred on nomenclature related to the respective 'legitimacy' of both sides: anti-treaty forces were always 'irregulars' or 'armed men' and were never to be given 'proper' military designations or be referred to as 'republicans'; the pro-treaty forces were to be called the 'Irish army', 'national army', 'national forces' or simply 'troops', while the provisional government was the 'Irish government' or simply 'the government'.[43]

Republicans lost their remaining mainstream newspaper mouthpieces in August 1922 when Cork fell to the national army. As republicans prepared to abandon Cork in the face of the Free State's advance, they destroyed the plant and machinery of both the *Examiner* and the *Constitution* as part of an orgy of destruction and sabotage across the city. This put paid to any chance of a return by the *Constitution*, and saw the *Cork Examiner* off the streets for three days and the *Echo* and *Weekly Examiner* for two weeks. Action against newspapers continued during the subsequent guerrilla phase of the civil war, with 'enemy' papers seized and destroyed and threats to editors continuing. On 1 September the last paper still publishing in Kerry, the Tralee-based *Kerry People*, was shut down by republicans who dismantled the printing presses.[44] In July the anti-treaty *Connachtman* had been suppressed by the provisional government, and in early August the editor and proprietor of the anti-treaty *Kerry Leader* were interned following the capture of Tralee by the national army, putting the paper out of business.

AFTERMATH

The end of the civil war in May 1923 ended the official censorship of, and direct interference with, the work of the regional press until the outbreak of the Second World War in 1939 and the advent of the draconian Emergency censorship regime (after which, incidentally, the press censors singled out E.T. Keane of the *Kilkenny People* as 'the most troublesome gentleman' with whom they had to deal).[45] Civil war animosities lingered, however, and in July 1924 the director of publicity at the Irish

---

43 'General instructions', July 1922, Desmond FitzGerald Papers, P80/282/12/2, UCDA. **44** M. Hopkinson, *Green against green: the Irish civil war* (Dublin, 2004), p. 131; *FJ*, 2 Sept. 1922. **45** D/J, Press Censorship Reviews: 'Provincial Papers', p. 12, NAI.

Free State's Department of External Affairs, Seán Lester, introduced the idea of a classic mechanism of press control: the withholding of government advertising from politically undesirable publications. The list of 'anti-state' (i.e. republican) weeklies drawn up by Lester included three regional titles – the *Waterford News*, *Waterford Evening News* and *Dundalk Examiner*. These were not only to be completely boycotted for the purposes of government advertising but were also, he noted, 'liable to prosecution on every edition'. A second list of titles that showed 'anti-state bias' and occasionally allowed their columns to be used by 'irregulars' consisted of the *Kerry Weekly News*, *Killarney Echo*, *Kerry Reporter* and *Donegal Vindicator*. These were to receive government advertisements only in 'exceptionable circumstances'.[46] This ban remained in place until the republican Fianna Fáil party came to power in 1932. That party's political ascendency initiated a new phase of political realignment in the regional press, reflecting (albeit more gradually) the pattern of the 1880s and after 1916, whereby a significant number of these essentially commercial enterprises followed rather than led public opinion for reasons of survival.

The Irish regional press had proven its resilience in the troubled years of 1914–23, with a large majority of papers either surviving the vicissitudes of conflict, including suppression and attack, or re-emerging in the aftermath. The primary sea change from the pre-First World War era to the newly independent Irish state was the near disappearance of the unionist/Protestant regional press in the twenty-six county area. At the turn of the twentieth century, there were almost thirty regional titles of this kind, but by the mid-1920s only the *Waterford Standard*, *Limerick Chronicle* and *Sligo Independent* remained. Direct interference in the revolutionary years had played a part, as in the cases of the *Cork Constitution* and *Cork County Eagle*, for example, but others, like the *Galway Express*, had arrived at commercial culs-de-sac and either sold up or shut down. The political redundancy of southern unionism and the loss of readership due to the sharp decline in the southern Protestant population, due primarily to emigration (conflict-related and otherwise), were the principal underlying causes of this phenomenon.

The fact that the Irish regional press was taken seriously by all the protagonists in the conflicts that marked the years 1914–23 was a backhanded compliment to its relevance and perceived influence. The general tendency of the commercial press to reflect dominant trends or shifts in public opinion was even more evident in regional papers, bound more intimately as they were – socially, culturally, commercially and politically – to their readership communities. This was shown in the pro-war consensus they reflected from 1914 to 1916, their shift towards republicanism from 1917 and the pro-treaty consensus in 1922–3. Efforts to control their political content were most successful in 1914–16, when public opinion was broadly supportive of the British war and recruitment effort. Once the tide turned after the Rising, however, and the regional press moved into

46 'Government advertising', 1924–36, D/T S4005, NAI.

an oppositional mode, these attempts became less effective and were ultimately counterproductive. The shift from conciliatory censorship to blatant coercion – from blue pencils to sledge hammers – like the broader British policy it reflected, failed to limit the advance of the separatist agenda, despite the partial muzzling of the regional press that was achieved. The attempts by the anti-treaty IRA to bludgeon a hostile press onto its side were equally futile, while the targeting by the Free State authorities of the small minority of titles that opposed them politically, both during and after the civil war, was but the final example in these years of the disregard held by all sides for the democratic principle of press freedom, despite their frequent, hollow claims to be its champions.

Thinking globally, acting locally: Irish regional newspapers and the Internet, 1994–2004

IAN KENNEALLY

The early to mid-1990s was a time of considerable uncertainty in the Irish newspaper industry, culminating in the collapse of the *Irish Press* in 1995.[1] That paper's demise left Independent Newspapers in control, directly or indirectly, of an increasingly large share of the Irish newspaper market. In addition, Irish-owned newspapers faced a growing commercial threat from British daily and Sunday papers. Such was the sense of crisis that the government formed the Commission on the Newspaper Industry in September 1995, which reported its findings nine months later. The commission was primarily concerned with issues such as the concentration of ownership within the media industry, the level of value added tax applied to newspapers and the need to encourage 'indigenous' Irish newspapers. Indeed, as John Horgan has noted, this period marked a 'watershed' for an Irish newspaper industry in which Independent Newspapers, later renamed Independent News and Media, was now the dominant player.[2] Yet, at the same time, Irish newspapers were facing a challenge that went far beyond that posed by the prevalence of British newspapers in the marketplace, or the potential monopolistic power of Independent Newspapers.

In 1989, Tim Berners-Lee, a computer scientist at the European Organization for Nuclear Research (CERN) in Switzerland, invented the World Wide Web, making it much easier to access information over the medium of the Internet. Two years later, Berners-Lee launched the first website, and, in April 1993, CERN released the relevant Web protocols and code into the public domain, allowing the nascent Web to spread internationally.[3] By the middle of the decade, Web browsers such as Mosaic, Netscape Navigator and Internet Explorer had been established, and the Web was rapidly developing as a means to communicate, share information and conduct business. Across the world, telecommunications companies started to offer fee-based Internet services, with IEunet, Ireland On-Line and Indigo

---

1 For an account of the paper's closure, see Ray Burke, *Press delete: the decline and fall of the Irish Press* (Dublin, 2005)   2 John Horgan, 'Newspaper ownership in Ireland and its effects on media diversity: the Commission on the Newspaper Industry re-visited' in Eoin G. Cassidy and Andrew G. McGrady (eds), *Media and the marketplace: ethical perspectives* (Dublin, 2001), p. 46.   3 An overview of these developments can be found at home.cern/topics/birth-web.

being among the first firms to provide Internet access to the commercial and public markets in Ireland.[4]

The societal and economic consequences of this new technology were still unclear, but many media commentators were not shy of extolling the benefits that they believed would accrue from the Web. During the mid-1990s, business and technology publications regularly promised that the so-called 'new economy' would revolutionize all aspects of life. A typical example of this thinking could be seen in the widely reproduced articles and books of Kevin Kelly, editor of the American magazine *Wired*, who opined that:

> The network economy will unleash opportunities on a scale never seen before on Earth [...] It is a unique phase of economic development, much like ado-lescence – a thrilling, disorienting, and never-to-be repeated time. The planet can progress only once through the stage when it is first completely wrapped by networks of thought and interaction. We are now at that moment when a cloak of glass fibers and a halo of satellites are closing themselves around the globe to bring forth a seamless economic culture. This new global economic culture is characterized by decentralized ownership and equity, by pools of knowledge instead of pools of capital, by an emphasis on an open society, and, most important, by a widespread reliance on economic values as the basis for making decisions in all walks of life.[5]

The accuracy, or otherwise, of Kelly's claims are beyond the scope of this chapter. However, his writings give a sense of the excitement that surrounded the new information technologies of the mid-1990s. In Ireland, similar sentiments were repeated in the print media. The basic message was expressed in a report from the *Irish Farmers Journal*, which warned that: 'Ireland must open up to information technology, the Internet is here and will impact on us. We must work with it, otherwise others will exploit us and we will risk an information poverty trap.'[6]

The new methods of communication and information transmission posed a special challenge to newspapers, and, in the remainder of this chapter, we will examine Ireland's regional press and detail how it reacted to these transformative developments.

'BRINGING WATERFORD TO THE WORLD'

The World Wide Web allowed businesses to have direct contact with potential customers, and perhaps even to bypass newspapers and broadcast media.

4 IEunet, founded in 1991 and partly owned by Trinity College Dublin, was Ireland's first commercial internet service provider (ISP). For the development of the Internet in Ireland, particularly in the 1990s, see the online database *Tech Archives*, a project that 'gathers the recollections of pioneers in computing, software development and networking': techarchives.irish/how-the-internet-came-to-ireland-1987-97. 5 Kevin Kelly, *New rules for the new economy: 10 radical strategies for a connected world* (New York, 1998), p. 156. 6 *IFJ*, 13 Apr. 1996.

Newspapers had long been a medium for advertising, but it now appeared that this lucrative and heretofore predictable source of income could be greatly reduced. Furthermore, the press, radio and television had largely controlled access to news and comment, but the Web afforded individuals and groups the opportunity to operate as alternative sources of news in competition with the traditional media. This was apparent even during the early days of the Internet, with the rise of the *Drudge Report* in the United States – a politically right-wing website. In 1995, journalist Matt Drudge began an email-based subscription service. Two years later, he added a website that, within months, had an average of 300,000 individual visitors per day.[7]

While it remained to be seen, if Drudge's website would prove to be a model or an outlier, his success raised the possibility that online news sources, operating independently of established media, could succeed in gaining huge readerships with, perhaps, deleterious effects for printed newspapers, both in terms of their sales and their ability to attract advertisers. Newspapers, internationally, had no option but to respond to the changing landscape. For example, John Hill, in his study of Britain's regional press, noted that:

> A popular response from publishers was to offer a digital version of their newspapers containing the advertising which at one time was carried exclusively in their print edition. Such a confrontational stance on the part of newspapers was designed to take full advantage of the fact that in the print version of the newspaper, they had an effective publicity vehicle in which to promote the digital form. However, the problem that this creates is that energetic promotion may drive readership away from the hard-copy product, which is significantly more profitable than the electronic version.[8]

Ireland's regional newspapers responded in a manner typical of their counterparts in other countries. The *Clare Champion*, in 1994, was the first Irish regional newspaper to establish an online presence (that year, the *Irish Times* became the first of Ireland's national newspapers to do so, using the domain irish-times.ie).[9] At the time, the *Champion*, which was quickly followed online by the Waterford-based *Munster Express* and the *Limerick Leader*, offered relatively little content

---

7 Initially, Drudge worked on his own, operating out of a one-bedroom apartment in Hollywood, but, by 1998, his site had gained international attention because of its role in breaking a story related to the scandal involving US President Bill Clinton and White House intern Monica Lewinsky. For an outline of the website's history, see Anthony Fellow, *American media history* (Boston, 2012), pp 372–3; Stuart Allan, *Online news: journalism and the Internet* (New York, 2006), pp 39–47; and Tony Harcup, *A dictionary of journalism* (Oxford, 2014), p. 88. As Harcup noted, the *Drudge Report* has often been cited as one of the success stories of 'journalism that exists outside the mainstream media structures, albeit one that relies to a large extent on linking to the work of others'. 8 John Hill, *The British newspaper industry: the future of the regional press* (London, 2016), p. 72. 9 *IT*, 14 Dec. 1998. See also *IT*, 28 June 2008, in which the paper announced the launch of irishtimes.com. The paper stated that it was the first newspaper in Ireland or Britain and 'one of the first 30 newspapers in the world' to establish a website. The *Irish Times* relaunched its website as ireland.com in 1999. In 2008, the paper changed to the domain irishtimes.com.

online – a fraction of what was in each paper's print edition.[10] The disparity between the print and online editions was, by the *Champion*'s own admission, a source of annoyance for readers but,[11] as detailed below, it would be the end of the decade before regional newspapers were able to more fully develop and expand their online facilities.

The *Munster Express* provides a case study of the process through which regional newspapers developed online editions. The paper launched its first website, munster-express.ie, during the summer of 1996, providing brief news, sports and entertainment items. Over the next six months, the site was developed to include opinion pieces and 'classifieds that would be of interest to a non-Waterford based readership'.[12] It was not, however, a rolling news service, and the site was updated once per week, usually on a Friday. The *Express*, according to its managing director, Kieran Walsh, aimed its website at readers 'outside the confines of our circulation area', especially among the Irish abroad. Walsh claimed that the site was visited by 'large numbers' each week, particularly by 'overseas-based Waterfordians':

> The *Munster Express* acts as that special link from an overseas location to their own local community here in Waterford. Whether it be in Nova Scotia or Newfoundland in Canada, New York or Chicago in the USA or Sydney, Australia, the emigrants all want to keep in touch with home, as our site visitors show.[13]

Indeed, the *Express* made little effort to promote the website among its local readers – such efforts were entirely directed 'to the diaspora'.[14] According to Walsh, 'the Internet is an ideal tool for publishing to an emigrant community from Waterford'.[15] At this stage, there was no charge for access to the website, as 'we see it as a way of opening up a new stream of readers, who are currently not receiving the *Munster Express*'.[16]

The website originated in discussions between the *Express* and Forbairt, a state body that would later be subsumed into Enterprise Ireland. Following these discussions, senior staff from the *Express* visited the United States, meeting with editors and journalists in various daily and weekly newspapers that produced online editions. During their journey, the *Express* team compiled enough

---

10 Examples of the *Clare Champion*'s website in 1994, as well as the websites of the *Limerick Leader* and *Munster Express*, can be found on archive.org/web. The site's Wayback Machine – a digital archive of the World Wide Web and other information on the Internet – provides snapshots of Irish newspaper websites, as they existed in 1994 and later years. 11 *CCh*, 2 Oct. 1999, web.archive.org/web/19991002203441/ http://clarechampion.ie. 12 *ME*, 20 Dec. 1996. 13 Ibid. 14 Between 1997 and 2000, the *Munster Express*' printed edition carried numerous advertisements for the paper's website, all of which were directed at emigrants. For example, see the edition of 8 Aug. 1997, which claimed that 'approximately 53.8 million adults worldwide' had access to the Internet: 'With the Munster Express Online, Irish living abroad can connect to their local newspaper 24 hours of the day. The Munster Express Online offers the latest news, sports, entertainment, classified and much more. So why not see for yourself.' 15 *ME*, 20 Dec. 1996. 16 Ibid.

information to 'get our graphic designers working on the project'. As Walsh explained, the new skills developed by the paper's staff signified the extent to which work practices within the regional press were changing:

> Now we have a situation where we have a number of staff competent to design for the Internet. Some even remember the days of hot metal. It is certainly a long way from hot metal in the 1970s. When the *Munster Express* changed to photocomposition, we were one of the first regional newspapers to do so. Now, we have gone down the digital road and are typesetting not only for the *Munster Express* paper edition – but also for the Internet and worldwide publishing via computer. We see it as a further development in the technology race and the *Munster Express*, as in previous generations, will be out there leading from the front in terms of technology.[17]

Although Walsh's comments contained an element of self-promotion, they were not inaccurate. In terms of technology, many regional newspapers were ahead of the nationals in the mid-1990s, with several papers carrying full-colour sections each week. Website development was one aspect of technological advancement, including electronic page make-up and Integrated Services Digital Network (ISDN) transmission of pages.

By 1998, the *Express'* website was routinely including colour photographs along with its news and sports stories, although the accompanying reports continued to be short summaries of the stories published in the print edition. The online version, during these years, could not be compared to the print edition in terms of scope and depth. The news and sport sections of the site provided a selection of around five stories each week. Another characteristic of munster-express.ie from 1996 to 1999 was that, as with the *Clare Champion*'s website, it doubled as a portal for tourist information, showcasing the county and providing information on local companies such as Waterford Crystal and Waterford Foods, bus and train schedules, shop hours, exchange rates and other information.[18] This focus on tourism and the associated desire to present positive stories on local areas was a feature among regional newspapers, and sentiments such as those expressed by the *Western People* were common:

> This newspaper is now on the Internet and exiles from this region all over the world can log in and get a sample of our news and sports stories each week within seconds. Positive developments in the region will be highlighted and stories which have particular appeal to those living away from home will be placed on the World Wide Web as part of the *Western People*'s policy of con-tributing in any way to networking contacts for the good of the region.[19]

There were a number of reasons that regional newspapers provided

---

17 Ibid. 18 For example, see https://web.archive.org/web/19980704172553/http://munster-express. ie (snapshot from 4 July 1998). 19 *WP*, 14 Feb. 1996.

relatively superficial news content online in the late 1990s. Public access to the Internet was a new phenomenon, and there were still relatively few people in the newspaper industry with the skills required to build and maintain websites. It seems that few newspapers were willing to engage in the research and development undertaken by the *Munster Express*. There was also confusion as to how best to use this new technology, and, at this time, regional newspapers viewed websites primarily as means to communicate with, and perhaps gain subscriptions from, the Irish diaspora. It appears that newspaper owners and editors believed that local readers would continue to prefer the printed version over the digital. Indeed the managing director of the Wexford-based *People* newspapers, Michael Roche, declared in December 1998 that 'the jury is still out on the tangible benefit of the online editions', although he was 'acutely aware that, other than buying the newspaper, the information we provide cannot be sourced elsewhere'.[20] Yet the biggest hurdle for website development was, as the *Clare Champion* declared, 'a lack of resources'.[21] However, this situation would change in late 1998, when the Regional Newspapers Association of Ireland (RNAI) announced a new strategy for website development among its members, and the creation of the Regional Media Bureau of Ireland (RMBI).

ALL TOGETHER NOW

The RNAI, which represented 51 papers in 1999, played a key role in establishing an online presence for the regional press,[22] with the foundation in December 1998 of the RMBI 'to oversee the transmission of the provincial press to the Internet'.[23] Member newspapers would no longer offer individual sites, but would become part of a portal – rmbi.ie.[24] From there, readers could click through to their preferred newspaper. To gain full access to the newspapers, readers would be charged a subscription of £50, £30 or £20 for one year, six months or three months, respectively. This subscription would, the RMBI promised, include access to the full content

---

20 *IT*, 14 Dec. 1998.   21 At this time, the *Champion*'s website had a weekly average of 800 readers, and the paper's webmaster claimed that the site had led to an increase in print subscriptions. Web.archive.org/web/19991002203441/http://clarechampion.ie (snapshot from 2 Oct. 1999).   22 The organization was originally founded in 1918 as the Provincial Newspapers Association of Ireland, before becoming the Regional Newspaper Association of Ireland in 1998: see *MC*, 16 May 1998.   23 *WE*, 19 Dec. 1998.   24 The site was fully operational by spring 1999, providing access to the following 28 newspapers: the *Anglo-Celt, Carlow Nationalist, Clare Champion, Clonmel Nationalist, Enniscorthy Echo, Enniscorthy Guardian, Gorey Echo, Kildare Nationalist, Kilkenny People, Laois Nationalist, Leinster Express, Leinster Leader, Longford Leader, Mayo News, Meath Chronicle, Nenagh Guardian, New Ross Echo, Northern Standard, Offaly Express, Offaly Independent, Roscommon Herald, Tipperary Star, Tuam Herald, Waterford News and Star, Western People, Westmeath Examiner, Westmeath Independent, Wexford Echo*. See web.archive.org/web/19991012151651/http://rmbi.ie:80/allpapers.shtml (snapshot of 12 Oct. 1999). The site stated that five other newspapers would soon join the portal: the *Connaught Telegraph, Leitrim Observer, Munster Express, Sligo Champion* and *Southern Star*. However, as detailed below, the rmbi.ie Web portal would close within months.

of each printed edition as well as archived editions, rather than merely shortened versions of news and sports items:[25]

> What is unique about the RMBI Internet site is that all copy and photographs of each newspaper are included and not just a selection of stories and pictures. In addition, because RMBI uses the same technology platform as the BBC for its digital development, they are able to offer subscribers a level of archival search unrivalled in Irish news.[26]

The RMBI website was developed through a partnership with Internet Ireland, a prominent Web development company, with the RNAI investing £500,000 to make the service fully operational by March 1999.[27] The RNAI's decision to create a single hub for regional newspapers was an effort to spread the risk and to lessen the costs that had prevented papers from offering more than a rudimentary online service. In the late 1990s, many regional newspapers were, as they had been since the nineteenth century, independent and often family owned. As Anthony Cawley has noted, the RMBI's hub 'would offer them a central technical resource and remove the need to develop the skills and architecture for online publication within each company'.[28] This fact was stressed at the launch of the RMBI by Jack Davis, then president of the RNAI:

> This is a landmark for local Irish news and the Irish abroad. As an association we saw the benefit of putting regional newspapers firmly on the Internet map as a collective industry grouping rather than individually. We know, from the many approaches to our titles, that the diaspora abroad want instant access to our news stories and pictorial coverage and that there is a market for our unique electronic news service.[29]

Davis suggested that the primary readership for this new service would be members of the Irish diaspora, who would 'be able to keep in touch with everything about their local areas – the jobs and housing situations, social and community developments, the courts and politics and how their sports teams are faring'.[30] It was on this basis that the RMBI, as the websites of the *Munster Express* and the *Clare Champion* had previously, targeted the Irish diaspora as its primary market:

> Ireland has the highest level of readership of local newspapers anywhere in the Western world. When this was viewed together with the long tradition of emigration that has deposited enclaves of Irish all over the globe, all hungry for local news from the homeland, we immediately saw the opportunity of working together to provide a special news service.[31]

---

25 *WE*, 19 Dec. 1998. **26** See, for example, *CN*, 18 Dec. 1998, in which the paper's managing director promised that 'all copy and photographs of each newspaper are included'. **27** According to the *Irish Times*, Enterprise Ireland also provided funding for the RMBI website, although the amount is unclear. The ultimate cost of the project was estimated to be £1 million: see *IT*, 14 Dec. 1998. **28** Anthony Cawley, 'Towards a historical perspective on locating online news in the news ecology: the case of Irish news websites, 1994–2010', *Media History*, 18:2 (2012), p. 230. **29** *WE*, 19 Dec. 1998. **30** Ibid. **31** Ibid.

The RMBI planned that newspapers would be only one aspect of its online offering. Barry Breslin, the company's director of information technology, promised that:

> Future developments will include meeting places, genealogy board, live audio broadcasts and a number of exciting merchandising opportunities. Market research shows that the diaspora is prepared to pay for local news properly presented and accessible.[32]

He also envisioned that the service could encompass an Irish digital television channel, providing subscribers with a single location for most, if not all, their media requirements.

Yet the RMBI portal would have a short existence. An undoubted innovation, it drew the attention of Independent News and Media (INM), which was searching for opportunities to develop its online presence, as well as to increase its share of the marketplace. In January 2000, INM acquired a 75 per cent stake in the RMBI (half of the remaining shares remained under the control of the RMBI, with the remainder split between the participating regional news-papers).[33] Out of this takeover a new company – Unison – emerged, which offered an online portal for the country's regional newspapers. The new portal, unison.ie, replaced rmbi.ie, promising to put up to 40 regional newspapers online.[34]

Unison would put many of the RMBI's ambitions into practice, in that it positioned itself as a digital content provider, rather than just a hub for local news. The company provided Irish consumers with a set-top box that could be plugged into a household phone line and then into the back of a television. The box could then be used to browse the Web, without the need of a personal computer. It also allowed the possibility of further upgrades, both in terms of software and hardware, which could further expand the content offered by Unison.[35] Indeed, as described by John Horgan, there were many other aspects to Unison's media content offering:

> International Network News, a Dublin-based radio news service, was not only providing timed news bulletins for the regional radio stations,

---

32 Ibid.   33 *SSt*, 12 Feb. 2000.   34 In June 2000, Unison listed the following 36 newspapers: *Anglo-Celt, Bray People, Carlow Nationalist, Carlow People, Corkman, Drogheda Independent, Enniscorthy Echo, Enniscorthy Guardian, Fingal Independent, Gorey Echo, Gorey Guardian, Kerryman, Kildare Nationalist, Laois Nationalist, Leinster Express, Leinster Leader, Leitrim Observer, Longford Leader, Longford News, Mayo News, Midland Tribune, Nenagh Guardian, New Ross Echo, New Ross Standard, Offaly Express, Offaly Independent, Roscommon Herald, Southern Star, The Argus, Tuam Herald, Tullamore Tribune, Westmeath Examiner, Westmeath Independent, Wexford Echo, Wexford People, Wicklow People*, see web.archive.org/web/20000613173722/ http://www.unison.ie:80/allpapers.php3 (snapshot from 13 June 2000). By the following year, the *Meath Chronicle* and the *Sligo Champion* had joined Unison. The number of participating papers declined thereafter, falling to 25 by June 2006 as newspapers developed websites individually. Both the *Munster Express* and the *Clare Champion* remained independent of Unison.   35 Initially, Unison gave away thousands of these boxes through promotions in participating regional newspapers, while the box retailed at £29.99; see *SSt*, 12 Feb. 2000.

but was acting as part of the platform for Unison and, additionally, was involved in creating a link for news from the Republic for UTV's website in Northern Ireland.[36]

DISRUPTION AND OPPORTUNITY

Unison, with headquarters in INM's Citywest offices in Dublin, earned an average of 10 million page impressions per month by 2002.[37] Part of its success was undoubtedly due to the wide variety of newspapers participating in the service, which meant that local news and sports was provided for most of the country. In addition, within months of going live, unison.ie offered sections devoted to international news, analysis, letters, arts, features, business, farming, education, weather, appointments and shopping, as well as crosswords and horoscopes. In short, Unison's online news service was moving closer in style and content to the print editions of the participating newspapers.[38] Another contributory factor may have been that, unlike rmbi.ie and previous individual newspaper sites, unison.ie provided readers with breaking news from January 2001, becoming a rolling news service.[39] Indeed, readers could also subscribe to the site's 'E-News' service, which would provide 'news headlines direct to your e-mail address'.[40] The website's design remained the same for much of the next six years.

The development of online editions by Ireland's regional newspapers replicated developments internationally, particularly in markets such as the US and the UK, where the successful newspaper business model was based on a monopoly of local advertising.[41] The challenges and opportunities of the World Wide Web would force newspapers to reconsider how they distributed their content, as well as the type of content they provided to readers. As newspaper companies realized, the Internet, potentially, allowed media brands to reach millions of consumers in a very cost-effective manner. For regional newspapers, particularly in Ireland, this offered the tantalizing possibility of making customers out of Ireland's vast diaspora. Yet the challenge was how to turn website readers into revenue, especially as the Internet, even by the late 1990s, provided a seemingly infinite supply of news and comment, most of it free of charge. Exacerbating this problem for regional newspapers was the fact that the increasing prevalence of Internet access enabled 'new sources of information to be created by lowering barriers in publishing to allow anyone to contribute to the Internet's collective

36 John Horgan, *Irish media: a critical history since 1922* (London and New York, 2001), p. 171. 37 Cawley, 'Ecology', p. 229. 38 Web.archive.org/web/20001204024700/http://www.unison.ie:80 /frontpage.php3?paper_name=Unison_News (snapshot from 4 June 2000). 39 Web.archive.org/web/ 20010118230200/http://unison.ie (snapshot from 18 Jan. 2001). 40 Ibid. Subscribers could select the number of stories that they wished to receive in a variety of categories. 41 Kimmo Lundén, 'The death of print? The challenges and opportunities facing the print media on the web', Reuters Institute Fellowship Paper (Oxford, 2009), pp 9–21.

knowledge base'.[42] In practice, this would see regional newspapers challenged by blogs and online-only news sites that would siphon readers and advertisers away from traditional media sources.

Online competition would grow increasingly fierce, a problem for online regional newspapers, since their audiences were, and are, relatively small and local content can be an overlooked niche in the broader Web. The landscape that newspapers inhabited after the arrival of the Web is illustrated in the complaints of a managing director of a regional English newspaper:

> We're competing with every other information and consumer choice that is out there, and that means that we're competing with Google when it comes to finding a local plumber or a local electrician, we're competing with the BBC when it comes to online journalism, we're competing with eBay when it comes to buying and selling items.[43]

The boom in Ireland's regional-newspaper industry that took place in the decade before 2008, as described by Anthony Cawley in the final chapter of this book, would see the regional press further develop its online offerings. Yet newspapers would continue to struggle with the problem of how to monetize digital content. This question would become increasingly vital to the regional press as the boom turned to bust and declines in revenues from print sources left many newspapers looking online for alternate sources of income. In the early years of the new millennium, it remained to be seen if focusing on online content as a commercial product would be a successful strategy for regional newspapers, both in maintaining their market share and in response to the changing media landscape of the Internet age.

42 Robert D. Atkinson, Stephen J. Ezell, Scott M. Andes, Daniel D. Castro and Richard Bennett (eds), *The Internet economy 25 years after .com: transforming commerce & life* (Washington DC, 2010), p. 52.   43 Roy Greenslade, 'Local newspapers' crisis: how managements have tried to cope', 9 May 2012, www.theguardian.com/media/greenslade/2012/may/09/local-newspapers-mediabusiness.

The changing relationship of Ireland's regional press with the national broadcaster, RTÉ, 1961–2018

RAY BURKE

Ireland's national broadcaster, RTÉ, has a close and enduring relationship with the country's regional press. Aside from a brief hiatus in the 1960s, this relationship has enabled RTÉ to continue to provide a truly national news service, despite revolutionary changes that have affected both newspaper and broadcast journalism over the past quarter century.

The importance of local news to Irish people both at home and abroad was reflected when Frank McCourt, author of *Angela's Ashes*, told the *Irish Times*:

> No, I don't understand that mysterious thing called sense of place. I don't understand why I trek all the way up to 42nd Street [in New York City] to buy the *Limerick Leader* ... why does my heart break when the Limerick hurlers lose to Offaly or Wexford in the final minutes, and when I read about the glorious deeds of the Young Munster, Garryowen and Shannon rugby teams why do I want to run into the streets and pubs of New York with the good news?[1]

Con Houlihan wrote similarly about local notes from Knocknagoshel in the *Kerryman*:

> I can't forget this: 'Mary and Eileen O'Connor, daughters of Dan C.D. O'Connor, our local publican, emigrated to Leeds last week. The village will never be the same again.' In those few words my friend said more about emigration than a thousand treatises.[2]

The Fleet Street newspaper magnate Cecil King, who was reared in Dublin, made an interesting observation about journalists in the late 1970s, when television was fast usurping the centuries-old near-monopoly of newspapers as the prime purveyors of daily news to people throughout the world. 'The brightest go to television', he declared, 'the rejects into magazines and the dregs into newspapers'.[3] King, who was chairman of the world's largest publishing firm, IPC, in the 1960s, died in Dublin in 1987, two years before the advent on television of twenty-four-hour rolling news and its ubiquitous offspring, ambient news.

---

1 Frank McCourt, *IT*, 24 Dec. 1996. 2 Con Houlihan, *Magill*, Feb. 2000, p. 53. 3 Author's note, undated (*c.*1977–8).

Porter Bibb, biographer of Ted Turner, the founder of CNN, wrote that the network had 'changed the definition of news from what has happened to what is happening'.[4] King's death also occurred in the last decade before the World Wide Web and the Internet sparked an even greater fragmentation, or 'disruption', of news dissemination, introducing online news and subsequently instant news and news via social media on smartphones and tablets. Within twenty years of King's death, the technology writer John Naughton noted: 'It took radio about thirty-seven years to build a global audience of fifty million. It took television about fifteen years to notch up the same number of viewers. The World Wide Web got to fifty million users in just over three years.'[5]

Donnybrook, in south Dublin, is where Cecil King spent his retirement years, and it is also where Teilifís Éireann and later Raidió Teilifís Éireann (RTÉ), grappled during those late-twentieth-century decades with its statutory duty to broadcast the news through the entirely new, or relatively new, medium that presented challenges that newspapers had not faced.

DEVELOPING THE NEWSROOM AND REGIONAL NEWS

RTÉ was formed in the mid-1960s when Teilifís Éireann (established in 1961) and Radio Éireann (dating from the 1920s) were combined. RTÉ initially had little choice but to employ journalists who had spent most or all of their careers on newspapers. (Ireland's first third-level journalism course was not established until the late 1960s in Dublin.) Direct entry to the trade by university graduates was strongly resisted at local and national level on the basis that theoretical knowledge was no match for practical experience. Trainee journalists could be paid less than graduates too. The nascent RTÉ, as a result of this strong print journalism influence, struggled for many years to present the news in an engaging way to a growing audience via the new audio-visual medium. Moreover, many of its viewers had been used to watching the news output of the BBC, ITV and UTV for much of the previous decade through the spillover of their signals onto Ireland's east coast and northern counties. (The BBC introduced daily news bulletins on television in 1954, followed within a couple of years by ITV and UTV.)

'When the television service was inaugurated, it inherited the old Radio Éireann newsroom, which now had the provision of a television news service added to its duties', noted the historian and long-time RTÉ employee John Bowman. He added:

> The newsroom at the time believed it had least to learn about television. They tended to think of television news as a radio bulletin read to a camera with occasional pictures. And since almost all newsroom staff had

4 Author's note, undated.   5 John Naughton, *Observer*, 14 June 1998.

come from the provincial press, they already thought of the radio bulletin as print news, read aloud to a microphone.[6]

A typical television news bulletin of fifteen minutes contained fewer than 2,000 words, equivalent to no more than two tightly packed columns on a broadsheet newspaper page. This demanded new disciplines from the former newspaper men – and over-whelmingly the initial intake of journalists were men – already grappling with having to write television scripts instead of reports. (The average number of words on the BBC 9 O'Clock News in the 1990s was 5,000 words, whereas the average number of words in the Daily Telegraph any day was 130,000.[7])

Any of the newspaper men who made the transition from the Dublin dailies to the fledgling Teilifís Éireann in its spanking new television building in Donnybrook, designed by prestige architects Scott Tallon Walker, would have empathized with the later comment of veteran Fleet Street tabloid journalist Kelvin MacKenzie. He reflected that when he joined Sky TV after stepping down from a very successful career as editor of the Sun: 'In the newspaper business, there would be very few people who could tell me how to run a newspaper', he recalled, 'however, when I went to Sky I knew nothing. Even the tea lady knew more than I did because at least she knew her way around the building.'[8]

The difficulties and failings of the first decade of Irish television news were addressed in an internal report produced in 1971 by two newsroom executives, Mike Burns and Eddie Liston, both, of course, former newspaper men. They said that the TV news bulletins largely ignored the Irish provinces and that foreign news was covered 'in a slap-dash, meaningless way'. They complained that there was 'a lack of discipline, rehearsal and pride' and a lack of analysis or even of any element of news-creation in the bulletins. The newsroom journalists, they noted, 'dressed badly, wore shaggy jackets, kept their hands in their pockets, and had poor diction'.[9]

Like the newly appointed provincial newspaper editor (name withheld to spare blushes) who wanted to jettison the pages of weekly local notes until he was persuaded of the folly of such a move, RTÉ recognized the error of pretending that nothing newsworthy was happening outside Ireland's capital city. It went back to basics and beefed up its network of 'stringers' – the regional newspaper journalists who supplied news copy from every provincial town and city – before gradually appointing its own staff journalists in the regions.

Many of RTÉ's initial intake of journalists and cameramen honed their skills in Northern Ireland, where the outbreak of sectarian violence in 1968 attracted worldwide attention. 'Northern Ireland was a world story on RTÉ's doorstep. As

6 John Bowman, Window and mirror: RTÉ television, 1961–2011 (Cork, 2011), p. 39. 7 Max Hastings, sometime Daily Telegraph editor, on Celebrity Choice, Classic FM, London, 9 Feb. 1997. 8 Kelvin Mac-Kenzie, quoted in Matthew Horsman, Sky high: the inside story of BskyB (London, 1997), extracted in the Guardian, 10 Nov. 1997. 9 Mike Burns, Eddie Liston, 'RTÉ News: 30 minute (television) bulletin feasibility study', May 1971, cited in Bowman, Window and mirror, p. 39.

a result many journalists were exposed to the challenge of covering live, volatile news stories,' said a later northern editor, Tommie Gorman.[10] The station's statutory remit as a thirty-two-county national broadcaster obliged it to deploy a generation of journalists and cameramen to report and record the escalating violence. 'Gratias for the verbal honesty of [RTÉ's] Liam Hourican ... day and night his integrity of words has sustained us,' wrote Paul Durcan in his poem 'Tribute to a reporter in Belfast, 1974', published on the 'New Irish Writing' page of the *Irish Press* in that year.[11]

Maintaining strong links with the local newspapers and their journalists was an imperative for RTÉ's first regional correspondent outside Belfast, Tom MacSweeney, when he was appointed Munster correspondent in the mid-1970s, with instructions to develop news coverage in Ireland's six southern counties from a base in Cork city. 'Using contacts in the local weekly papers was vital', MacSweeney recalled, 'as was purchasing and reading every local weekly paper every weekend'. He continued:

> The local papers were published on Fridays so my weekends were spent poring over them to find storylines. I also used friendly colleagues in the regional papers throughout Munster to establish a 'stringer' network that also included the weekly paper photographers, some of whom acquired wind-up Bolex [film] cameras to take pictures, but without sound![12]

Before his appointment as RTÉ's Munster correspondent, MacSweeney had worked in Cork for the *Cork Examiner* and *Evening Echo*, and the *Southern Star*, where he was the editor, based in Skibbereen. He had then spent ten years in Dublin and Northern Ireland, reporting for the *Irish Press* and RTÉ. Returning to Cork, MacSweeney immediately re-established links with former colleagues in the *Cork Examiner/Evening Echo* newsroom, and established links with 'stringers' in west Cork. 'That meant the "morning coffee" with the local journalists in the alternative newsroom of the Chateau pub on Patrick Street,' he said.[13]

Broadcasting facilities, however, were 'a bit of a shock', MacSweeney found:

> I found that the news facilities at the RTÉ studios, then on Union Quay, comprised a small desk in a small, shared office and a shared phone line, unavailable for news usage when required by the studio for 'other radio programmes'. The studio technical boss added to the limitations by telling me that there could be no live news reportage into the main radio bulletins at 8 a.m. and 9 a.m. or at 1:30 p.m. or 6:30 p.m. – the very times of the main radio news bulletins in those days – because 'we only work 9–1, lunch is 1–2 and we close at 5.[14]

MacSweeney was able to record news reports in Union Quay, 'but for live inserts battle had to be waged with the technical boss to get on air'. TV news reporting

10 Tommie Gorman, e-mail to author, 5 Aug. 2016.   11 *IPr*, 20 July 1974.   12 Tom MacSweeney, e-mail to author, 27 July 2016.   13 Ibid.   14 Ibid.

was even more difficult. 'News packaging for TV had to be literally "canned" before 2:30 p.m., that is put into a can and onto the afternoon train to Dublin, to be collected at Heuston Station and taken to the studios in Montrose for processing.'[15] Despite these constraints, one of MacSweeney's first assignments as Munster correspondent was an instruction from a news editor in Dublin to 'hop down to Castletownbere and get a piece back for the 1:30 radio news'.[16] He had to rely on his regional newspaper colleagues to get the information before filing his report. He then sent a map of west Cork by surface mail to the news desk in Dublin, showing that in the largest county in the country, Castletownbere was 90 miles from Cork city on bad roads.

Tom MacSweeney's pioneering work in Cork, which would not have been possible without his network of contacts with the regional newspapers throughout Munster, set the template for all future RTÉ regional reporters and correspondents. At the same time, the RTÉ news editors in Dublin developed and nurtured their own network of 'stringers' around the country in competition with all the national newspapers, whose executives maintained similar lists of 'contacts'.

Before the mushrooming of third-level undergraduate and post-graduate courses in journalism, and before the establishment of licensed independent radio stations around the country in the final decade of the twentieth century, almost every reporter in RTÉ's newsroom and in the national newspapers' newsrooms came from a regional newspaper. Most of them maintained strong links with the paper they had first worked on, and with the contacts they had made there.

RTÉ's first three heads of news – Pearse Kelly, Jim McGuinness and Wesley Boyd – were former newspaper journalists who began their careers on regional titles. It was not until 1990 that RTÉ appointed a career broadcaster, Joe Mulholland, as head of news. Mulholland had made his name as a producer of current-affairs programmes within the station, notably *Today Tonight*. His successor from 2002, Ed Mulhall, built a newsroom team that won multiple awards for coverage of banking scandals, tribunals of enquiry and the economic collapse, and on which former newspaper journalists were for the first time outnumbered by colleagues from broadcast-only backgrounds. 'It was ... Joe Mulholland and Ed Mulhall – both with a wealth of experience in current affairs – who finally modernized the newsroom and comprehensively brought television production values to its output,' wrote John Bowman.[17] Mulhall, who was head of news, and later also of current affairs, for a decade from 2002, recalled: 'Regional content has been an important part of RTÉ's development and remains an important strategic advantage for RTÉ News.'[18] He added:

> From the start of the television service, sourcing stories from the regions was an important part of the role, with *Newsbeat* as the main output vehicle. This was edited by Frank Hall and it had Bill O'Herlihy and Michael

15 Ibid.   16 Ibid.   17 Bowman, *Window and mirror*, p. 202.   18 Mulhall, e-mail to author, 10 Aug. 2016.

Ryan among its reporters. It was in those days very much a news-features programme. Later, what started as quirky stories from the regional newspapers presented by Hall developed into satire, and the programme became *Hall's Pictorial Weekly*. The regional news features were taken over by the newsroom and enhanced by the development of the regional correspondent network, but with features staff in Dublin. By the later 1980s these stories were presented on television in a half-hour slot at 6 p.m.

RTÉ's *Six One News*, which was devised by Rory O'Connor and developed by Mulhall, merged the regional news with national and international news, sports and business slots in an hour-long bulletin. This broadcast was regularly watched by over half a million viewers over the succeeding decades. The *Six One News* evolved by expanding its hard-news elements and by introducing live interviews and reports, including from regional locations, where editing and live transmissions became possible through the acquisition of mobile satellite units.

'It was the development of the *Nationwide* programme as a separate strand immediately after *Six One* that eventually settled the tension between hard and soft content from the regions,' said Mulhall.[19] He added:

> By having these two major vehicles, *Six One* and *Nationwide*, with large audiences, RTÉ maintains a connection with the wider national audience, and this is best shown by how big cross-regional stories such as bad weather, traffic accidents and suchlike impact. Another important factor was having regionally based staff originating the content, which involves better contact with the local communities and local media and also a more rapid response and broader range of cover.[20]

Nonetheless, until well into the new century every regional newspaper published in Ireland was delivered every week to the RTÉ newsrooms, along with the national newspapers, where an idle reporter, or a graduate of that paper, would scrutinize it for potential stories or leads. RTÉ News, like the national dailies, continued to rely heavily on reporters on all the regional newspapers for news from the provinces after it established its own regional network. RTÉ News now employs four staff journalists in Cork and Kerry alone – three for News and one for Nuacht – and the other Munster counties are covered by the mid-west and south-east regional correspondents. All of these journalists regard reading the local and regional newspapers as an essential weekly duty.

FACING THE FUTURE

Two developments over the years since 1992 or so have, however, weakened the links between the regional newspapers and RTÉ, which remains the national

---

19 Ibid. 20 Ibid.

public-service broadcaster (or multimedia, platform-neutral, digital-first news provider, in its latest incarnation). The first development was the growth in popularity of local radio. The second was the better payments that the imported Fleet Street tabloids, and later the Anglo-Irish tabloids (if the *Daily Star* and the *Irish Daily Mail*, *Irish Sun* and *Irish Mirror* can be so described), offered local journalists to supply them with exclusive copy.

Today RTÉ News has its own network of staff in all the regions and all but one of its regional correspondents began their careers on regional newspapers. Working clockwise from the Waterford regional studios, they are: South-East Correspondent Damien Tiernan, whose first full-time jobs were on the *Wicklow People* and the *Wexford People*; Southern Editor Paschal Sheehy, who cut his teeth on the *Kerryman* in Tralee and who was later news editor of the *Cork Examiner*; Mid-West Correspondent Cathy Halloran, who started on the *Connacht Tribune* in Galway and whose late father Danno had begun his career on the *Western People* before joining RTÉ, where he worked on the news desk and established the Oireachtas Unit; North-West Correspondent Eileen Magnier, who began work on the *Wexford People*; North-East Correspondent to 2018 Richard Dowling, who started on the *Waterford News and Star,* as did his father and grandfather before him; and Midlands Correspondent Ciaran Mullooly, who first worked for the *Longford Leader*. The only RTÉ regional correspondent without any local newspaper experience is Western Correspondent Pat McGrath, who began his career on a local radio station, Clare FM, before moving to the short-lived newsroom on RTÉ Lyric FM in Limerick.

Pat McGrath is likely to represent the beginning of a new trend. The first and second generations of journalists employed by RTÉ came, without exception, from regional newspapers, usually after an intermediate few years on a national daily or weekly. However, RTÉ has not directly recruited a journalist with regional newspaper experience for more than a decade. The last reporter to have been recruited directly from a regional newspaper was *Morning Ireland*'s Cian McCormack, who joined from the *Clonmel Nationalist* in 2005, over ten years ago. He has recalled that after university he did a nine-month internship at TV3, but that that in no way equipped him with the skills and knowledge he needs for his current job. He said it was the years he spent at local council meetings, district courts, GAA matches and agricultural shows for the *Clonmel Nationalist* that prepared him properly for the award-winning work he now does.[21] Although RTÉ News these days recruits its journalists mostly from local radio stations or from the BBC or TV3, it could not properly fulfil its public-service remit without maintaining close links with the regional press. This is principally through daily contact between its own regional correspondents and their local-newspaper colleagues. And the local papers are also a very fertile source of leads and stories for RTÉ's current affairs radio and TV programmes, and for the thirty-minute

21 Cian MacCormack, interview with author, 21 Nov. 2014.

Nationwide programme which attracts 300,000 viewers three evenings a week, immediately after the *Six One News*.

Two of the best-known and best RTÉ journalists over recent decades, Jim Fahy and Tommie Gorman, are products of small-town newspapers in the west of Ireland. Jim, who retired as RTÉ's western editor just over five years ago, got his first job on the *Tuam Herald* in 1965, and he was the first reporter to be hired from outside the family that owned that paper. He worked there until 1974, when he joined RTÉ as western correspondent. On top of his day job as a news reporter, Jim also recorded and broadcast the memorable RTÉ radio series *Looking West*, which comprised more than 450 programmes on the lives and stories of notable and interesting west-of-Ireland people. *Looking West* remains a priceless resource for anybody interested in west-of-Ireland lives, not just in the twentieth century but also in the nineteenth century. Many of the programmes arose from contacts Jim had made in his early days on the *Tuam Herald*. Jim was usually the first correspondent the news editor spoke to every morning. Each of the regional correspondents and specialist correspondents speak to the news editors before nine o'clock each morning, and several times throughout the day.

RTÉ's current northern editor, Tommie Gorman, was previously RTÉ's European correspondent and earlier RTÉ's north-west correspondent. He began his career in 1977 on the *Western Journal*, a paper established by John Healy, who became a household name in Ireland in the 1960s through his work for the *Irish Times* and on RTÉ television's politics programmes. By the age of 21, Tommie Gorman was managing editor of the *Western Journal*'s sister paper, the *Sligo Journal*, in charge of a staff of thirty-five people. 'Everything was easy after that,' he has recalled. 'I had to dodge the bank manager when I went out for my lunchtime sandwich because I was writing cheques for which there was no cash and then I had to report on neighbours who were in court for drink driving or suchlike. That was a hard-swallow for a young journalist.'[22] Tommie's first boss, the aforementioned John Healy, who also wrote two important books, *Nineteen acres* and *No one shouted stop*,[23] had started work in 1948 on the *Western People*, in Ballina, Co. Mayo. On the staff there at the same time was Aidan Hennigan, who later served as London editor of the *Irish Press* group between 1972 and 1995. Also on the staff was Michael Finlan, who worked for the *Irish Press* and the *Irish Times*, notably as western correspondent of the *Irish Times* from the early 1970s until the mid-1990s.

Jim Fahy's first newspaper, the *Tuam Herald*, was also a remarkable journalism nursery, although it is based in a west-of-Ireland town even smaller than Ballina. Now the fifth-oldest newspaper on the island of Ireland, published every week since May 1837 (with the exception of a few weeks in 1930 when publication was

---

22 Tommie Gorman, interview with author, 28 Nov. 2014.   23 John Healy, *Nineteen acres* (Galway, 1978); John Healy, *No one shouted stop! The death of an Irish town* (Achill, 1988).

suspended as the paper changed hands),[24] the *Tuam Herald* is unique in that two
of its former cub reporters became rival editors on Ireland's two biggest-selling
national dailies – namely Kevin O'Sullivan, until recently the editor of the *Irish
Times*, and Gerry O'Regan, former editor of the *Irish Independent*. The *Tuam
Herald* was also the launchpad for Tracey Hogan and Martin Breheny of the *Irish
Independent*, Eithne Donnellan of the *Irish Times*, Jerome Reilly of the *Sunday
Independent*, and Michael Lyster and Jim Carney of RTÉ Sport. Carney, who has
passed his sixty-fifth birthday, still writes for the *Herald* every week.

It is unlikely that RTÉ will ever again employ a journalist whose career began
on a regional newspaper. It is even less likely that it will recruit one whose first
day at work was as eventful as that described in the memoir of the late journalist
James Downey. He began work on the *Sligo Champion* in the middle of the last
century before moving to the *Carlow Nationalist* and later the *Evening Press*
and the *Irish Times*, where he narrowly missed out on being appointed editor.
While working as a young reporter on the *Carlow Nationalist*, Downey was dis-
appointed to be overlooked for promotion to district correspondent in Portlaoise,
to succeed Michael Finlan. The editor, Liam Bergin, instead appointed another
young reporter, Pat Nolan, later a well-known industrial relations correspondent
on the *Irish Times*. According to Downey:

> When Nolan arrived in Portlaoise, Finlan was still 'working out his notice',
> and he showed his replacement around the district. He introduced him to
> contacts in Mountrath, ten miles from Portlaoise. The trip ended in a pub,
> where Nolan drank too much and started to smash bottles and glasses. The
> owner, a widow, appealed to Finlan and asked him what she should do. He
> replied in his strangely Americanized accent: 'Call the cops.' Many years
> later, in conversation with me, he denied this version of the story, saying
> that he was in another room when the incident occurred and someone else
> called the police. One way or another, the Gardaí arrived, arrested Pat
> Nolan and threw him in a cell for the night. Soon afterwards he attended
> his first session of the Mountrath District Court in the dual capacity of
> reporter and defendant. He sent an item to the *Nationalist* to the effect
> that 'Patrick Nolan, a reporter, of the County Hotel, Portlaoise' had been
> fined forty shillings (say, one-fifth of a week's wages) for being drunk and
> disorderly. It was greatly to his credit that he wrote the item, and equally
> to Bergin's credit that he published it.[25]

But the twenty-first century successors of Liam Bergin, Pat Nolan, James
Downey and their ilk are unlikely ever to benefit from the regional-newspaper
experience of their twentieth-century counterparts. Irish newspapers and broadcasters are today employing journalists who are younger and with much narrower

24 Hugh Oram, *The newspaper book: a history of newspapers in Ireland, 1649–1983* (Dublin, 1983), p. 169.
25 James Downey, *In my own time: inside Irish politics and society* (Dublin, 2009), p. 43.

experience, no matter how good their third-level qualification or social media skills may be. Some 68 per cent of Irish journalists are in the 25 to 44 age group, compared to 55 per cent less than a decade ago, according to the most recent study.[26] While 80 per cent have a third-level qualification, nearly two-thirds of them specialized in courses in journalism and/or communications, it found.[27] 'The young age profile, matched with decreasing career opportunities, cannot but have an impact on how journalists report the news,' wrote one of the authors, Kevin Rafter, professor of political communications at Dublin City University.[28] 'Given the pivotal role played by the media in "educating and informing" the public about societal issues, there must be concern about the ability of younger journalists to offer serious editorial context when reporting and contextualizing major news stories,' he added. The dangers are, if anything, underestimated by Rafter, according to a young *Irish Times* journalist, Ciaran D'Arcy. 'This experience deficit is exacerbated by the fact that young reporters tend to be confined to the office,' he wrote in response to Rafter's article, adding:

> They are shorn of the opportunity to go out and glean a deeper understanding of the events they are being asked to cover and are, in many instances, expected to simply regurgitate content produced by competitors as per the nauseating mantra of 'aggregation' being employed by certain media brands.[29]

Nor is 'aggregation' – a polite word for the way that the online outfits plagiarize the hard-won stories of journalists, including local newspaper journalists – the only emerging threat. Most people still get their news, particularly during general election or referendum campaigns, from television bulletins, where politicians' 'soundbites' have shrunk sharply and where the public interest is in danger of being trumped by what's deemed to be of interest to the public. 'TV news now is rife with cat, dog and baby videos, weather stories and narcissism,' wrote Maureen Dowd recently in the *New York Times*. She added: 'The mighty news anchors are not figures of authority. They're part of the entertainment, branding and cross-promotion business.'[30]

An even more scathing summary of television news, albeit from another newspaper veteran, was offered by the former *Guardian* editor and *Observer* columnist Peter Preston, following the 2015 British general election. He wrote:

> The infantile video Polyfilla of people who aspire to run the country playing ball with infants or lecturing small crowds of extras on industrial estates? They – the politicians – only do it for you, the TV producers: weeks of photo ops without point or human content except a few eyeball minutes on the TV news each night. But it isn't news. It's the precise opposite. It's

26 Kevin Rafter and Stephen Dunne, 'The Irish journalist today', part of the Worlds of Journalism project, http://www.worldsofjournalism.org/, reported in the *Irish Times*, 27 July 2016.   27 Ibid.   28 Ibid.   29 *IT*, 28 July 2016.   30 Reprinted, *IT*, 9 Feb. 2015.

political spam. Why not give it up for a few days next time and see whether anyone applauds? No non-news might be very good news.[31]

In his *Irish Times* article, Ciaran D'Arcy painted an even bleaker picture for journalists and for citizens. He wrote:

> The experience of modern journalism is that many young graduates or would-be graduates are offered internships in major titles and broadcasters that are unpaid or offer derisory remuneration. Where these enthusiastic interns expect it will be the start of a long career in the writing game, the culpable companies in effect operate a revolving-door system where the young professionals are taken in for a short period of time to fill a gap before being dropped.[32]

And the international trends suggest that the outlook may get even worse for Irish journalists and the citizens they serve. D'Arcy was able to report that 'Irish publishers have so far eschewed the pay-per-view model or paying or retaining journalists based on how many clicks their articles get, which has gained popularity in England.'[33] In the United States, President Barack Obama's 'foreign-policy guru', Ben Rhodes, the White House deputy national security adviser on strategic communications, told the *New York Times*: 'The average reporter we talk to is 27 years old, and their only reporting experience consists of being around political campaigns. That's a sea change. They literally know nothing.'[34]

Ed Mulhall, who recently retired after fifteen years as RTÉ's head of news, did not agree that the challenges now facing RTÉ are as acute as those confronting national broadcasters and newspapers abroad. 'The main challenge is digital developments and the economic model, not expertise or experience,' he said.[35]

> The simplistic sound bites and showbiz fixation of the US is not an inexorable trend, but there are dangers that if there is not a sound economic model that could be the direction that online pulls us towards, particularly if it is decided that mobile platforms are the drivers.[36]

He added:

> No matter where they are working the challenge for present-day jour-nalists is between processing and origination. Recognizing the ongoing importance of what they call in the United States 'the beat' is to me the real issue and this is where I believe there still is an important role for the national public service broadcaster or quality newspaper – it is important for trust and connection. In RTÉ terms this means the specialist cor-respondents, regional and foreign correspondents and desk reporters. To be authoritative as specialists requires expertise, not dumbing down. Processing on all platforms is vital in getting to the audience, but striking

31 *Observer*, 10 May 2015.   32 *IT*, 28 July 2016.   33 Ibid.   34 *New York Times Magazine*, 5 May 2016. 35 Ed Mulhall, e-mail to author, 9 Aug. 2016.   36 Ibid.

the balance will determine success ... Whether there is an economic model that sustains quality is the dilemma, but that strengthens the case that the public good requires that these key investments are made for public funding of public service media.[37]

Many of the journalists in the early days of RTÉ had learnt their trade in Ireland's regional newspapers. After a slow start in the 1960s, from the 1970s the organization and its correspondents took the broadcast news skills they had honed covering the Troubles in Northern Ireland into developing regional 'beats' for the national broadcaster. As was with the early experience of Tom MacSweeney in Cork, effective connection and cooperation with their regional print colleagues, and staying up to date with their reporting was, and is, central to the role of an RTÉ regional correspondent. To this day the majority of RTÉ's regional correspondents started their careers in the regional press. But this is changing, and it is over a decade since a journalist was recruited directly from a regional title. The challenges posed by evolving means of news production and consumption are felt across Ireland's print and broadcast media; and precarious employment and training opportunities present challenges to the next generation of journalists, and by extension the news organizations they report for. Despite this, the ties between RTÉ and Ireland's regional press remain strong and close. How they face the future and continue to serve the Irish public is a shared challenge.

37 Ibid.

Boom to bust: corporate perspectives on Ireland's local newspaper industry since 2000

ANTHONY CAWLEY

For about a decade from the late 1990s, Ireland's local newspaper industry was among the narrative strands threaded through the economic success story that was the Celtic Tiger. A national economy that traditionally had been underdeveloped, moribund and insular was infused with a neo-liberal zeal and transformed into a dynamic, open and highly globalized marketplace. Tracking a similar trajectory, the country's local press was shaken out of its historical structure of small, often family owned publishers with strong community connections.[1] Nested within a booming economy, local titles that were generating robust advertising revenues came to be viewed by group publishers as investment opportunities and cash-generation units. The valuations attached to local mastheads were inflated rapidly amid an acquisition scramble among a small number of corporate media groups, including British-based Dunfermline Press, Scottish Radio Holdings and Johnston Press, as well as, on the island of Ireland, Alpha Newspapers and Thomas Crosbie Holdings. By the mid-2000s, the industry had been reshaped along the lines of other media sectors in Ireland, with amplified consolidation and internationalization of ownership and a sharpened sense of commercial priorities.[2]

The boom in Ireland's local-newspaper industry was, to a degree, counter-intuitive, as it coincided with the advancement of online platforms to distribute news. Even by the late 1990s it was a well-worn prediction that the World Wide Web and the growing dominance of digital would overrun print publications. When, in the early 2000s, a wave of online enterprises crashed in the international dotcom downturn, one of the responses of the newspaper industry was to flag the resilience of print publications in the face of unproven digital platforms. It was in this context that Tony O'Reilly, then chairman of Independent News and Media, proclaimed newspapers to be the 'ultimate browser'.[3] He was not alone in thinking that newspapers had faced down an existential threat. In the

---

1 John Horgan, Paul McNamara and John O'Sullivan, 'Irish print and broadcast media: the political, economic, journalistic and professional context' in John Horgan, Barbara O'Connor and Helena Sheehan (eds), *Mapping Irish media: critical explorations* (Dublin, 2007), pp 33–48. 2 Roddy Flynn and Paschal Preston 'Media ownership and concentration in Ireland' in Eli Noam (ed.), *Who owns the world's media* (Oxford, 2016), pp 142–74. 3 INM, *Annual Report* (Dublin, 2000), p. 8.

years after the millennium, newspaper companies in the United States, the United Kingdom and Ireland were producing strong – and sometimes record – revenue returns and operating profits, and print titles were trading hands for premium prices.[4] Internationally, these performances were being squeezed out of print markets that overall, in circulation volumes, were shrinking.[5] Publishers' operating profits were being maintained principally through increased industry consolidation, which facilitated cost savings in editorial production, printing, distribution, administration and back-office functions.[6]

In broad terms, such strategies increasingly characterized the profitable operations of Ireland's local press during the Celtic Tiger. And with greater urgency, they have also underpinned publishers' efforts to survive in the tough trading conditions that have prevailed since 2008, when, in sync with the wider economy, Ireland's local newspaper industry descended into crisis. The overinflated prices that publishers had paid for local titles were quickly exposed when boom-time circulation and advertising revenues crumbled.[7] Circulations across the industry were estimated to have dropped more than a quarter between 2007 and 2011.[8] (Gauging current circulation levels is difficult, as in recent years most Irish local newspapers have been withdrawn from Audit Bureau of Circulations scrutiny.)

Since the crash, trading conditions have remained harsh for Ireland's local publishers. In large part, this has been because of enduring weakness in regional and local economies across the country. But a critical factor has been an accelerated migration of audiences from print to digital platforms, in particular for consumption of news and social-media content through smartphones.

In response, newspaper publishers have been placing greater stress on raising the commercial returns from their digital activities, especially online advertising. However, the experience in Ireland, as it has been internationally, is that since the late 2000s publishers have been struggling to replenish deep losses of print revenues with digital income.[9] A consequence is that publishers' diminished capacity to generate revenues is eroding the commercial sustainability and resourcing of their news production. In Ireland, this is raising serious concerns about the vigour with which local newspapers can perform their traditional informed-citizenry and watchdog roles in covering local politics, courts, business, culture and sport.[10]

This chapter, through the lens of corporate annual reports and registered financial accounts, will examine the shifting operational and market contexts of

4 John Soloski, 'Stability or rigidity: management, boards of directors, and the newspaper industry's financial collapse', *International Journal on Media Management*, 17:1 (2000), pp 47–66. Also: Johnston Press, *Annual Report* (Edinburgh, 2005); INM, *Annual Report* (Dublin, 2002).   5 George Brock, *Out of print: newspapers, journalism and the business of news in the digital age* (London, 2013).   6 John Mair, Neil Fowler and Ian Reeves (eds), *What do we mean by local? Grass-roots journalism: its death and rebirth* (Bury St Edmunds, 2012).   7 Kevin Rafter, 'When the "Wild West" came to the local newspaper market' in Mair et al. (eds), *What do we mean by local?*, pp 34–40.   8 Tom Felle, 'From boom to bust: Irish local newspapers post the Celtic Tiger' in Mair et al. (eds), *What do we mean by local?*, pp 41–50.   9 Brock, *Out of print*, p. 96.   10 Felle, 'Local newspapers post the Celtic Tiger', p. 46.

four media groups that played key roles in shaping Ireland's local newspaper industry during and after the Celtic Tiger: Independent News and Media (INM), Thomas Crosbie Holdings (TCH), Celtic Media Group and Johnston Press. It will consider their commercial performances and organizational responses as the industry slipped from boom to bust in the aftermath of the country's financial crisis in 2008. Further, it will assess the scope for publishers' digital activities to reinvigorate the industry in a challenging post-boom environment. Although the analysis will primarily focus on financial returns and operational strategies, the research recognizes that publishers' difficulties and decisions in these areas can have significant repercussions for the resourcing and public-good value of Irish local journalism.

THE FINANCIAL PERFORMANCE AND OPERATIONAL RESTRUCTURING OF LOCAL NEWSPAPER PUBLISHERS DURING AND AFTER THE CELTIC TIGER

Independent News and Media (INM)

Consolidation of the local newspaper industry among Ireland-based media groups had been gathering pace since the mid-1990s. But a move by British publisher Mirror Group to purchase the *Donegal Democrat* in 1998 was 'the first time that a foreign company [had] bought into the Republic's regional press'.[11] Scottish Radio Holdings entered the market soon after, which among other developments, prompted INM's annual report for 2000 to note 'the vigour with which other companies [were] buying up regional papers'.[12] Despite an obvious contraction of local press ownership, INM positioned the acquisitions as measures of 'diversity'.[13]

Energised by the booming economy of the time, INM's eleven local titles were returning strong results, achieving an aggregate circulation rise of 3.6 per cent and posting an operating income of €5 million. Having built up its regional portfolio prior to the Celtic Tiger, INM spoke of the 'inherent value' in local mastheads and declared that 'the provincial press is thriving'.[14]

The following year, INM highlighted the 'vitality' of the local market in which its titles had 'performed very well in terms of advertising and core circulation'.[15] Confirming itself as the country's largest local publisher, INM pointed to 'further consolidation in the regional sector by other local and foreign groups', which the company interpreted as validating the importance of 'local franchises, both in value and earnings terms'.[16]

By 2002, INM was, in the form of a 'challenging' advertising market, feeling the impact of a brief downturn in the Celtic Tiger.[17] Nevertheless, the company

11 *IT*, 9 July 1998. 12 INM, *Annual Report* (Dublin, 2000), p. 10. 13 Ibid., p. 24. 14 Ibid., pp 10, 24. See also: Rafter, 'Local newspaper market', p. 36. 15 INM, *Annual Report* (Dublin, 2001), p. 17. 16 Ibid. 17 INM, *Annual Report* (Dublin, 2002), p. 22.

reported 'record' operating profits of €74.9 million and noted the contribution of its local titles to the achievement.[18]

The Irish economy had returned to strong levels of growth by 2004. As a second phase of the Celtic Tiger gained momentum, INM informed shareholders the company's local portfolio would be 'a focal point for expansion as the prosperity of Ireland grows over the next decade'.[19] The company highlighted the favourable commercial and strategic location of its titles along the 'fast-growing east corridor from Louth to Wexford', which increasingly during the boom formed part of Dublin city's economic catchment area.[20]

In 2005, British media group Johnston Press superseded INM as the country's largest local publisher when it paid more than €200 million to acquire the Leinster Leader Group, Local Press and Score Press. INM acknowledged the 'record prices' paid for titles as 'corporate activity in regional newspapers in Ireland continued apace'.[21] The company, once more, viewed the premium prices as benchmarks of 'inherent value'. INM assured shareholders that its local titles, supported by 'strong cost containment', would benefit from 'continuing growth prospects'.[22]

Although INM highlighted repeatedly the formidable performance and 'inherent value' of its local titles, the company had been a bystander as other media groups bulked out their holdings. This would change in 2007, when it agreed to purchase the *Sligo Champion* for €25 million. So strong was the board's confidence in the regional market that INM was planning to expand not only by acquisition but also by launch. By February 2008 it had established two new titles: the *Waterford People* and the *Dungarvan People*.[23]

The 2008 annual report demonstrated that the company had expanded its local operation just as the country's economic crisis had hit and the industry's boom was dying. INM reported a 22.9 per cent drop in Irish operating profits to €75.8 million, which resulted from a 15 per cent decline in advertising income, 'mainly due to significantly reduced property and recruitment'.[24] The accounts did not separate out the relative drops for national and local print advertising revenues.

The following year, INM reported that its local titles had 'performed well', but this was in the context of 'difficult market conditions' in which the company's overall revenues in Ireland had fallen by 14.8 per cent to €357.5 million.[25] Again, INM did not separate out specific financial figures for its local holdings, but it did describe their circulation performance as 'exceeding that of the market' in the second half of 2009.[26] In light of circulation figures at the time, exceeding the market could be interpreted as meaning that INM's titles were losing sales less quickly than the publications of competitor companies. This would certainly

18 Ibid. 19 Ibid. 20 Ibid., p. 24. 21 INM, *Annual Report* (Dublin, 2005), p. 26. 22 Ibid. 23 INM, *Annual Report* (Dublin, 2007). 24 INM, *Annual Report* (Dublin, 2008), p. 20. 25 INM, *Annual Report* (Dublin, 2009), p. 10. 26 Ibid.

have been the case when measured against the accumulated circulation loses of Johnston Press' titles. Between the first six months of 2008 and the last six months of 2009, the combined audited circulations of INM's regional paid-for titles dropped from 120,716 to 112,056, a decline of about 7.17 per cent. In the same period, Johnston Press' paid-for titles fell from 136,095 to 125,995, a slide of 7.42 per cent.[27]

In 2010, INM informed shareholders that its local newspapers remained profitable but had suffered through 'the more difficult economic backdrop prevalent in regional Ireland', a message that was echoed in the 2011 and 2012 annual reports.[28] The annual reports for 2013, 2014 and 2015 made no specific reference to the financial performance of the group's local titles. However, in 2016 INM reported that advertising revenues across its local titles had 'remained strong', but without isolating financial figures.[29] The company highlighted that, subject to regulatory approval, it intended to purchase seven local titles owned by Celtic Media Newspapers Limited.[30] However, in June of the following year, INM and Celtic Media issued a joint statement that they had 'agreed by mutual consent to terminate the transaction'.[31]

Thomas Crosbie Holdings (TCH)
Among Ireland-based media groups, TCH was embarking on one of the more aggressive strategies of local-title acquisition when it gained control of the *Western People* in 1995.[32] The following year it acquired the *Sligo Weekender*, with the company posting a turnover of £25.5 million and an operating profit of £1.8 million.[33] During the Celtic Tiger, the company's managing director said TCH was expanding under the philosophy of 'rather than be acquired, we are acquisitive'.[34] Pursuing this strategy, TCH bought the *Nationalist and Leinster Times* in 2001.[35]

By 2004, TCH was reflecting the economic boom in its operating profit, which at close to €10 million almost equalled the price it paid that year for the *Roscommon Herald*.[36] More eye-catching was the group's profit before tax of €45 million, although the bulk of the figure came from an 'exceptional item' that related to the proceeds of a property sale.[37] Indeed, the company's flagship newspaper, the *Irish Examiner*, included in its headline over the story that the deal would add '€30m to [TCH's] acquisition war chest'.[38] At this stage, TCH was benefiting from a much improved debt profile, carrying no bank loans in 2004, as against a figure of €10 million for 2003.[39] The group's turnover, bolstered through acquisitions and boom-time revenues, indicated that TCH had grown significantly as

27 Audit Bureau of Circulations, *Island of Ireland Report, June 2009* (Berkhamsted, 2009). 28 INM, *Annual Report* (Dublin, 2010), p. 12. Also: INM, *Annual Report* (Dublin, 2011); ibid. (Dublin, 2012). 29 INM, *Annual Report* (Dublin, 2016), p. 14. 30 Ibid. 31 Celtic Media Group, 'Celtic Media not to proceed with newspaper sale to INM', celticmediagroup.ie/blog/?ss=290, accessed 27 Feb. 2018. 32 *IE*, 7 Mar. 2013. 33 TCH, *Annual Accounts* (Dublin, 1996). 34 *IE*, 7 Mar. 2013. 35 *IT*, 28 Feb. 2001. 36 TCH, *Annual Accounts* (Dublin, 2004). Also: *IT*, 23 Mar. 2013. 37 TCH, *Annual Accounts* (Dublin, 2004). 38 *IE*, 1 June 2004. 39 TCH, *Annual Accounts* (Dublin, 2004).

a commercial entity since 1996: in eight years its turnover had stretched from £25.5 million (about €32 million) to more than €83 million.⁴⁰

In 2006, TCH added the *Wexford Echo* group of newspapers to its portfolio, for €15 million.⁴¹ It was also a significant year for another reason: the group exceeded €100 million in turnover for the first time, reporting a figure of €106 million.⁴² Out of this, the company secured an operating profit of more than €12 million and a profit before tax of €6.7 million. In 2007, the figures for turnover and profit before tax climbed to €112 million and almost €12.5 million, respectively. Operating profit dipped slightly, to €11 million. The year's accounts stated that the company's strategy remained 'focused on maximizing shareholders' returns through organic and acquisition growth'.⁴³ Notable in the company's risk assessment, however, was the statement that 'the health of the economy is reflected in the revenue generated by the group's newspaper titles';⁴⁴ 2007 was the final year that TCH recorded a profit before tax.

In 2008, as Ireland's economy collapsed, the company's key financial indicators began to slide: turnover was posted at €106 million and operating profit at €5.6 million.⁴⁵ But when exceptional items (investment write-downs) and restructuring costs were factored in, TCH recorded a loss before tax of €3.5 million. Also, the company's debt profile had deteriorated significantly since 2004, with bank loans having risen to €22.3 million and overdrafts to €4.8 million.⁴⁶

Key financial indicators deteriorated at a faster rate in subsequent years. Turnover declined more than 20 per cent to €82.5 million in 2009 and a further 13 per cent to €71.8 million in 2010.⁴⁷ The group also began to file operating losses – of more than €2.9 million in 2009 and €3.1 million in 2010.⁴⁸ In the same years, under the strain of exceptional items and restructuring charges, TCH reported losses before tax of €38.2 million and €6.37 million. Bank loans declined gently in this period, from €19.3 million in 2009 to €19.1 million in 2010, but overdrafts rose to €7.9 million and then €9.2 million.⁴⁹ The overall effect was that the group's heavier debt burden was being supported by a weaker revenue base.

TCH's accounts for 2010 highlighted that, in response to withering revenues and the 'trauma to the Irish economy', the company had implemented a cost-reduction programme in 2010 and would carry it forward to 2011.⁵⁰ The accounts said that some €12 million of costs had been taken out of the business in 2010, while €4 million of costs had been removed in the first half of 2011. The group acknowledged the 'acceptance of pay and other benefit reductions' by employees.⁵¹ The accounts did not specify the scale of the reductions, but reports in the *Irish Times* suggested that after staff had accepted a 5–8 per cent pay decrease early in the year, the company later returned with proposals for an additional 10 per

40 Ibid.   41 *IE*, 7 Mar. 2013.   42 TCH, *Annual Accounts* (Dublin, 2007).   43 Ibid., p. 3.   44 Ibid.
45 TCH, *Annual Accounts* (Dublin, 2008).   46 Ibid.   47 TCH, *Annual Accounts* (Dublin, 2010).   48 Ibid.
49 Ibid.   50 Ibid, p. 3.   51 Ibid.

cent cut and a pension contribution 'holiday'.[52] The company sold the *Sligo Weekender* and the *Newry Democrat* in 2010.[53] The divestments marked a significant about-face from the company's strategy of acquisitive growth during the Celtic Tiger.

The depth of TCH's financial difficulties was revealed in March 2013, when the company effectively collapsed and a receiver was appointed to manage its holdings. Soon after, the company's key assets, including the *Irish Examiner* as well as local titles and radio stations, were sold in a 'pre-packaged restructuring' deal to a new company, Landmark Media Investments.[54] The assets may have ceased to be owned by Thomas Crosbie Holdings, but they maintained a connection to some members of the Crosbie family, who were involved with Landmark Media. The new group was incorporated about a month before TCH went into receivership.[55]

Landmark Media's first set of accounts, covering March to December 2013, showed an operating profit of €67,255 from a turnover of about €37 million. But when exceptional items and interest charges were considered, the group recorded a loss before tax of close to €700,000. Acknowledging 'continued financial support' from Allied Irish Bank, the accounts revealed that the group was carrying some €20 million in loans.[56]

The accounts that Landmark Media filed for 2014 reported turnover of more than €47.6 million, although making a direct comparison to the previous year's revenue was difficult as the 2013 figure of €37 million was based on only nine months' trading.[57] The group achieved an operating profit of €19,000, but posted a loss before tax of €57,000. The two figures were slender, and they stood in the shadow of the group's bank loans, which had increased by almost €2 million to €21.3 million. The company again highlighted 'continued financial support from its main bank, AIB'.[58]

The accounts noted the allocation of 'capital investment in order to reduce the cost base of the group', which funded new systems for editorial production and centralized facilities for advertising, finance and administration.[59] That year, the *Irish Examiner* reported that Landmark Media was seeking fifty redundancies, in areas including editorial production, and added that 'approximately half of the redundancies will be in the regional titles'.[60]

In their accounts, neither TCH nor Landmark Media showed financial figures either collectively or individually for their local titles. However, the accounts did illustrate the difficulties being experienced by the wider group entities, of which the local titles were a significant part. In December 2017, The Irish Times DAC announced its intention to acquire Landmark Media's seven regional newspapers, along with the *Irish Examiner* and three radio stations.[61]

52 *IT*, 4 Sept. 2010. **53** *IE*, 2 Dec. 2010. See also: *BNL*, 2 Sept. 2010. **54** *II*, 7 Mar. 2013. **55** Landmark Media, *Reports and Financial Statements* (Dublin, 2013). **56** Ibid., pp 4, 23. **57** Landmark Media, *Reports and Financial Statements* (Dublin, 2014). **58** Ibid., p. 4. **59** Ibid. **60** *IE*, 17 Apr. 2014. **61** *Irish Times*, 6 Dec. 2017. The Irish Times DAC (Designated Activity Company) is the corporate entity that publishes the *Irish Times*.

Celtic Media Group / Celtic Media Newspapers Limited

Scotland-based publisher Dunfermline Press, which would trade in Ireland as Celtic Media Group, acquired the *Meath Chronicle* for €30 million in 2002.[62] Over the next couple of years it added the *Anglo-Celt*, *Offaly Independent*, *Westmeath Independent* and *Westmeath Examiner*.[63]

The group's first full trading year as owner of all five titles was 2005. It posted turnover of €22.3 million, operating profit of €7.3 million and profit before tax of €5.1 million.[64] Intangible assets were valued at €44 million. In its risk assessment, the company identified 'potential migration of advertising revenues' (without specifying the Internet), 'erosion of circulation revenues' as well as 'decline in overall economic activity levels in [titles'] main markets'.[65] Against the backdrop of a still-vibrant Celtic Tiger, the group assured shareholders that it had 'comprehensive strategies in place to deal with any such issues'.[66] However, the accounts also revealed that the group was carrying bank loans of €51 million.[67]

By 2009, Celtic Media Group's revenue was much diminished. Noting the 'significant impact' of the economic crisis on local markets, the company described the year as 'a very difficult one for the group, with a significant decline in advertising revenues'.[68] To mitigate the effects, the group said it had 'implemented a number of cost-saving strategies'.[69] Turnover had fallen to €14.6 million, operating profit had dipped to €1.8, and profit before tax was down to €265,000. As in 2005, intangible assets were still being valued at €44 million. The group continued to carry heavy bank debt of €42.6 million.[70]

In 2012, at a time when its Scottish parent company was financially stressed, Celtic Media Group entered receivership and was bought out by local management in a 'pre-packaged' restructuring deal.[71] Celtic Media Group's final set of accounts ended in the year to 30 June 2012. In the previous twelve months, turnover had fallen to €11.3 million (about half the 2005 level) and the company returned an operating loss of €2.85 million.[72] However, in the eighteen-month period to June 2011, the group had recorded a loss of €43.3 million, the bulk of which related to a write-down in the value of intangible assets. In the same period, as the group edged closer to receivership, it was holding bank debt of €42.6 million. After the receivership restructuring, this amount was listed as €22.3 million.[73]

A new corporate entity, Celtic Media Limited, was established to manage the portfolio of local titles. In its first full trading year, to June 2013, the group posted turnover of €10.4 million and generated an operating profit of €880,000.[74] For the year to December 2015, turnover was almost €11.3 million, but operating profit had slipped to €296,767.[75] The following year, INM announced its intention to purchase Celtic Media's local titles, justifying the proposal to shareholders

62 *II*, 19 Dec. 2002.   63 Ibid., 29 June 2012. Also: *IT*, 19 June 2012.   64 CMG, *Annual Accounts* (Dublin, 2005), p. 11.   65 Ibid., p. 3.   66 Ibid., p. 3.   67 Ibid., p. 30.   68 CMG, *Annual Accounts* (Dublin, 2009), p. 3.   69 Ibid.   70 Ibid.   71 *II*, 29 June 2012.   72 CMG, *Annual Accounts* (Dublin, 2012).   73 Ibid., p. 22.   74 CML, *Annual Accounts* (Dublin, 2013).   75 CML, *Annual Accounts* (Dublin, 2015).

on the basis that 'quality, trusted and relevant [local] journalism remains very popular with customers'.[76]

Johnston Press

In 2005, Edinburgh-based publisher Johnston Press spent at least €200 million to acquire fourteen local titles, scattered across Ireland's four provinces, to displace INM as the largest local publisher by circulation volume.[77]

Johnston Press' move, as the Irish industry's boom was nearing its peak, followed years of debt-funded acquisitive growth in the group's home UK market. In 2006, the company's Irish titles out-performed their UK equivalents in growing advertising revenues. Johnston Press Ireland, a subsidiary entity established to manage the company's Irish interests, recorded a profit before tax of €13.6 million for the year.[78] It is perhaps not surprising, therefore, that the Johnston Press board affirmed its willingness to seek further investment opportunities in Ireland's local market.[79]

But in 2007, the company reported signs of trouble emerging in the Irish economy, which was reflected in a downturn in advertising revenues.[80] The next year, Johnston Press Ireland reported a turnover slip of more than €9 million, from €46.3 million to €37 million.[81] The subsidiary was still profitable, returning a profit before tax of almost €4 million, but the key financial indicators were deteriorating. Only three years after entering the market, Johnston Press announced that it was willing to sell its Irish titles if it could fetch a price that would represent shareholder value and reduce the group's debt.[82] In 2009, however, the board revealed that it had halted attempts to sell the Irish titles after failing to attract an acceptable price.[83] Johnston Press Ireland would be loss-making for 2009 and 2010.

The company's turnover in Ireland fell from a peak of €46.3 million in 2006 to a low of €15.1 million in 2013.[84] In trying to maintain an operation that was financially sustainable, Johnston Press implemented in Ireland key aspects of the organizational and commercial strategies that had lowered its cost base in the UK: centralizing back-office functions (such as administration, finance and Web maintenance), consolidating printing facilities (which eventually entailed the closure of printing operations in Limerick and Kilkenny), layoffs, restructuring of management, reorganization of editorial teams and news production processes, and outsourcing of newspaper distribution.[85]

---

76 INM, *Annual Report* (Dublin, 2016), p. 8.   77 JP, *Annual Report* (Edinburgh, 2005). Johnston held this position while regional publishers continued to submit their titles to the Audit Bureau of Circulation, exiting the market in 2014. It has subsequently become very difficult to say which publisher has the largest circulation, because very few regional newspapers now submit their titles to the ABC.   78 JPI, *Annual Report* (Dublin, 2006).   79 JP, *Annual Report* (Edinburgh, 2006).   80 JP, *Annual Report* (Edinburgh, 2007).   81 JPI, *Annual Report* (Dublin, 2008).   82 JP, *Annual Report* (Edinburgh, 2008).   83 JP, *Annual Report* (Edinburgh, 2009).   84 JPI, *Annual Report* (Dublin, 2006). Also: JPI, *Annual Report* (Dublin, 2013).   85 Anthony Cawley, 'Johnston Press and the crisis in Ireland's local newspaper industry, 2005–2014', *Journalism*, 18:9 (2017), pp 1163–83.

From 2008 on, these measures may have softened the impact of advertising and circulation declines, but the underlying challenge of revenue erosion persisted. Johnston Press sold the titles in 2014, to Iconic Newspapers, and the value lost from its original 2005 investment of at least €200 million was clear in the final sale price: €8.5 million.[86] On finally leaving Ireland, Johnston Press stated that the deal represented an opportunity for the group to refocus on its home UK market and to concentrate on raising its digital revenues.

The titles continue to trade in Ireland through Formpress Publishing, a subsidiary of Iconic Newspapers, both of which ultimately are owned by UK-registered company Mediaforce. In 2016, Formpress Publishing posted a turnover of €13 million and an operating profit of just over €1 million.[87]

Online revenues of Irish local publishers

Johnston Press, in its annual reports, had been outlining its ambitions to generate higher levels of digital income since before the company entered the Irish market. In absolute figures, the company realized the ambition as group (UK and Ireland) digital income grew, in sterling, from £11.3 million in 2006 to £24.6 in 2013.[88] But this was in the context of overall group turnover being £602.2 million in 2006 and total underlying revenues being £291.9 million in 2013.[89] Digital income, proportionately, represented 1.88 per cent of 2006 turnover and 8.4 per cent of (the reduced) 2013 revenues.

Narrowed to the Irish market, Johnston Press Ireland reported its digital income for the years 2010, 2011 and 2012 as €229,000, €308,000 and €457,000.[90] But as a percentage of the subsidiary's diminishing revenues for the three years, digital income represented only 0.99 per cent, 1.58 per cent and 2.66 per cent.[91] These figures were returned at a point when the Johnston Press board had identified digital as the company's 'real opportunity for growth' in the face of print decline.[92] Formpress Publishing did not specify digital-revenue figures for the former Johnston Press titles in its 2015 or 2016 accounts.

There is little evidence in the documents examined for this chapter that other Irish local publishers generated significant proportions of their income from digital activities, either during or after the Celtic Tiger. In recent years, INM has highlighted rises in its digital income, with online revenues jumping from €6.4 million in 2013 to €15.1 million in 2016.[93] But even as a growing figure, it remained a small proportion of overall revenues for both years: 1.99 per cent of €322.4 million in 2013 and 4.67 per cent of €323.4 million in 2016.[94] INM did not separate out the online advertising figures attributable to its national and

86 JP, *Annual Report* (Edinburgh, 2014).   87 Formpress, *Directors' Report and Financial Statements* (Dublin, 2016).   88 JP, *Annual Report* (Edinburgh, 2006). Also: JP, *Annual Report* (Edinburgh, 2013). 89 JP, *Annual Report* (Edinburgh, 2006). Also: JP, *Annual Report* (Edinburgh, 2013).   90 JPI, *Annual Report* (Dublin, 2011); ibid. (Dublin, 2012); ibid. (Dublin, 2013).   91 JPI, *Annual Report* (Dublin, 2011); ibid. (Dublin, 2012); ibid. (Dublin, 2013).   92 JP, *Annual Report* (Edinburgh, 2011), p. 1.   93 INM, *Annual Report* (Dublin, 2014), p. 82; INM, *Annual Report* (Dublin, 2016), p. 134.   94 Ibid.

local titles. But neither did the company suggest that local titles were fuelling growth in digital revenues.

Celtic Media's accounts identified none of the group's principal revenue streams as deriving from digital, even though the websites of its local titles carried advertising and offered e-paper subscriptions. Neither were there signals of strong digital-revenue performance in the accounts of TCH or, later, Landmark Media. During the Celtic Tiger, and in the immediate years after, TCH identified its principal activity solely as the publishing of newspapers. By 2011, in its final set of registered accounts, TCH had added 'investment in new media' to its principal-activity statement, but without specifying whether these areas were news-related.[95] Landmark Media, in its 2014 accounts, committed to 'revenue-improvement plans' for online activities, but without specifying any plan details or isolating digital-revenue figures for its local newspapers.[96]

Challenging times

Foreign investment in the Irish media market was 'quite limited' at the beginning of the 1990s.[97] But such was the scale of market transformation and upheaval in the following decades that among thirty countries examined for a major international study published in 2016, Ireland returned the 'highest concentration of foreign media ownership'.[98] The restructuring of the Irish media market was reflected in the local-newspaper sector through the 'extraordinary increase in merger and acquisition activity' in the early and mid-2000s.[99] In part, this was driven by the acquisition strategies of Ireland-based media groups. But crucial, also, was the expansion of UK-based media groups into the Irish local-news market. Despite the contraction of ownership diversity accompanying industry consolidation, Irish regulators tended to approve the acquisitions on the basis of narrow economic criteria, to the neglect of plurality and diversity considerations.[100] In particular, Irish provincial newspapers tended already to hold monopolistic or oligopolistic positions in their respective local areas, which regulators viewed as mitigating the potential for group ownership to distort the market.[101]

As suggested by the media groups considered for this chapter, a consequence of this was that the local newspaper sector experienced a more transient and group-oriented model of title ownership than had been the case historically. In addition, and reflecting developments in local-news provision in the UK media market, ownership of provincial newspapers tended to be further removed from communities the titles served.[102] By 2008 it was apparent that

95 TCH, *Annual Report* (Cork, 2011), p. 3. 96 Landmark, *Annual Report* (Cork, 2014), p. 4. 97 Wolfgang Truetzschler, 'Foreign investment in the media in Ireland', *Irish Communications Review*, 1:1–3 (1991), p. 1. 98 Eli Noam and Paul Mutter, 'Ireland – data summaries' in Eli Noam (ed.), *Who owns the world's media* (Oxford, 2016), pp 175–81, at p. 175. 99 Flynn and Preston, 'Media ownership Ireland', p. 148. 100 Ibid. Also: Colum Kenny, 'A double-edged sword: Irish media merger policy in transition', *Journal of Media Business Studies*, 6:3 (2009), pp 93–108. 101 Ibid. 102 Bob Franklin, *Local journalism and local media: making local news* (London, 2006).

some of the factors that had fuelled the Celtic Tiger, while also creating the conditions for the crash, were recognizable in the local-newspaper industry. The pattern of unsustainable debt in the wider economy was traceable in the loans publishers amassed to buy local titles. And across the economy and among publishers was a widespread assumption that boom time levels of income would continue unchecked.

It is unsurprising that the local newspaper industry has shown few signs of significant recovery while weakness endures in Ireland's regional and local economies. But the industry's challenges run beyond the immediate economic environment. They track an international trend where declines in print sales are eroding the dual-market business model of circulation and advertising revenues that historically has sustained local journalism.[103] The trend was partly manifest during Ireland's economic boom. Even as advertising revenues were buoyant, readership of local newspapers was declining as a proportion of the country's growing population.[104]

The principle strategies that the publishers examined for this chapter adopted to survive after the Celtic Tiger were extensions of the approaches they used to support profitability during the boom. First, benefit from economies of scale and scope through maintaining a portfolio of newspapers, as the efficiencies gained by sharing resources across several publications allowed individual titles to be produced at a reduced cost.[105] Second, protect operating margins through cost-cutting in the form of redundancies, new technological systems for editorial production, centralized back-office functions and reorganized or outsourced printing and distribution. Under the weight of debt, the strategies eventually were insufficient to support the Dunfermline Press-owned Celtic Media Group and TCH, although the latter had commercial interests outside of local publishing. Yet the industry's principal operational strategies have remained unchanged. The reliance on consolidation was evident again in 2016, when INM announced a deal to purchase Celtic Media's local titles, and in 2017, when The Irish Times DAC moved to acquire Landmark Media's local newspapers.[106] A gnawing concern is that, year on year, publishers are relying on these strategies to carve commercial and journalistic sustainability out of progressively smaller revenues bases.

Since the crash there has been an accelerated migration of audiences from print to digital platforms. Irish local publishers have endeavoured to keep pace through embracing social media, apps and mobile devices as platforms to engage audiences and distribute and promote news content. However, it would appear that many publishers neglected, or at least failed to prioritize, digital investment when resources were more abundant during the Celtic Tiger. For instance, in

103 Jim Chisholm, 'The industry in context – and how we can rediscover it' in Mair et al., *What do we mean by local?*, pp 8–17.   104 Felle, 'Local newspapers post the Celtic Tiger', p. 42.   105 Gillian Doyle, *Understanding media economics* (London, 2013). Also: Robert Picard, *The economics and financing of media companies* (New York, 2011).   106 *Irish Independent*, 10 Sept. 2016. *Irish Times*, 6 Dec. 2017.

2002 INM described its investments in digital as 'tempered' at a time when it was the country's largest local publisher.[107]

Since the late 1990s, the online activities of Irish local newspapers have focused primarily on generating revenues through subscriptions to digital editions and advertising, or on using the website as a promotional tool for the print product. Notwithstanding the addition of social media and apps to the mix, local publishers' online approaches have remained fairly static and indicate that across the industry digital innovation has stalled. Indeed, as Felle highlights, it is difficult to detect signals of a coherent and potentially profitable digital strategy among local publishers.[108] That argument chimes with the financial and corporate evidence examined here. The documents suggest that the declining print product remains the primary revenue generator and that publishers which remain viable are doing so more through restructuring and cost cutting than digital revenue growth. Social media is siphoning off potential digital income. Facebook, Google and Twitter are not only rival distribution systems for content that is of community interest, they also have had significant success in soaking up digital advertising revenues that otherwise might have been available to local publishers.[109] The digital economy, thus far, has proven unfavourable to local newspaper publishers, weakening their revenue-generation capacities both in print and online.

It is important to acknowledge that Irish local journalism has always operated on limited means. Even so, it is apparent that editorial resourcing is not immune to the increasing pressure on the industry's revenues.[110] Traditionally, freedom of the press in Irish local journalism has been equated with market freedom (local news as a for-profit informational commodity produced by private companies, which themselves can be traded for profit – as happened frequently during the Celtic Tiger). But as well as serving a commercial imperative, local newspapers have also performed a public-good function in maintaining an informed citizenry and acting as a watchdog on power. The evidence examined in this chapter would suggest that traditional print business models and attempts to transition to digital platforms are struggling to generate the revenues necessary to resource a market-based Irish local journalism that is critical, investigative and deeply embedded in communities.

---

107 INM, *Annual* Report (Dublin, 2003), p. 23.   **108** Felle, 'Local newspapers post the Celtic Tiger', p. 41.
109 Robert McChesney, *Digital disconnect: how capitalism is turning the Internet against democracy* (New York, 2013).   **110** Felle, 'Local newspapers post the Celtic Tiger', p. 46. Also: Rafter, 'Local newspaper market', p. 39.

Abbreviations

AC	*Anglo-Celt*	ETC	Exchange Telegraph Company
AFIL	All-for-Ireland League	FA	football association
AFP	Agence France-Presse	FC	football club
AGM	annual general meeting	*FH*	*Fermanagh Herald*
AP	Associated Press	*FJ*	*Freeman's Journal*
BMH	Bureau of Military History	*FM*	*Fermanagh Mail*
BNL	*Belfast News Letter*	GAA	Gaelic Athletic Association
BUP	British United Press	*GE*	*Galway Express*
CC	*Cork Constitution*	GL	Guildhall Library
CCCA	Cork City and County Archives	GPO	General Post Office
CCh	*Clare Champion*	HC	House of Commons
CE	*Cork Examiner*	ICA	Irish Citizen Army
CFP	*Cork Free Press*	IDGC	Irish Distress and Grants
CI	chief inspector		Committee
CJ	*Clare Journal*	*IE*	*Irish Examiner*
ClM	*Clare Man*	IFA	Irish Football Association
ClN	*Clonmel Nationalist*	*IFJ*	*Irish Farmers Journal*
CM	*Connachtman*	*II*	*Irish Independent*
CMG	Celtic Media Group	*IM*	*Irishman*
CML	Celtic Media Limited	INA	Irish News Agency
CN	*Carlow Nationalist and Leinster Times*	INM	Independent News and Media
CO	Colonial Office	*IP*	*Irish People*
CS	*Connacht Sentinel*	IPP	Irish Parliamentary Party
CT	*Connacht Tribune*	*IPr*	*Irish Press*
CTe	*Connaught Telegraph*	*IR*	*Impartial Reporter*
CWE	*Cork Weekly Examiner*	IRA	Irish Republican Army
CWN	*Cork Weekly News*	IRB	Irish Republican Brotherhood
DC	*Daily Chronicle*	ISDN	Integrated Services Digital
DD	*Dundalk Democrat*		Network
DI	*Donegal Independent*	*IT*	*Irish Times*
DJ	*Derry Journal*	ITGWU	Irish Transport and General
DNB	Deutsches Nachrichtenbüro		Workers' Union
DoD	*Donegal Democrat*	*IV*	*Irish Volunteer*
DORA	Defence of the Realm Act	IV	Irish Volunteers
DPA	Deutsche Presse Agentur	JP	Johnston Press
DrI	*Drogheda Independent*	JPI	Johnston Press Ireland
DRR	Defence of the Realm Regulations	*KE*	*Killarney Echo*
DV	*Donegal Vindicator*	*KJ*	*Kilkenny Journal*
EE	*Enniscorthy Echo*	*KM*	*Kerryman*
EH	*Evening Herald*	*KMo*	*Kilkenny Moderator*

KN	*Kerry News*	RIC	Royal Irish Constabulary
KP	*Kilkenny People*	RMBI	Regional Media Bureau of Ireland
KS	*Kerry Sentinel*	RNAI	Regional Newspapers
LE	*Leinster Express*		Association of Ireland
LeL	*Leinster Leader*	RP	Redmond Papers
LG	*Leitrim Gazette/Advertiser*	RTÉ	Raidió Teilifís Éireann
LL	*Limerick Leader*	*SC*	*Sligo Champion*
LO	*Leitrim Observer*	*SE*	*Skibbereen Eagle*
MC	*Meath Chronicle*	SF	Sinn Féin
ME	*Munster Express*	*SI*	*Sligo Independent*
MG	*Manchester Guardian*	*SIn*	*Sunday Independent*
MN	*Mayo News*	*SlSt*	*Sligo Star*
MS	manuscript	*SN*	*Sligo Nationalist*
MT	*Midland Tribune*	*SSt*	*Southern Star*
MVF	Midlands Volunteer Force	*ST*	*Sligo Times*
NAI	National Archives of Ireland	TCH	Thomas Crosbie Holdings
NAUK	National Archives, UK	*TH*	*Tuam Herald*
NG	*Nenagh Guardian*	*TS*	*Tipperary Star*
NLI	National Library of Ireland	UCC	University College Cork
NV	*National Volunteer*	UCD	University College Dublin
OI	*Offaly Independent*	UCDA	University College Dublin Archive
OPC	Office of the Press Censor	*UH*	*Ulster Herald*
PA	Press Association	*UI*	*United Irishman*
PCMR	Press Censorship Monthly Report	UIL	United Irish League
PD	Parliamentary Debates	UVF	Ulster Volunteer Force
PNS	Provincial Newspaper Society	*WI*	*Westmeath Independent*
PRONI	Public Record Office of	*WP*	*Western People*
	Northern Ireland	*WS*	*Waterford Star*
RH	*Roscommon Herald*	WS	witness statement

Contributors

JOHN BURKE obtained his PhD in NUI Galway. He is the author of numerous articles and two books, the most recent of which is *Athlone, 1900–1923: politics, revolution and civil war* (2015). He is currently working on the Roscommon contribution to the Four Courts Press series The Irish Revolution, 1912–23.

RAY BURKE has been a news editor at RTÉ News since 1996 and chief news editor of RTÉ News since 2007. He is the author of *Press delete: the decline and fall of the* Irish Press (2005) and *Joyce County: Galway and James Joyce* (2016). He is a member of the executive committee of the Newspaper and Periodical History Forum of Ireland.

ELAINE CALLINAN has recently completed a PhD in Trinity College Dublin on the topic of 'Electioneering and propaganda in Ireland, 1917–1920'. She lectures in modern Irish history at Carlow College, St Patrick's. She has published public-history works and journal articles, and she has peer reviewed books for journal reviews.

ANTHONY CAWLEY is a senior lecturer in media at Liverpool Hope University. His research interests include media history, media industries and innovation, Ireland's provincial press, and news-media framing of financial crises. His research has been published in books and peer-reviewed international journals.

CONOR CURRAN is Irish Research Council post-doctoral research fellow at Trinity College Dublin and has taught sports history at De Montfort University, Leicester. He has published two books, *The development of sport in Donegal, 1880–1935* (2015) and *Irish soccer migrants: a social and cultural history* (2017).

CHRISTOPHER DOUGHAN obtained his PhD from Dublin City University in 2015 following completion of his thesis 'The printed word in troubled times: the Irish provincial press, 1914–1921'. He is currently finalising this thesis for publication.

JOHN HORGAN is emeritus professor of journalism at Dublin City University. He joined DCU in 1982 following a career as a journalist, and as a member of Seanad Éireann, Dáil Éireann and the European Parliament. He served as Ireland's first press ombudsman (2008–15) and is the author of a number of books on Irish politics and media, most recently *Irish media: a critical history* (2018) with Roddy Flynn.

ANTHONY KEATING is a senior lecturer in psychosocial analysis of offending behaviour at Edge Hill University, Lancashire. Having completed his PhD at Dublin City University in 2003, on the abuse of children in the care of the Irish state, Keating continued his research there as a Government of Ireland post-doctoral research fellow, 2004–6, researching sexual crime in Ireland, 1922–72. His interest in journalism in the Irish Free State arose directly out of his research on the reporting of sexual crime in Ireland.

IAN KENNEALLY is editor of *The Revolution Papers, 1923–1949*. Among his books are *The paper wall: newspapers and propaganda in Ireland, 1919–1921* (2008) and *From the earth, a cry: the story of John Boyle O'Reilly* (2011). He has also contributed to many edited collections and journals, especially in the area of media history.

ALAN McCARTHY is a PhD candidate and head tutor at the School of History, University College Cork. He was the recipient of an Eoin O'Mahony Bursary from the Royal Irish Academy for 2017 and is the holder of the Diarmuid Whelan Memorial Scholarship awarded by UCC for 2017/18.

MARK O'BRIEN is senior lecturer in the School of Communications at Dublin City University and the author of *The fourth estate: journalism in twentieth-century Ireland* (2017), *The* Irish Times*: a history* (2008) and *De Valera, Fianna Fáil and the* Irish Press*: the truth in the news?* (2001).

JAMES O'DONNELL teaches history at NUI Galway. His research interests include news agencies as transnational media organizations and the role of news and media in the formation of national identity. He is secretary to the Newspaper and Periodical History Forum of Ireland and editor of the *Irish bibliography of press history*.

DONAL Ó'DRISCEOIL is a senior lecturer in history at University College Cork. He has published widely on modern Irish history, and recently co-edited the award-winning *Atlas of the Irish revolution* (Cork, 2017).

REGINA UÍ CHOLLATÁIN is associate professor and head of the School of Irish, Celtic Studies and Folklore, University College Dublin. She has published widely on media, print culture and language revival. Her most recent publications as co-editor include the study of urban Irish-language writing in Ireland in *Saothrú na Gaeilge scríofa i suímh uirbeacha na hÉireann, 1700–1850* (2016) and the first comprehensive study of Irish-language literature in a global context, *Litríocht na Gaeilge ar fud an domhain* (2015).

MARK WEHRLY worked as a journalist for fifteen years. In 2008, he received his PhD from Maynooth University, and he has taught history at Maynooth

University and journalism at the University of Limerick. He currently works for the Golfing Union of Ireland as event director for the 2018 World Team Championships.

AOIFE WHELAN lectures in modern Irish and in Irish studies in the School of Irish, Celtic Studies and Folklore, University College Dublin. She is an active member of the Newspaper and Periodical History Forum of Ireland and is an adviser to the *Irish bibliography of press history*. Aoife served as deputy editor of *The Revolution Papers* in 2016.

Index